The End of
GENDER

The End of GENDER

A PSYCHOLOGICAL AUTOPSY

SHARI L. THURER

Routledge
Taylor & Francis Group

NEW YORK AND LONDON

Published in 2005 by
Routledge
Taylor & Francis Group
270 Madison Avenue
New York, NY 10016

Published in Great Britain by
Routledge
Taylor & Francis Group
2 Park Square
Milton Park, Abingdon
Oxon OX14 4RN

Printed in the United States of America on acid-free paper
10 9 8 7 6 5 4 3 2 1

International Standard Book Number-10: 0-415-92770-6 (Hardcover) 0-415-92771-4 (Softcover)
International Standard Book Number-13: 978-0-415-92770-3 (Hardcover) 978-0-415-92771-0 (Softcover)

Library of Congress Cataloging-in-Publication Data

Thurer, Shari.
    The end of gender : a psychological autopsy / Shari L. Thurer.
        p. cm.
    Includes bibliographical references and index.
    ISBN 0-415-92770-6 (hardcover : alk. paper) -- ISBN 0-415-92771-4 (pbk. : alk. paper)
    1. Gender identity--Philosophy. 2. Gender identity--Psychological aspects. 3. Homosexuality--Philosophy. I. Title.

HQ1075.T495 2005
155.3--dc22   2004030615

Taylor & Francis Group
is the Academic Division of T&F Informa plc.

Visit the Taylor & Francis Web site at
http://www.taylorandfrancis.com

and the Routledge Web site at
http://www.routledge-ny.com

For everyone on the gender continuum

CONTENTS

ACKNOWLEDGMENTS

In lieu of combat pay, I wish to thank my family for putting up with me during the thirty-five dog years it took me to write this book. I could not have done so without the calming presence of my husband Bob Thurer, the intellectual provocation of my daughter Sally, the affectionate support of my brother Gary, and my parents Lilly and Sidney Lehrer. Thanks are also due to my friends—Brenda Star, Susan Haskell, Beth Wharff, Karen Taylor, Penny Thurer, and Kathleen Miller —a veritable Greek chorus of positive (if bemused) reinforcement. Their willingness to peruse chapters and allow me to bounce ideas off them has been invaluable.

Appreciation is owed to Cary Friedman for his critical reading of an early draft. He and Catherine Kimble led a fascinating seminar on gender and sexuality in 2003 at the Boston Psychoanalytic Society and Institute that provided a sympathetic forum for my thinking and a potent stimulant for my writing. I am also grateful to the ongoing Discussion Group on Sexual Orientation and Gender Identity sponsored by the Boston Psychoanalytic Society and Institute and the Fenway Community Health Center, as well as the Lacan Seminar led by Judith Feher-Gurewich at the Harvard Center for Literary and Cultural Studies. Thanks, also, to my intrepid editors Michael Bickerstaff, Amanda Rice and their patient team.

My ideas have been shaped by the ideas of others, some of whom I have communicated with—Lynne Layton, Lois Shawver—and many whose writings I have read and cited. I hope I have done justice to their thinking.

Above all, I thank my many patients whose stories inspired—no, incited—me to write. The clients I describe in the pages of this book have been portrayed in such a way as to be unidentifiable. I do not mean to project my interpretation of issues as the final word. I offer this book not as an answer to the enigma sex/gender identity, but merely as a provocation for more questioning.

PREFACE

Let's face it, sexuality has changed—all sorts of deviations have been "outed"—but theories about them haven't caught up. They have arrested in moth-eaten bias—the conviction that there are two, and only two, normal versions of gender. Biologists are still apt to look for the origins of homosexuality in lesions or biochemical abnormalities, as if gay and straight sex were absolutes; and the former were a faulty version of the latter. Psychologists still try to "fix" sissy boys, as if effeminacy were bad. Behaviorists continue to blame sexual nonconformity on poor parental shaping, and psychoanalysts persist in regarding transgendered individuals as character disordered.

Yet, even as scientists, psychological theorists, and practitioners display archaic prejudice, there are other theorists of sexuality—those that hail from the realm of French cultural theory—who leapfrog 180 degrees away from hierarchical thinking, who view all sexuality as okay. But while postmodernists, the French-inflected theorists, are politically correct, they sometimes lack common sense and are insensitive to people in pain. Here we have two hyper-educated, presumably reasonable groups of people with opposing viewpoints, neither of which is sufficient for explaining erotic desire. You would think they would cross-pollinate ideas and build a better theory. The problem is they do not talk to each other. While they grapple with similar topics, they barely cross-reference. Their jargon is mutually impenetrable. It is as if they are speaking in tongues.

I wrote this book as an antidote to this Tower of Babel. My intent was to synthesize and critique the various theories about sexual orientation and gender identity. I focused on psychoanalytic theory and postmodern gender theory, but included biology, evolution, data-based psychology, anthropology, sociology, history, and linguistics, as well as inferences from art, literature, and pop culture. These disciplines can never entirely cohere because there are vast differences among them about what constitutes evidence and truth. Nevertheless, they do suggest ways that psychoanalytic theory—my home—might be modernized, or "postmodernized," to shed light on our "new" reality.

Here is a road map of my intellectual journey. Chapter 1 overviews the demise of binary sex/gender categories and introduces postmodern gender theory (aka "queer theory") as a possible way of sorting out some of the contradictions in our understanding of sexuality. Chapter 2 takes a closer look at postmodernism and the cultural landscape, zeroing in on recent queer history, and culminating in a case description in which I incorporate some postmodern ideas. In Chapter 3, I critique some of the premises employed in the "harder" sciences—neurophysiology, genetics, hormonal studies, anatomy—as well as some of the "softer" ones—data-based psychology, anthropology, sociology, and evolution. Chapter 4 is a history of queer theory, from its origins in feminism, gay theory, and French philosophy, to its status today in literature, arts, and philosophy departments. In Chapter 5, I review psychoanalytic theory, incorporating some ideas from postmodern gender theory. By using queer theory in selective ways—by smashing the binary—psychoanalytic therapists might be able to make their brilliant insights about the unconscious relevant to the twenty-first century.

1

PSYCHOANALYSIS MEETS POSTMODERN SEX

"We're born naked, and the rest is drag."[1]

Drag queen RuPaul

Once there were only two genders: male and female. Males, typically, were the big hairy ones who left the toilet seat up. Females were the smaller, less hairy ones who put the toilet seat down. They had eyes only for each other. It was easy to tell them apart. These days it's not so easy. Men sport ponytails and earrings and teach nursery school; women flaunt their tattoos and biceps and smoke cigars. Everywhere we look—on television, at the movies, in glossy magazines, in self-help books—we see not two genders, but something more like a crossbreed, a point on a continuum. There she (he? it?) is in a Pepsi commercial, ogling the sculpted torso of a male construction worker, appropriating the macho gaze with uncanny ease. There he (she? it?) is again in the TV hit *The Sopranos*, where Mafia boss Tony talks about—of all things —his feelings to a female psychiatrist; and there he (she? it?) is yet again in my own psychotherapy consulting room, this time in the form of a male college football player neurotically obsessed with dieting, a preoccupation that used to be exclusively a girl thing. With the turn of the millennium we have sequined female ice skaters who beat up their opponents and pumped-up male opera divas who sing soprano. The genders are leaking into each other. And these are just the most obvious examples.

1

The demise of discrete gender categories goes deeper, well beyond the relaxation of fixed gender codes for roles and behaviors. Not only is each sex playing with each other's toys, wearing each other's clothes, and adopting each other's neuroses—each is usurping the other's lovers. In many circles it is no longer expected that sexual preference be for the opposite gender. Men are openly attracted to men, and women to women. Homosexuality has become downright reputable. Same-sex commitment ceremonies are now routinely announced in the *New York Times*, and Massachusetts recently tentatively legalized gay marriage. In 2000 Vermont allowed gay couples to form civil unions, and in 2003 The U.S. Supreme Court affirmed gay privacy and opened the way to a revolution in family life. Indeed, there are so many gay characters on prime time that their presence no longer feels sensational, it merely shows that television programming is catching up with real life. When both the daughter of the conservative Republican vice president and the wily winner of TV's first *Survivor* (mother of all "reality" television and de facto barometer of mainstream taste) are unabashedly "out," we can only assume that a homosexual is a person one might conceivably want to be.

If the new visibility of homosexuality derails our conception of orderly gender arrangements, then the new visibility of bisexuality amounts to an intellectual train wreck. The obvious ease with which so many folks are switching sexual scripts seems to defy an eternal verity, that we are either straight or gay, attracted to men or women—but never both. Apparently, a person's sexual orientation may not be fixed after all. In a few ZIP codes, one's erotic preference for a person of a certain gender has become as malleable as one's hairdo, and about as serious. The necessity for a permanent and exclusive sexual orientation seems to have become obsolete.

Joining the list of gender archaisms may soon be the requirement that a gender identity cohere with your genitals. These days it's not unusual to be one gender on the Internet and another in bed. All attributes once considered specific to a particular sex, including the very feeling of being either male or female, are now, for some, up for grabs, and may yo-yo back and forth. Gender-bending is the new beat of pop stars, Olympic athletes, fashionistas, perfume makers, and young intellectuals, many of whom have taken to flaunting a self-styled potpourri of male and female characteristics. Regarding attributes like gender role, identity, and sexual preference, we're apparently more smorgasbord than *menu fixe*.

The contemporary art world has been supplying the visuals for what the whole culture is obsessing about. Recent installations at the

Pompidou, the Guggenheim, and the Brooklyn Museum are chock full of randomly situated penises and vaginas. Trends in fashion and cosmetics—boxer shorts (with a fly!) for women, hair coloring for men—reinforce the gender blur. Obviously, marketers have discovered the allure of androgyny. We are bombarded with advertisements featuring partially nude models of ambiguous sex curiously draped and intertwined—but who desires whom?—juxtaposed against consumer goods. Images like these, which once might have evoked disgust, instead produce an inclination to shop. Presumably, deviance sells. In a radical reversal of sensibility, that which used to cause some folks to lose their lunch—the depiction of so-called perversion—now pushes product. Here is an idea worth pondering.

Let me disentangle some of the nomenclature. The term "sex" refers specifically to a person's anatomy or to an erotic act, like sexual intercourse. In up-to-date social science usage, sex is distinguished from "gender," the latter of which refers to the social expectations for a person's sex. "Gender identity" or "sexual identity," an individual's sense of being a gendered self, is not always congruent with society's expectations for that individual's biological sex, and neither is sexual orientation. Complicating the matter is the fact that a person's anatomy may be ambiguous, and so may a so-called erotic act. Recall the infamous oral-genital encounter between Monica Lewinsky and Bill Clinton: Clinton steadfastly refused to call it sex.

These terms seem positively precise when compared to the newly minted vocabulary used to describe our changing sex/gender reality. Prominent in this new gender-speak is "gender-bender," which is an inclusive term referring to all gender nonconformists, from female bodybuilders to the straight male lovers of men who cross-dress—anybody who defies gender expectations. The term "queer" is synonymous with gender-bender but is sometimes used politically, and therefore may include so-called normal individuals and, indeed, anyone, as long as they are willing to label themselves queer and are openly doubtful about the existence of a hardwired gender and/or sex binary.

Among the diverse people living under the big gender-bender tent are "transgenders," those folks whose mental gender does not synchronize with their congenital anatomy. In other words, transgenders' physical bodies aren't consonant with their disposition. These individuals feel they were truly meant to be a different anatomical sex and/or they wish to engage in cross-gender behavior at least some of the time. Transgenders include in their midst, but are not limited to, "transvestites" (cross-dressers or practitioners of drag); "transsexuals" (those who medically "correct" their genitals to match their gender identity); and "intersexuals" (people with various physical conditions in which the genital or reproductive organs do not fit into the standard category of male and female).

The prevalence of gender-bending broadly conceived is not trivial. Statistics are slippery things, but the most comprehensive study done in the United States so far indicates that 9 percent of the women and 10 percent of the men surveyed reported homosexual behavior, desire, or identity since turning age 18.[2] The incidence would be about half if you counted only those men who sleep exclusively with men and women who sleep exclusively with women on a regular basis and admit it to a survey taker. Comparably reliable statistics do not exist in this country for the percentage of people who yearn for, seek, or undergo a sex change. In the Netherlands, where accurate records are maintained, it was found that that 1 in 30,400 persons born female and 1 in 11,900 persons born male had taken hormones to change their sex.[3] The Dutch data are a decade old and probably represent a conservative estimate of prevalence today.

Individuals under the tent may be gay, straight, bisexual, or asexual, regardless of the shape of their genitals. In fact, about one third of male-to-female transgenders, including post-operative transsexuals, go on loving women—hardly the most parsimonious route to get a woman if we presume that most women prefer to have sex with people with penises. Obviously, these particular transgenders' wish was not to be conventional women, but to be lesbians.[4] Their basic identity is female and gay, not male and heterosexual. Contrary to the simplicities of everyday thinking, a person's physical body, gender identity, and sexual orientation are not necessarily yoked together but may vary somewhat independently of each other and over time. Yet they remain incorrectly yoked together in the public mind, which stubbornly wants to pigeonhole a person as either permanently male or female, replete with attendant clichéd attributes. (This tendency to obsessively compartmentalize gender has been hilariously parodied by Pat in TV's *Saturday Night Live*, whose deliberate sexual ambiguity irresistibly frustrated all onlookers.) As advances in medical technology and hormone replacement enable future generations to fashion their own sex/gender as they wish, the boundaries between categories will become vaguer and vaguer. So will nomenclature.

The current conspicuousness of gender-bending is part of a global cultural shift in thinking about gender deviants: that they are, like, say, left-handers, a very ordinary minority. While not quite welcomed in polite society, gender-benders are gaining respectability. Once ghettoized in the seedy venues of the demimonde, cross-dressers such as Dame Edna or Eddie Izzard have become fixtures of the mainstream. Drag is now the current entertainment of choice for upscale Bar Mitzvahs and Broadway shows (e.g., the current hit *Hairspray*). Publicly voiced acceptance of gender nonconformity is still rare, but there has been an observable positive tilt in the media, exemplified by a 1995 account in the venerable *New Yorker* of a well-known cross-dressing businessman in Nashville. This popular Tennessee Republican had a habit of showing up with his wife at restaurants wearing a tuxedo jacket, along with a skirt and high heels. Apparently, no one seemed to mind.[5]

These days, even flaming transgenders like RuPaul are not automatically reviled, let alone jailed or forced to undergo a "cure." The arrival of the twenty-first century has been accompanied by a rise in queers' approval rating as well as a rise in gender-bending as a subject of intense academic interest. In only one year (2002), transgenderism was seriously explored in a historical study published by the Harvard University Press (*How Sex Changed*), a collection of thoughtful essays by novelist/psychotherapist Amy Bloom (*Normal*), and a critically acclaimed novel by Jeffrey Eugenides (*Middlesex*).[6] Two years before, Hilary Swank won the Academy Award for her realistic portrayal of true-life murder victim Brandon Teena, a female-to-male transgender, in *Boys Don't Cry*. Unlike Hollywood's typical depiction of a transgender individual, Teena was not presented as repugnant or outrageous, but as sympathetic and gentle; it was his brutal murderers who were repugnant and outrageous.

Transgenders like Teena are becoming so apparent, so bourgeois, that they are actually organizing to demand political equality. Far from flouting norms, they are creating new ones, like the acceptance of themselves into the natural order of things. A few are lobbying for the right to marry or adopt children, requests that hardly signal a wish to tweak bourgeois convention but rather a wish to join it. Herein lies a new market niche for etiquette books. Such was the conclusion of a clever *New Yorker* staff writer who had fruitlessly perused existing etiquette guides in search of a recommendation for appropriate attire for a member of a wedding who happened to be in between sexes at that moment.[7] Recently, when an NPR radio researcher asked male-to-female transgender teens in Los Angeles what they wanted most in the world, he found them to be, well, just like their "biologically correct" female adolescent counterparts. Their responses: "a cute steady boyfriend"; or, if the transgender teen's orientation happened to be lesbian, "a girlfriend."[8]

The law is trying to keep up with the new social reality. Most states now permit transsexual persons to change their drivers licenses and birth certificates to conform to their new status. In 1977, the New York Supreme Court ruled that Renee Richards, a transsexual, could play in women's tennis tournaments despite being genetically male. So, except for the fact of their gender identity and/or sexual orientation, queers may not be so queer after all, at least in the human, if not the numerical, sense. Their increased exposure has shown them to be pretty much indistinguishable from everybody else. They crave ordinary lifestyles. They are not freaks. Maybe it's "normal" to be queer.

Many twenty-somethings think so. What was perverse for baby boomers has become mainstream for their offspring, who have been surfacing in my practice over the last decade—such as the male college student who realizes he is bisexual but, after a brief period of adjustment, shrugs his shoulders and plans to get on with an otherwise mundane life. Bisexual young women are so common on college campuses as to merit their own acronym: l.u.g. = lesbian until graduation. In the current atmosphere, it's practically obligatory for a new TV ensemble show aimed at the youth demographic to offer a gender-blending character. Take the lyrics of a pop song by the band Astrid (used in a 2001 Target commercial)—"Are you a boy or a girl? Either way you rock my world!" These lyrics tend to puzzle an over-forty cohort but are entirely obvious to one that is under thirty. They resonate with contemporary youths' sensibility.

Indeed, the routine paraphernalia of today's young people—their zines, online "handles," comics, underwear, haircuts, body decoration, ornaments, icons, and so on—can be aggressively androgynous. If we were to seriously consider the implications of these artifacts instead of casually dismissing them as the ritual rebellious stuff of youth, we would realize that they confound our habits of gender typecasting, which reinforces our need to rethink our habits. To be sure, there is a lot of sex going on among young adults, probably as much or more than their predecessors, but, unlike that of their predecessors, their sexual activity may not involve the convergence of a penis with a vagina. I am not suggesting that erotic desire is not alive and well, but that it is not necessarily deployed in the way it used to be. For a whole generation, the meltdown of gender categories is a given and not a problem. We are witnessing the end of gender, or at least the end of gender in the way it has been customarily defined.

But it's funny about gender categories. Even as we notice the fineness of the line between the sexes—we'd have to have been asleep for the last thirty years not to—we just don't get it. We're mired in doublethink.

Most of us are gender fundamentalists, believing that gender and sexual orientation come in two, and only two, varieties. Even those who profess tolerance for all manner of sexual behavior construe the blending of gender as a trend, a trivial phenomenon that goes on only in New York or San Francisco, in the movies, or among people in arty professions—certainly not among people who drive SUVs and own suburban real estate. We stubbornly resist acknowledging the implications of the obvious: that if gender and sexual orientations are continuums (as many claim to think), then we shouldn't be quite so surprised when biological females indulge in "potty" humor and make rude noises or when biological males wish to wear open-toed stilettos. It should follow that those kinds of behaviors would be somewhat expectable, not shocking or morally tainted. Yet to many folks, even to those who proclaim the opposite, gender-bending remains disturbing and outrageous, equivalent to mucking around in swampy waters. There is a serious disconnect going on between our thinking and our believing. In their hearts, many otherwise intelligent people cling to a rigid sex/gender paradigm.

We have only to look at pop sensibility—at sitcom-style girl-bonding; at the allegedly hardwired "boys will be boys" mentality that excuses activities such as those of Bill Clinton and the NFL; or at the frightened, triumphalist rage of a certain strain of women's rock music—to realize the insidious reach of this segregationist mentality. Take humor: Caricaturing sexual genres is a veritable staple of stand-up comedy, of greeting cards, of comic novels like *Bridget Jones's Diary*, and of the joke spam that clogs our computers. In typical e-list fodder, every configuration of human coupling is assigned a blatantly stereotypic trademark conflict. For straights, it's the Venus/Mars thing, the gist of which goes something like this: men are aggressive, competitive, selfish boors; women are their moral superior and also their dupes. They speak in different languages. Gay men, on the other hand, are said to complain that they can't find a good man with whom to settle down. Sex for them is as impersonal as going to the gym. Lesbians' problematic issues are—to wit—the "urge to merge" and "lesbian bed death" (the so-called tendency for lesbians to lose sexual interest in their partner even as they sustain an emotional bond). And "bis" wonder if they exist, as does everyone else (buttressed, no doubt, by the heterosexual disclosures in 2001 of once-bisexual icon, actress Anne Heche). Sexual humor like this depends for its effect on an apartheid-like mentality that presumes discrete, inviolable boundaries between genders and sexual orientations. Good fences make good neighbors. Without boundaries, there would be no group identity, no exclusivity, no sense of superiority, nor, importantly, tribal behavior of which to make fun. To be sure, the joke teller, like the rest of us, is unaware of this presumption. The belief in neat, binary divisions of gender and orientation is so ordinary, so internalized, and so implicit, that, like air, it is not noticed.

Of course, popular thinking, not being subject to the demands of conceptual rigor, may well accommodate two diametrically opposing ideas without noticing a contradiction, especially if it has no impetus to do otherwise. A pop mentality has a notoriously high tolerance for cognitive dissonance. With regard to gender categories, most people manage to live quite comfortably with a tidy illusion of duality because the great majority of people are content with their sexual orientation and biological sex. They take them for granted and assume everyone else does too. At the heart of their belief may be a kind of hubris, albeit an inadvertent one: the conviction that their own inclinations are ordinary for everyone, that if they prefer heterosexual sex, then it's normal to prefer heterosexual sex. Their perspective is limited to their own reflection in the mirror. Or perhaps some people are victims of their own thought police; that is, they are so threatened by any awareness of sexual or gender deviance that they banish it from consciousness.

But science, with its imprimatur of truth and objectivity, is supposed to be immune to common prejudice. Presumably, it adheres to a higher standard—the uncompromising belief in only what can be seen, measured, and proven in randomized, double-blind tests. Yet it, too, has fallen prey to the assumption of discrete gender categories, thereby lending that notion undue intellectual respectability. The field of evolutionary psychology (viewed as a science by some) is a case in point. Basking in the reflected glory of exciting new advances in genetics and molecular biology, this discipline is receiving especially widespread press at the moment, along with anything to do with chromosomes, heredity, or the human genome. But while recent studies in genetics may have resulted in new cancer treatments, better forensic evidence, and disease-resistant crops, those in evolutionary psychology seem to have revived an interest in an exclusively biological explanation for virtually all human actions or feelings, including depression, homosexuality, religion, and consciousness. Never mind our soul, spirit, imagination, or the subterranean forces swirling around in our psyche—the very qualities that make us human. Typical of evolutionary psychologists' thinking is their Neo-Darwinian rationale for rape—that men rape women because sexual assault is favored by natural selection to give sexually dispossessed males the chance to have children. The implication is that men can't help it: it's encoded in their DNA. Blame your genes, they seem to be saying. (But a biological explanation undermines social and political reform: genes are impervious to legislation). It is rarely pointed out that these researchers may be offering skimpy evidence, misconceiving how genetics works, and/or employing circular reasoning; that is, committing the tautological error of assuming in their research design that which they are attempting to explain, namely, sex/gender difference.[9]

Alas, it is in psychology, the field from which I hail, that this line of thinking receives its fullest elaboration. Developmental and educational psychologists, in particular, have razed forests with their publication of empirical evidence describing differences between gays and straights, males and females. Even though many researchers explicitly caution that they are talking about socialized characteristics, their accounts have a way of slipping into essentialism, that is, biological inevitability. Quite apart from their contents, the sheer quantity of data about difference, in and of itself, stacks the deck against a perception of similarity. Most researchers are looking for difference (not sameness) and are therefore apt to find it and exaggerate its importance—like looking for distinguishing characteristics in identical twins, discovering a mole or two, and concluding that the twins are not identical. They deduce too much from too little. The way these studies have been designed obscures the fact that gender and sexual orientation may be continuums. We too readily infer from them that men and women (and likewise, homosexuals and heterosexuals) are members of completely dissimilar categories, not variations of a common category—that they are essentially different, not fundamentally the same. Never mind the fact that, genetically speaking, every human being on the planet is 99.9 percent identical.

Even more demoralizing to me is the realization that the specialty of psychological practice in which I was trained, psychoanalytic psychotherapy, derived from the very theory that took sex out of the closet, is one that has done much until recently to keep it in (all but straight sex, that is). Originally revolutionary, the *agent provocateur* of the avantgarde (who took dream life very seriously), psychoanalysis was literally mind altering and antibourgeois. Psychoanalysts and creative types used to have an affinity for each other. Art and therapy circles seriously overlapped. The Hogarth Press, founded by the bohemian writers and thinkers known as Bloomsbury, for example, was the first publisher of Freud in English. Anaïs Nin, famous for her scandalous diaries, was analyzed by Otto Rank. Salvador Dali, for whom eccentricity was a stock in trade, painted the dream sequences reported by the psychiatric patient in Hitchcock's *Spellbound*. And lay analyst Lou Andreas-Salome was the intimate of both philosopher Friedrich Nietzsche and poet

Rainer Maria Rilke. The list goes on. Visual artists like Rene Magritte and Man Ray and modernist authors like James Joyce and William Faulkner purposely tapped into the swirling taboo thoughts and impulses of the unconscious; and architect Richard Neutra, like Freud, blurred the lines between exterior and interior. Intellectual incest reigned. Artists and psychoanalysts were mutually attracted allies in the cultural revolution.

But that was the art/psychoanalytic scene of the first half of the last century. Psychoanalysis has calcified over the years into a theory that, until ten years ago, had been interpreted as sanctioning one, and only one, line of human development—that which leads to the heterosexual marital bed. It no longer smashes the status quo. Even today the theory is less reflective of the once-scandalous thinking of its founders than the conservative sexual politics of its heyday, the "I Like Ike" years. Accordingly, it is now most often understood as presupposing two complementary genders, each of which has an appropriate role and distinctive proclivities, ergo the gender binary and, in poet Adrienne Rich's words, "compulsory heterosexuality." The myopia of this view might not have been so damaging had parochial mid-century psychoanalytic thinking held less sway over the collective imagination. At the time, it powerfully influenced social science, education, child rearing practices, and the law, as well as the psychotherapy business itself and the very formation of psychiatric diagnostic categories. With its enormous prestige, it served to define what was healthy, good, and right, and deviant sexuality did not qualify. Queer inclinations were deemed pathological. In the decades that followed, these ideas hardened. Ironically, what was once a liberating paradigm shift had itself become a repressive one. Today's artists are more likely to take Prozac or do yoga than engage in orthodox psychoanalysis or look to it for inspiration.

Aroused from its moral and conceptual torpor by the women's movement and the sexual revolution, society at large became more sensitive to issues of gender and sexuality in the late sixties, but many psychoanalysts kept their heads stubbornly buried in the sand. Oblivious to the bias in their own backyard, few managed to notice that their gay clients were no sicker than the rest of the population. Or if they did, they did not broadcast their thoughts. For too long psychoanalysts and other psychoanalytically trained therapists maintained a fastidious distance from the second half of the twentieth century. They were well behind the bell curve in dealing sensibly with these issues. It took them twenty years longer to okay homosexuality than even garden variety psychiatrists, who themselves had lagged behind mainstream culture when, in 1973, they finally removed the eighty-one words describing homosexuality from the *Diagnostic and Statistical Manual of Mental Disorders* (DSM), thereby making it normal to be gay. By the early '80s, most research psychologists, following the lead of psychiatry, had purged homophobic bias from their methodology, but the psychoanalytic institutes remained oblivious.[10] During this time, non-heterosexuals were considered untreatable and were denied access to psychoanalytic training. I should add that "gender identity disorder" is still categorized as a pathological condition in the 1994 DSM, continuing the psychiatric habit of masquerading a social judgment as a medical fact. But on a positive note, its inclusion in the DSM does facilitate financial reimbursement by insurance companies for pricey gender reassignment procedures.

It is currently common among analysts to minimize their dark legacy with regard to gender nonconformity or to assign it to a far distant past. Their ideas may have been calamitous to many people, but why dwell on your mistakes? Other analysts, perhaps out of professional courtesy, have muted their criticism. These are difficult times for psychoanalysts. Besieged by managed care and a vogue for quick-fix biological treatments, they are necessarily more preoccupied with self-preservation than in delivering a *mea culpa* or repairing theory at the behest of a stigmatized minority. I suspect their resistance is driven less by homophobia than by being otherwise engaged. But their reluctance to publicly acknowledge the full measure of their past error serves to compound it for those tarnished. It also amounts to self-serving historical revisionism. You merely have to glance at psychoanalytic journals of only a few years ago to find homosexuals described as overly narcissistic, perverted, arrested in their development, and/or incapable of mature love. It is hypocritical of psychoanalysts, the consummate debunkers of self-delusion, to hesitate to grapple with their own closeted skeletons or to proceed in critiquing their ideas so quietly that the world at large is unaware.

To be sure, there is a small groundswell of analysts working to revise theory to accommodate modern sexual reality; committees have formed, a few journals have been created dedicated specifically to sex/gender issues, and works representing different points of view have been added to the canon. But most of the people doing the talking and writing are gay themselves (and/or living in New York or San Francisco), and they are mostly talking to each other.[11] "Lesbigay" analysts counsel each other to keep a low profile. "Queer" issues, they warn, are still political hot potatoes in a number of psychoanalytic circles, some of which are stuck in a time warp. As a result, psychoanalytic theory, despite its enormous potential for understanding human nature, has practically arrested in its usefulness for explaining gender identity and desire.

The gap between theory and reality puts psychoanalytically oriented therapists like me in a no-win situation: to summarily eschew theory would oblige us to wing it, to proceed in performing psychotherapy without a roadmap, to discard much of which we know in our bones to be true. It reduces our method to chaos. But, alternatively, to selectively partake of theory when convenient, to unsystematically pick and choose, and to employ psychology models as we do garden tools such as spades and shears, employing or discarding them based on their usefulness (the *modus operandi* of most seasoned therapists), renders us prone to bias and arrogance. It strikes me as lazy, sloppy, subjective— too dismissive of our potential for finding coherence.

Yet, to do otherwise, to wholly embrace the theory without criticism, would force us to falsely conclude that gender nonconformity is less than optimal, if not outright sick. We are in a conceptual mess. As specialists in human behavior, we are in the unenviable position of being expected to shed light on a subject about which we know very little. Obviously this lack of understanding limits our effectiveness as caretakers. Granted, we probably get closer to an understanding of peoples' experiences of sexual preferences and gender identity than other professionals (if for no other reason than we have the luxury of time to pay scrupulous attention to what clients say). Yet we can no more explain why certain persons are queer (or not) than why they may prefer Indian food over Thai. Many of us are doing a lot more guesswork than we let on. We simply do not yet comprehend the causal chain of events or variables that lead to sexual orientation or gender identity. Neither do neurologists, evolutionists, behavioral psychologists, geneticists, or anyone else in the scientific or social science disciplines. There is a story here that we are all missing.

But there may be a glimmer of hope in a recent intellectual movement that has been taking place in the arts and humanities—postmodern gender theory, known sardonically (and probably to its detriment) as "queer theory." Queer theory is effusive about precisely those subjects in which psychoanalysis is tongue-tied: the modern sexual scene. The fingerprints of these maverick scholars are all over the place these days in fields like philosophy, literature, anthropology, film theory, or cultural studies. In fact, the literature pouring forth from this hybrid young discipline is so voluminous that it practically constitutes its own publishing niche, although its readership tends to be limited to itself. In academic circles, these scholars are known as the "lit-crit" crowd, those aggressively cerebral social and cultural critics who consider all universal explanations, all taken-for-granted truths—such as religion; the progress of civilization; a unified sense of self; all absolute political theories; the legitimacy of categories such as dirt, disability, gender, beauty, and so on—to be corrupted by power politics, and it is their job to root it out, like a chef boning a fish. This process is famously called deconstruction, after which the good postmodernist pokes fun at the exhumed categories in order to expose their coercive nature. So, if the chef were to ironically call attention to the fish bones by, let's say, reassembling them, painting them purple, and mounting them on a stand, the chef would be mischievously suggesting that the fish skeleton no longer overwhelmingly signifies food, but also art—leading to the very postmodern conclusion that there is no such thing as a single meaning for fish bones, or, as postmodern (PoMo) theorists assert, for anything. Meaning is socially constructed and subject to change.[12] Unlike Freudians, postmodernists never consider a cigar just a cigar.

What queer theorists argue, with their tongues resolutely out of their cheeks, is that there is no missing story about gender difference because there is no such thing as gender. They contend that dividing people up into two groups based on the shape of their genitals is but a cultural invention, and a poor one, for it creates a false dichotomy. Such a division is much too crude, linear, tunnel visioned, coercive. The gender binary, according to queer theory, is not writ in the stars, the primordial soup, the collective unconscious, or our genes. It was created by a privileged class, the demographically dominant, those people whose numbers and social status entitled them to define the world according to their own blueprints (in Western culture: straight, white men). Put differently, those in power get to assign meaning. So our particular idea of what constitutes gender is just that: an idea, not an eternal verity. Our predecessors followed a pattern different from our own, and our descendants may hew to one that is no less different.[13]

As absurd as it sounds, queer theory is actually just giving academic credence to something that sex/gender nonconformists have known all along (and the rest of us may have forgotten): that the imagination is promiscuous; the unconscious wants what it wants, uncategorically. Desire cannot be pigeonholed into male and female: it is much too diffuse, wanton, extreme, aggressive, satisfied with nothing less than everything. The psychoanalyst Robert Stoller, who devoted his career to pioneering studies of sexuality, observed that "humans are not a very loving species—especially when they make love." While we might prefer to think that the sexual allure of one person for another is exclusively fueled by the possibility of a tender-hearted merger with the person's opposite half, we have only to log onto the Internet or glance at cable TV to disabuse ourselves of these sanitized notions. What becomes apparent is that sexual excitement may result as much from teasing, illusion, mystery, risk, artifice, challenge, tension, dissonance, transgression (especially, it seems, in France), up and down, here and there, top and bottom as the shape of one's partner's genitals. It is far darker, more contradictory, more of a maelstrom of impulses and passions, of cruelty, ecstasy, and madness than it is billed by polite society. Note that I am talking mostly about sexual excitement, not love. The two may be different and, much to many folk's frustration, may work against each other. Years of listening to peoples' fantasies in the privacy of my own psychotherapy office have convinced me that Stoller was right—the same irrational dynamics, though in different mixes and degrees, are found in almost everyone.[14] Queer theory reminds us of our polymorphous perversity.

But even as queer theory is old news, it is also radically new, because it challenges the very starting point of most scientific and social science inquiry. Try to recall a survey or psychological instrument that doesn't begin: "M or F?" It is nearly impossible, because a request to indicate one's gender is a conventional feature of almost all standardized forms. We seem to be unable to collect information without automatically requiring a rupture between males and females. So it is hardly surprising that when we tabulate data, we tend to find an absolute difference between genders, not a relative one. It's preordained. Without thinking about it, we organize our knowledge around the sex/gender binary. This is precisely what queer theorists are undoing. As part of the "queering" endeavor, scholars are eliminating the distinction between males and females (and gays and straights) as a central organizational principle in all fields—a sexual revolution that, ironically, has been absent in psychoanalytic theory. It is ironic because by interrogating (to borrow their word) preconceived gender categories, postmodernists are using one of the major tools of psychoanalysis—interpretation of that which is encoded. But psychoanalysts, according to queer theorists, did not take interpretation far enough; they stopped short of using their tool on themselves, they failed to interpret some of the deep-seated biases in their own ideological structures. Feminists started doing this to psychoanalytic theory in the '70s when they found sexism at every turn; but from the queer theory perspective, the feminist project was seriously incomplete.

Despite their differences, both queer and psychoanalytic theorists operate in much the same heady universe. Both are attracted to irresolvable ambiguities; both take enormous pleasure in the play of multiple mean-ings; and both are inherently skeptical. You would think that a cross-pollination of ideas would have occurred instinctively. But, pre-posterous as it seems, these groups do not talk to each other. Basically there is no conversation. There is hardly even a debate. Instead, they speak in different languages to entirely different constituencies. Worse, they sometimes use the same language (words like "unconscious," "hysteria," or "phallus") to mean entirely different things, making mutual understanding tricky. As a result, there dwell within the groves of academe two opposing camps: the experimental scientists and psy-choanalytic practitioners (odd bedfellows, but united in this instance) on one side and the queer theorists (mostly humanities and arts profes-sors) on the other, and when they look at one another all they see are cartoons.

Let's think of them as they might think of each other when caught off guard: as regressive sticks-in-the-mud on the one side, or out-of-touch pedants on the other. Each caricature has its turf, divided up, very broadly speaking, according to its position on the origin of so-called sex/gender difference. The scientists and practitioners, the sticks-in-the-mud, whose feet are firmly planted on the ground, take gender categories seriously. They tend to be biological determinists. Males, they argue, are inherently different from females, as are gays from straights. People are born, not made. In former times, this group would have supported the "nature" side of the famous nature/nurture controversy. Today they are dubbed "essentialists" because they believe that gender categories are naturally occurring phenomena with an "essence" that is independent of time and place. In contrast, queer the-orists, the pedants, whose feet are planted in the clouds, assert that gen-der categories are made, not born; that is, they are an effect of culture, not a cause. Gender is an artifice, a delusion, an ideology—a social construction—and those who hold that view are known as "construc-tionists." According to them, gender may look real, but it is actually just a pose, a masquerade. Take away gesture, language, dress, movement, and action and there's no such thing as gender, no pristine category that stands behind society's invention of it. In fact, there is no compel-ling reason why the gender types should be two (correlated to the biological sexes) rather than three, or five, or infinitely many.[15]

Each side comes with baggage. The scientists and practitioners, who deal with actual people, set the research bar considerably higher than the queer theorists, who, as academics in the humanities or the arts, are exempt from the inconvenient claims of reality—such as the need to ameliorate suffering or pay attention to plain matters of fact. They are much more taken with the patina of high-altitude abstractness. Queer theorists delight in playing with ideas and symbols, in dazzling their audience with convoluted logic and clever turns of phrase. They are armchair philosophers, not bean counters. Given the rarified atmosphere in which postmodernists operate, it is no wonder that their theory has turned out to be a bit decadent. Their writing is heavily loaded with self-referential jargon and peculiar neologisms, with allusions to esoteric French philosophers and unfailingly ironic titles (my favorite: *This Sex Which Is Not One*), often further obscured by artfully placed parentheses.[16]

As a result, postmodern theory is mind numbing to the ordinary psychologist and virtually impenetrable to the average mortal. Not surprisingly (and perhaps not undeservedly), it has become the object of a right-leaning, anti-intellectual backlash and a nearly irresistible subject for satire. But mangled language is an all-too-easy target for criticism. Obscurity is an annoyance, not an indictment, and may be an inevitable consequence of dealing with an elusive subject for which there is no precise vocabulary. Besides, the scientists and clinicians of the first group are not exactly user-friendly. They are guilty of their own brand of obscurity. They too have been known to numb the nonexpert with statistics, graphs, unintelligible jargon, and dense case studies.

For all their clotted language and ivory-tower pomposity, queer theorists may be on to something. Their theory has appealing face validity and resonates culturally with our times. Ironically, these pointy-headed intellectuals have been able to capture the mood of the modern, freewheeling sexual scene in ways that the more observation-based and clinical theorists have not. In one conceptual move, the PoMo camp has obviated a problem that has plagued the essentialists for three decades: accounting for the kaleidoscope sexual psyche of the postmodern citizen without pathologizing or criminalizing it. By banishing the sex/gender binary, postmodernists make all romantic permutations possible—everything becomes okay. Bisexuals may unabashedly go both ways; Hedwig needn't be angry; male swishing may be legitimized instead of mocked. There would be no fixed models, no archaic formulas, and no coercive standards that stigmatize some behaviors and valorize others. Hypothetically speaking, a binary-free world would be refreshingly democratic. Indeed, postmodernism makes a compelling political argument.

Of course, political correctness is not a justification for embracing a theory. As we shall see, the explanatory power of "pure" postmodern theory is limited. It cannot supply a causal chain of factors that accounts for peoples' sexual orientations or gender identities. It cannot get into any one person's head. The clinical value of a postmodern "take" is, in and of itself, nearly nil. But, it does jolt us out of our inadequate knee-jerk explanations for what is going on. Postmodern theory presents therapists and scientists with a new set of hypotheses, an opportunity for a "dialectical moment." Why not throw caution to the wind and seize the moment? Why not ponder the existence of the gender binary as one would a Zen koan, with the goal of blowing ourselves out of our narrow conceptual grooves?

By weakening the binary's hold on our rote thinking, we inextricably force ourselves to shift our conception of human desire and its objects. This shift may enable us to overcome our theoretical impasse and forge new ground. It may allow us to discern some predictive factors of queerness (or dampen our desire to predict; hypothetically speaking, all sexual orientation and gender identity outcomes would be equally valued). We finally might be able to understand *why*—instead of just noting *that*—ours is an age of fluid boundaries. At the very least, we will be able to construct a theory that is more inclusive and that revokes some painful inequities. But first there needs to be a dialogue across disciplines. I hope to facilitate that conversation—to translate partisan points of view to opposing partisans. My goal is to perform a cross-disciplinary debriefing, to sort things out, to arbitrate among the contradictions so that we may learn from each other and from our mistakes.

That, baldly, is what I plan to do. I am aware at the outset that sexuality is an inherently fuzzy subject that is probably irreducible to theorems. But by engaging myself in this endeavor, I aim to provide a clearer picture of a very fuzzy subject.

You could say that I came by my ideas honestly in that they derived from my clinical practice, not from personal erotic inclinations. This disclosure may discredit my comments in some circles, but hopefully serves to convey that I have no particular ax to grind. As I performed psychotherapy over the years, I discovered that the dreams and ruminations of my patients stubbornly refused to conform to traditional concepts of gender. No matter how I stretched my patients' stories, I could not make them fit neatly into the Procrustean bed of a binary. The more I listened, the more contradictions I found—the more I began to question the assumption that a certain set of desires and behaviors are always associated with a certain set of body parts. Most of the time, of course, my patients' gonads and proclivities were synchronized in the usual manner. To be sure, my typical patient with a penis was just that—typical. He felt he was male, had male chromosomes, male hormones, preferred a female as a sexual partner, and was reluctant to express wimpy emotions in public; and my typical patient with a vagina felt she was female, and so on. But for a number of individuals these attributes did not link up in the expected way. This variability occurred too often to be considered trivial or dismissed as a descriptor of an insignificant lunatic fringe. It is the predicament of many real people. Here are a few recent vignettes from my practice and cultural snooping that triggered my thinking.

> Liz came to me wondering whether she was really a lesbian, or even a bisexual. It wasn't the sex—she enjoyed sex with women— it was the aesthetic. Liz was a 23-year-old hairdresser in an upscale salon who realized three years ago that she was in love with her best girlfriend from childhood. They had been living together romantically (and amicably) for over a year when Liz came to see me. Both young women had enjoyed previous sexual relationships with a few males and females but felt that their relationship with each other transcended that of previous lovers, and they wished to make it permanent and monogamous. Since both came from the same small town in New Hampshire, which is far removed from any homosexual scene, they had been unaware of lesbian cultural norms and politics. Now that they were living in an urban center, they were beginning to explore the implications of their sexual orientation and wish to commit to each other. It was the fallout from this exploration that had prompted Liz to visit me. She could not "relate" at all to the Doc Martens, pinkie rings, large bodies, and cropped hair of the women she met in the gay community. Liz reported that she did not wish to look like these women, nor was she "attracted" to them. (This was also true of her girlfriend.) She preferred "cute" women and even "cute" guys to butch women. Did that mean she wasn't truly gay? Would she wake up one day and discover that she was no longer "turned on" by her girlfriend and had become straight?

Liz's seemingly simple question—one commonly heard by therapists these days—opens up a Pandora's box of confusion. For a start, it assumes that there is a bright line between lesbians (or bisexuals) and heterosexual women and that, among other things, the erotic contemplation of women by women differs from that of women by men. According to conventional wisdom (which Liz shared), when she chose her intimate partner, she should somehow have absorbed lesbian social norms—baseball skills, for example, and an affinity for certain hair removal patterns, underarm deodorant, and manner of sartorial display. Yet, Liz wanted to look like a Barbie doll—with which, by the way, she played as a child—and not G.I. Joe. She did not fit neatly into any unambiguous and predefined category. She experienced herself to be somewhat "off." But what if it is our labeling system that is "off," and not Liz? Perhaps it is possible to develop a more precise classification system that could accommodate Liz. Perhaps we could create better nomenclature. But wouldn't that be an infinitely regressive process? Wouldn't we be forced to construct more and more categories, more and more surgically refined? Where, for example, would we put the putatively straight woman who is exclusively attracted to gay men? Or the queer man who never had sex? Ultimately, all people are individuals, each of whom would require his or her own category...in which case, a truly accurate classification system would be *reductio ad absurdum.* It is tempting, then, to invoke the postmodern imperative—to abolish all categories. But wouldn't that seriously disturb our understanding of the world? If we cannot split people up according to sexual orientation, for example, how can we go about setting up our sexual liaisons? Why, if groups are not truly differentiated entities, do sex/gender attributes insistently cluster—such as urination positions or body piercing or gym bodies? And why, if there are no distinct categories, do groups of people seemingly deliberately parody each other—such as girly boys who ape frilly girls and butch dykes who ape macho men—instead of adopting random group stereotypes? The so-called genders need each other to butt up against in order to define themselves. But wouldn't that suggest that there are distinct groups and bright dividing lines after all? We have come full circle.

Of course, Liz had not come to therapy to discuss the philosophy of labeling but rather her own personal labeling issues. A managed care provider's dream, she was not inclined toward deep exploration. She reported feeling much relief after only a few sessions, during which I reassured her that she could be herself and pointed out that conventional heterosexuality was no guarantee of sustained sexual attraction to one's mate either. Happily, she had a sense of humor and managed to construct a comfortable category for herself that seemed to resolve her affiliation wishes, at least for now. The term she coined—"lipstick bi"—combines the pop lingo phrase "lipstick lesbian" (lesbians who display "feminine" codes of dress and manner) with the abbreviation for bisexual.

Ivan, a long-term patient, also had a playful sense of humor, but one tinged with mischievous irony, mock naivete, and melodramatic complaints about social anxiety, mood swings, various physical maladies (such as backaches and tiredness), and existential despair. Picture a brooding Raskolnikov crossed with Woody

Allen. Ivan, like Liz, had sexual orientation issues. Was he gay, bisexual, or straight? He was attracted to both men and women but had no sexual experience with the former and little experience with the latter ("only" three women). When Ivan was young, his schoolmates considered him girlish and he recalls feeling closer to his nurturing, he-man father than his cold, hypochondriac mother, who dominated the small household of three. He embarrassingly told me that once when little Ivan had been bouncing on his father's lap he had had an erection. He also recalled feeling terrified when he was unwillingly fondled by a tram driver and wondering why the conductor chose him. Did he give out a feminine aura? As a preadolescent he worried that he might fall into the "black hole" of being gay.

But sexual orientation was only one source of identity confusion. Having immigrated to this country from Eastern Europe at the age of 18, he wondered at age 27 (when he began twice-weekly treatment) if he was American enough. Did he dress right? Should he cut his hair and/or color it? (He experimented with both.) A voracious reader, Ivan longed to be a sophisticated intellectual but feared that he was really just a boy who loved fart jokes and *Star Trek*. Maybe he was an imposter, a poseur who carried around highbrow books for effect. He wondered whether he should become a bourgeois capitalist like his parents' friends, or a Marxist-leaning feminist like his American fiancée, a Wiccan nine years his senior who had been his college instructor in psychology. Was he, in his heart, more of a computer technician, a professional librarian, a rock musician, a novelist, a folk singer, a cellist, or, god forbid, a boring nerd? Born Jewish but hardly aware of it, Ivan regularly tried out religious convictions and dabbled in mysticism, the teachings of the Gnostic Jesus and Merlin, Hinduism, paganism, yoga, the Buddha, and crystal balls. An irrepressible seeker, he even made bids for "truth" from me. But, notably, when he talked about his interest in magic and the otherworldly, he did so with a wink and a great deal of puppy-dog charm, playing, I think, to his audience—me, his earthbound, skeptical therapist.

Ivan claimed that these days his attraction to men did not bother him in and of itself—he liked the idea of being an erotic nonconformist—but insofar as it might interfere with sexually satisfying his fiancée, a prospect he found daunting. She was far more sexually experienced than Ivan (with both men and women), explicit about her sources of pleasure, and candid about his performance. He was surprised and dismayed to discover that her libido did not equal his, at least with regard to frequency. They did have pleasurable, orgasmic encounters, but in the back of Ivan's mind was a nagging worry that he was not as "good" as her previous partners.

A year into treatment, Ivan married his fiancée in a Wiccan ceremony during which they donned medieval garb. By then he was happily employed at a prestigious academic library managing its computer system. He talked to me of flirting lightly and chastely with a few gay male colleagues and his older female supervisor, but these interactions did not dominate his fantasies and, far from harming him, served to ingratiate him with the library staff. Subsequently he obtained a master's degree in library science, a promotion at work, and started singing in his wife's Renaissance folk band and taking lessons on the cello, an instrument he had studied as a child. Regarding marital life—he was generally quite content, suffering nothing more than the routine grievances of early marriage, like division of labor disputes and money allocation. They "processed" their relationship a great deal; that is, they engaged in many soulful discussions about it, which mostly worked in its favor.

After a year of marriage Ivan animatedly reported a rapturous sexual encounter with his wife—the best ever. He had placed his ear on her vagina, between her legs, and she did the thrusting. He was very aroused. He recalled feeling that he was both a man and a woman because his ear is both convex and concave. He reported thinking that if a male were in bed with them, he could insert his erection into a male, or, alternatively, come all over the pillow and make a big mess (but not mess his wife). In fact, he did "mess" his wife, in that he ended up having intercourse with her in the ordinary missionary position, which he enjoyed very much.

What struck me about this encounter, apart from its mechanical versatility, was its "genderlessness." Or, perhaps we might more accurately characterize the encounter as "omni-gendered," which seemed to describe Ivan himself. Who or what was male or female here, or homosexual or heterosexual? Even the sexual valence of Ivan's ear was fluid—first male, then female. If one's ear may be variously assigned a gender, may one's other body parts? Must a vagina, then, always signal female, and a penis, male? This thought is not so crazy when one considers transgendered individuals, persons with ambiguous genitalia, persons with cognitive impairment, blind people raised in homes where they do not encounter the genitals of another, and, arguably, the very young. To continue this line of reasoning: If Ivan felt for an instant that he was a she, does it make the sex act Ivan was performing at that instant a lesbian one? Recall the infamous moment in the 1992 film *The Crying Game*, when the camera lowered its gaze to the naked crotch of glamorous Dill, only to reveal a penis. Heretofore the audience and the protagonist himself had thought he was making love to an anatomical woman. Must we now categorize the interaction as gay? In other words, does a sexual act have a fixed sexual orientation? Can we separate the dancer from the dance? Is it true, as we once thought, that insertion and aggression are male, and passivity, receptivity, and masochism are female? Who are we *really* when we make love? Should sexual conduct be defined by measurable, observable behavior or by what is going on in the participants' heads (in which case we are all probably adulterers at some point)? What if the participants' views of what is going on are different? This brings us back to the celebrated question posed by the notorious Cinton/Lewinsky episode—is oral sex "sex"? What are sexual relations, after all?

Early on in treatment, it seemed to me that Ivan might be more distressed by the androgynous aspects of his personality than he admitted. He had been brought up in a famously macho country and felt closer to his once-athletic father than his difficult mother. But his identification with his father was problematic: While Ivan envied his father's manliness, he also disrespected him for caving in to his mom. I suspected that some of Ivan's boyish "innocence" and charm were defensive compromises that served to ward off self-inquiry, circumvent his anxiety about identifying with his parents, and win favorable attention. Eventually he believed this to be true. Over the course of therapy Ivan became less histrionic, less moody, more willing to take on adult responsibility. He comfortably solidified his playful, multifarious identity, although, importantly, it remained playful and multifarious. We were able to trace some of his sex/gender identity fluidity back to life events—his mother's manipulation, his father's submission to her, his early effeminacy, his cultural uprooting, his conflation of semen with messiness, and so forth—but it ceased to be a problem when, along with increasing insight, he found a like-minded partner and he joined a community in which bookish men were the norm. More problematic were his dependency wishes and insecurity, issues that seemed to have lives of their own quite apart from sex/gender anxiety. Perhaps it is naive to suppose that Ivan's sexual orientation and gender practices might never have been conflicts to him at all if his culture of origin had been more permissive, but it is reasonable to speculate that they may have held less sway. At this writing, Ivan seems happy being in between. He is contemplating fatherhood. His cheerful, wholesome gender leakage suggests that the death knell of categorical imperatives may some day toll for us all, perhaps not as individuals, but as a culture.

Chris, a large, hulking individual with the broad shoulders of a football player, is visually alarming and knows it. Chris hunches over and seems to hide behind his/her long, brown stringy hair, baggy shirts and pants, and large glasses. His/her voice is deep but soft, his/her demeanor oddly recessive given his/her great height. I use the pronoun "his/her" intentionally because that is Chris's preference. Chris is an intersexual—an individual who was born with ambiguous genitalia, one of the many congenital abnormalities that blur male and female characteristics. Lumped together, these conditions occur in about 1 in every 2,000 births.[17] In Chris's case, the abnormality was a micropenis (sometimes called an enlarged clitoris, depending on your perspective). Like most children born with ambiguous external genitalia in the past forty years, Chris was subjected to surgery to "correct" them during infancy. And like most such babies, Chris was given a preliminary vagina because, as some pediatric surgeons' joke: "It's easier to dig a hole than to build a pole." Chris was raised as a girl and not told of the surgery in accordance with the medical advice at the time, which assumed gender identity to be pliable. That was in the late 1960s, but largely holds true today.

Although not a patient of mine, Chris was eager to talk with me in service of my research. Chris's misery and bitterness were palpable. He/she was enraged at the medical profession for "mutilating" him/her and for compounding that affront by failing to disclose the fact. In a nutshell, Chris never was and never became a "normal" girl. Despite being reared as a girl and undergoing additional surgeries and hormonal treatment, despite a heroic effort to be "cute," Chris never felt female. It was not until Chris's teens that Chris discovered his/her hermaphroditic history, which was finally revealed to Chris by his/her repentant mother. At that point, Chris ceased all treatment. Chris was left with feminine breasts, an attraction to women, an incomplete vagina, a lot of scar tissue, many infections, and an inability to have orgasm—and later on, masculine musculature and an abundance of body hair. Throughout his/her life, Chris felt the cosmic aloneness of being a freak. He/she attempted suicide once during adolescence, is phobic of doctors and hospitals, and distrustful of others. Now in his/her mid-thirties, Chris is still sexually attracted to females but despairs of finding a life partner. Nevertheless, Chris has achieved professional success as a scientist and assures me that he/she finds meaning and connection in nature and wildlife and in telling his/her story to convey to the world that intersexuals are real people.

At first glance, Chris's unhappy predicament would seem to affirm a gender binary—that there are two genders and that Chris was inadvertently assigned the wrong one; hence, Chris was miserable. If there were no gender categories or the categories were truly blurred, as queer theorists claim, then Chris's gender assignment would have been irrelevant. Any so-called gender would have done. Being retrofitted with a preliminary vagina should not have mattered to Chris. But, in fact, it did matter. While Chris did not feel quite male, he/she very definitely felt not female. His/her proto-vagina and enlarged breasts felt alien. Presumably, if the surgeons had constructed a penis Chris might have felt more normally male, albeit a cosmetically enhanced male.

But would creating a penis for Chris be enough to manufacture a male identity? Common sense dictates that Chris would also have to be raised as a boy (even though being raised as a girl did not produce the desired effect). Then, too, he/she would have to take hormones. But when would medical intervention stop? At what point would he/she feel male? What are the necessary and sufficient conditions for gender identity? Is it in our chromosomes, central nervous system, gonads, endocrinology, locker-room appearance, psychic reality—all, some, or none of the above? Chris's abnormality makes us question normality, which, if we are honest, renders us tongue-tied. We simply do not know. And if we cannot define normal gender, how can we presume that there are discrete genders, or that there are two?

So, on deeper reflection Chris's situation may not really confirm a "two-party" sex/gender system after all. Chris's body, both before and after surgery, was disconnected from his/her gender identity. Intersexuals like Chris, as well as transgendered individuals, suggest that genitals do not mean gender. Hermaphrodites and other intersexed people are embodiments of the idea that sex and gender identities reside more in your head than in your ancillary cavities and protrusions. In a sense, they are at the forefront of gender evolution. But let us not sugarcoat their predicament. Intersexuals are not joyous proponents of multiple erotic possibilities. Relentlessly stigmatized by his/her peers, Chris, for example, was palpably wretched and lonely, as are many persons with gender variations, which is why they resort to surgical alteration. Certainly most parents of infants born with ambiguous genitalia presume future difficulty for their children and actively seek surgical reconstruction as soon as possible. Interestingly, this has become ethically dubious, as we have come to realize that Chris's troubled outcome is not unusual. It is turning out that a number of these infants, as they mature, are greatly displeased with their sexual assignment—which is not to say that they should never undergo sexual reassignment. But surely they should have been given the right to decide for themselves about their own bodies.

A person with gender deviance may sensibly decide that it is worth enduring repeated surgical trauma in order to become "at one" with his/her body. Their very existence flies into the teeth of nearly everything the dominant culture dictates and they invariably produce great discomfort in others, which may account for their long-standing treatment as circus anomalies and sex workers. Understandably, many intersexuals may wish to embrace the gender binary and leave social pioneering to someone else, especially as they did not elect to be deviant or participate in a social experiment in the first place. From their perspective, the conventional might look pretty good. But it is important to realize that much of their shame and sorrow may be socially induced. It is the toll inflicted by society's insistence on a rigid sex/gender binary and the lack of a permitted category. Just as many persons with disability refuse the definition of themselves as handicapped, and instead regard society as handicapping, intersexuals might resist society's view of themselves as defective. Indeed, some intersexuals are organizing to promote an "intersexual identity" in support of those among them who choose not to undergo surgical "correction." In effect, they are bidding for respectability, for the legitimization of a label that would allow them to be themselves in their manifold incarnations. This is an idea shared by various anthropologists, biologists, philosophers, and psychologists. I will revisit these themes later. Here, I just wish to show how intersexuality creates another "category crisis," to borrow a postmodern term that conveys the panic that is sometimes induced by blurry boundaries.

The borders between the genders are porous these days; yet many heterosexual psychotherapists of a certain age have so internalized the old dichotomy that we don't get it. We want to be permissive, yet we retreat into denial. (If the unconscious were a politically correct place, it would not have to be unconscious.) The result is a landscape characterized by superficiality and double-think: Like the observers of the emperor with no clothes, we are bewildered by what we see and have adopted an uneasy passivity.

To do otherwise, to aggressively pursue a more sophisticated understanding, to embrace the radical possibility that the genders are not discrete and that our sexual orientation might be more fluid than fixed, is deeply worrying. It would seem to lead us down a slippery slope. It threatens to undermine the very foundation of our social structure, of monogamy, intimacy, family. Such ideas also play havoc with some of our most sacred tenets of psychoanalytic thinking—the conflation of gender stability with mental health, a core sense of self.

But today the ideals of wholeness, fixedness, and unity have largely been retired. Talk about fragmentation of culture and consciousness is commonplace. We all know about the vigorous intermixing of black culture and white, high culture and low, humans and robots, early Madonna and late, Eastern cuisine and Western (aka fusion), TV drama and comedy ("dramedy"), and so on, all resulting in wholes that may be greater than the sums of their parts. Think of the renowned beauty of actress Halle Barry. Cultural multiplicity is no longer seen only as a problem, but as a solution—a solution to the confines of identity. Multiple consciousness, once a disorder, may now be a cure. This, in my view, applies to sexual orientation and gender identity.

Let us upgrade our psychological theories to catch up with the obvious. A theory that is prima facie out of touch with reality is hardly useful. Besides, denial is a brittle defense, highly prone to disintegration. And it renders us oblivious to new sources of knowledge that could, ironically, undo some of our massive anxiety. Let us review new sources of knowledge, particularly the stubbornly opaque ideas that derive from queer theory. By re-visioning postmodern theory through the more accessible lens of a discipline that engages with actual people, as opposed to one that merely deconstructs texts, I suspect that we will be better able to explain why gender categories are withering, why now, and what it all means.

2

POSTMODERNISM FOR THOSE WHO MISSED IT

Postmodernism is the theory everyone loves to hate. Pointing to its virtues is a little like championing Roquefort cheese. Both are acquired tastes and both tend to expose you to accusations of being a cultural snob. Neither is easily accessible to the uninitiated, which, at least with regard to the theory, includes most psychotherapists. But if we are to unravel the mystery of gender identity and amorous inclinations—popularly crazy-glued together and known, of course, as "sex"†—we might do well to unravel some of the intricacies of postmodernism. For sex and postmodern theory, in my view, have a much stronger family resemblance than sex and reason, the usual mechanism for understanding what is going on in the world. Erotic desire can hardly be accused of conforming to something as orderly as, say, the laws of algebra. Sex is absurd; but then, so is postmodernism.

Here are some ways they resonate. Both straddle the line between rationality and chaos. (The Marquis de Sade once noted that "some swollen little vessels can instantly send someone out of his wits.")[1] Each is fluid, frustratingly disobedient, mentally kaleidoscopic, and morally oblivious. Preposterous as it seems, both are simultaneously deep and shallow; that is, they are heavily layered with meaning yet ignited by surfaces. In the case of sex, the trigger for the process might be a peek

---

†For convenience, and only in this chapter, I use the word "sex" in the colloquial sense, collapsing identity, anatomy, and nature of erotic preference and/or behavior into each other...although they are discrete characteristics.

of hidden flesh; in the case of postmodern theory, it might be a double entendre, like the name "Hole" for a feisty bad-girl band. Once stirred, there is, for both, a propulsive ripple effect. Postmodernism might be considered the cognitive equivalent of sex (except that actual sex sometimes culminates in orgasm, while postmodernism seems to have arrested in endless foreplay). But the most significant parallel is that they defy logic in similar nonrandom ways: they are associative, allusive, fluid, and fickle rather than linear, precise, predictable, and fixed.

So it turns out that sex and postmodernism may be better analogues to each other than either is to common sense. No wonder our long-standing attempt to understand sexuality via rationalism or empiricism was doomed to failure. Who can explain passion exclusively in terms of deduction or induction? What about emotion, memory, poetry, our gonads? Freud, of course, recognized the futility of this endeavor and inserted a primary process mode of thinking—symbolism, displacement, and condensation—into his paradigm. But he limited its operation. He did not take it far enough to explain erotic desire. Freud's genius was to create a box; unfortunately, it was a box outside of which later analysts tend not to think. Or, more accurately, later analysts focused on only a part of the box, the part that emphasized the importance of the body on sexuality. Perhaps a tincture of postmodern analysis may help us break through the container.

POSTMODERNISM, BROADLY CONCEIVED

But we are getting ahead of ourselves. First we have to figure out what postmodernism is before we can use it to help explain sexual orientation and gender identity; to do that, we must confront the rampant PoMo phobia that exists everywhere except, perhaps, among postmodernists themselves. But fear not. You don't have to be a rocket scientist to understand postmodernism. Indeed, it helps if you're not, because scientists are notorious believers in facts, and postmodernists question that very thing—the validity of facts, the implication that the world is knowable. As a result, they tend to delight in things that play with facts (dubbed "simulacra" by theorist Jean Baudrillard)—reproductions, parodies, faux icons, simulations, especially copies of things that brazenly call attention to themselves as fakes—like the infamous hotel casinos of Las Vegas.[2]

These soaring colossi, triumphs of visual hucksterism, exemplify the postmodern sensibility and are a good way to introduce the topic. Situated loosely in an area known as the Strip, each hotel tries to outdo the other in knocking us out with a gaudy, neon-lit caricature of a real or imagined place like Monte Carlo or New York. Ironically, the impact of these outrageously saccharine replicas may stunt that of the actual locations, in much the same way that silicon-enhanced breasts induce a thrill. (Later I discuss a patient who was obsessed with women's augmented breasts as well as with exhibiting his penis, which was also prosthetic.) Simulacra are not unreal, according to PoMo theorists. Rather, they replace reality. They are more than real: the illusion trumps the reality. We've been so brainwashed by media images that the firsthand experience of actual things feels trivial.[3]

Epitomizing this dynamic, the Venetian Hotel recently incorporated into its midst a branch of the Guggenheim Museum, containing, of course, bonafide highbrow art. Perhaps the hotel was attempting to upgrade its campy image. Whatever the owners' intent, they certainly succeeded in amplifying the hotel's postmodern quotient because most visitors consider the real art in the museum to be no artier than the kitsch building in which the museum is housed. This juxtaposition of "good" and "bad" art produces an exquisitely PoMo circumstance; it calls into question the definition of art. Complicating the matter is the fact that much of the art on display is itself postmodern; that is, the art's goal is more cultural critique than aesthetic, and it frequently draws inspiration from ordinary, mechanically reproducible commodities. The museum's debut exhibition, for example, consisted of a display of motorcycles. But if a motorcycle is art, why isn't the Venetian Hotel? If you can't tell the difference between true art and schlock, or prefer the schlock, why does it matter? When you strip away the definitions we've inherited for art, what's left? All this suggests that our belief in the intrinsic value of "real" places and "original" art is mere sentimentality, or, as postmodern theorists imply, emotional bric-a-brac. True to the spirit of postmodernism, this section is a work of inspired imitation, as I borrow from others' outlines of postmodernism, though the material is filtered through my own clinical sensibility.[4]

By now you are realizing that you can't get a fix on postmodernism—that one of its major themes is that there is no fix. Truth can't be pinned down. Reality just isn't out there. We continually make it up; that is, we organize "reality" into arbitrary categories according to our own unconscious blueprints, which is how we give it meaning. So, for example, we designate one plant a weed and another a flower; or, we assume that the Eiffel Tower in Paris is "better" than its knock-off in Las Vegas; or we define a human with a convex genital as male and one without as female. But is all this classifying and ranking legitimate? Is the convexity of a genital truly a powerful distinguishing feature of personality, more so than, say, a preference for poodles over pit bulls?

Might not one person's weed be another person's flower? Unfortunately, our blueprints are contaminated by our contexts—such as our social status, IQ, moment in history, personal experience, and/or the limitations of language. How can we know something, or communicate it to another, if there are no mutually understandable words to say it or grammar in which to conceive it?

To confuse matters further, postmodernists are victims of their own theory. Not only is there no consensus about what constitutes reality, there is also no consensus about what constitutes postmodernism. The term is so bandied about that it has devolved into a cliché. Serious culture critics apply it mostly to ideas or things that are ironic and self-referential and/or deliberately splice genres or pilfer styles from various historical periods, especially if the ideas or things are wacky or over the top. These constructions usually involve pastiche or parody and are knowingly in bad taste. But few people can say with assurance what they actually mean when they call something "postmodern." Some media pundits arbitrarily assign the term to anything in bad taste, whether it is knowingly tasteless or not. No wonder postmodernism raises eyebrows outside its niche in the ivory tower—it is maddeningly inexact.

POSTMODERNISM, PRECISELY CONCEIVED

But along with its incarnation as a buzzword, postmodernism was concurrently assigned a somewhat more precise meaning in the realm of philosophy in late twentieth-century France, where it referred, unsurprisingly, to an intellectual movement that is "post" the cultural perspective known as modernism. That is, it grew out of, and responds to, modernism, about which it is mostly (but not completely) skeptical. So it questions Reason, Science, Truth, and the steady march of Progress—all those Enlightenment articles of faith that underscore modernism. These sacred tenets understandably lost their luster after the horrors of World Wars I and II, the bomb, the Kafkaesque nightmare of "rationally" administered death camps, human-made ecological disasters, and the persistence of rampant injustice despite our best efforts at social engineering—events that hardly could be construed as Progress. Add to this the recent failure of modern hi-tech to prevent low-tech terrorism (which, in fact, may have been provoked by hi-tech's hubris) and you can understand an intellectual backlash. This is not to say that postmodernists returned to embracing magic or superstition, but that they seriously question top-down, unifying explanations of how the world works, like the Marxist certainty that the working class will revolt; the connoisseur's certainty about the importance of an actual, flesh-and-blood, artist's hand in the production of art; or the Freudian certainty about the occurrence of an Oedipal complex.

Put differently, postmodernists are radically uncertain. They democratically skewer all the big certainties (which Jean-Francois Lyotard famously calls "metanarratives").[5] These include those certainties mentioned above, but also such old saws as the belief in the virtue of Christian salvation, or Manifest Destiny, or the presumption that only valuable objects deserve to be exhibited in museums, or the idea that there are but two genders, or that our sense of self is coherent and stable, or, indeed, all the overriding principles that claim to explain our universe. Far from thinking that history follows an inevitable progressive trajectory, postmodernists argue that history follows no overall pattern. To illustrate their point writ small, consider something as quotidian as fashion, which, with the benefit of a second look, is never just about itself. It turns out that in the late '90s, wealthy Japanese youths took their fashion cues from American inner-city black kids; that is, "homeboys." But according to modernist verities, this shouldn't have happened. The commodities of the elite are supposed to be fetishized, not the commodities of the poor. Yet, affluent Japanese teenagers, to their parents' chagrin, insistently paraded around the streets of Tokyo with artificially darkened skin, frizzed hair, carefully torn apparel, and branded footwear, as if they were members of a stigmatized American underclass. The irony did not stop there. Apparently the fashion trends of these young Japanese were scoped out by paid scouts, who communicated their findings to Euro-American couturiers, who then incorporated them into their designs for rich Western adults. So we not only had the bourgeoisie studiously aping the so-called unwashed masses, we had grown-ups imitating children, and haute couture copying *pret-a-porter*. Marx, Freud, and Christian Dior must have turned over in their graves. Their views no longer seem to apply. Perhaps no metanarrative of whatever kind can ever apply to a world that has become as hopelessly fractured and heterogeneous as our own. Accordingly, postmodernists argue that one overarching cultural certainty may be as good as any other. Down with all "isms"! There is no Big Picture.

The scent of French theory wafted onto American shores in the late '70s and permeated just about everything in the humanities, arts, and culture. In the studio art and music world, it was midwife to the aforementioned hodgepodge style that radically blurs the distinction between high and low culture; hence, the motorcycle exhibit in an art museum and other crossover phenomena such as "sampling" in music, fusion food, and scholarly reviews of graphic novels (formerly known as comic books). Cultural relativism reigned. Consider the recent play on

Broadway by Edward Albee, *The Goat or Who Is Sylvia?* In it, Martin, the financially successful, married, middle-aged protagonist, falls in love with a goat (a goat!)—not your standard infidelity. Ordinarily you would expect the audience to be repelled by Martin's bestiality, but, interestingly, Martin elicits sympathy from the audience. The play was not a farce: Martin was truly enthralled with the goat and had purportedly engaged in actual sex with her. I suspect that Albee, in what only could be described as a postmodern state of mind, crafted his play to suggest that love, regardless of its manner of expression, is a matter of soul rather than the mechanics of a body, that objects of desire might be as fluid as our categories for good and bad art. Desire, Albee implies, is culturally determined.

In academia, postmodernism morphed into cultural studies with such controversial areas of specialization as the media, postcolonialism, race studies (originally black studies), and gender studies (an expansion of women's studies). The latter gave birth to queer theory, which in turn infiltrated the political arena and begot various activist organizations promoting the acceptance of sexual nonconformists, such as Queer Nation and ACT-UP, the AIDS Coalition to Unleash Power. In technology, postmodernism gave us cyborgs (hybrids of men/women and machines) and cyberspace, which soon begot cyberpunks and cybersex, spawning a profusion of new sexual "perversions" (and an enhanced income stream for psychotherapists).

The scent of postmodernism even managed to drift into the privileged domain of pure science, once enshrined as the exclusive way to Truth. To be sure, its influence was felt not so much on scientific practice—understandably most people want their bridges built (and Prozac prescribed) by people who take objective facts very seriously—but on the social studies of science, where it wisely suggested that scientific knowledge is culturally constructed, not discovered. Much of scientific knowledge depends on who's asking the questions, what questions are asked, the way they are asked, and who benefits from the answers.

POSTSTRUCTURALISM††

The postmodernist thinking that was absorbed into ordinary, standard-issue American academic departments, such as philosophy and

---

†† The term "poststructuralism" is sometimes used as a synonym for the broader term "postmodernism," but, strictly speaking, refers to a specific branch of postmodernism—postmodern linguistic theory. Poststructuralism evolved from "structuralism." Interestingly, the term is rarely used in France, its putative place of origin.

French, had by then taken a linguistic turn evolving into an arcane, subversive way of critiquing ideas, texts, and images, the previously described "deconstruction." Deconstructors—people who engage in deconstruction—are "poststructuralists," and, like their forbears, the "structuralists" from whom they derive their name, they excavate the camouflaged structures and tacit rules that slyly govern all language and all social phenomena—such as kinship systems, the intrinsic characteristics of all myths, and codes in advertising. These structures determine how we interpret things. But, according to deconstructors, they are ideologically contaminated and must be exposed in order to grasp how we are being manipulated. For example, the subliminal coercers used in advertising—e.g., coloring a product green to imply that it is "natural"—may cause us to desire things that we might not ordinarily want, like astroturf or toothpaste or color-enhanced (but tasteless) vegetables. With such hidden persuaders we might be coaxed into prizing certain dungarees over others, a shirt with a Prada label, a clunky SUV, or, even, as Albee suggests, a goat.

But unlike structuralists, poststructuralists believe that deconstruction is an exercise in futility. Ironically, this does not prevent them from endlessly engaging in the endeavor—which is precisely what makes them postmodern. According to poststructuralists, you can't freeze-frame meaning. The structures that underlie words and social phenomena perpetually break down and collapse into each other. Words are unable to stop evolving, revolving, resolving, and dissolving into other terms and concepts. "Green," for example, may connote nature in one instance and sickness or decay in another. Meanings are slippery. Interpretation can never be definitive. Recall the fish carcass (Chapter 1). The bones may signify a dead fish, but they also may signify art, or whatever. There is no final signification for fish bones.

Structualism, poststructuralism, deconstruction—I can see readers' eyes roll as I write this. Of all the manifestations of postmodernism, poststructuralism is probably the most off-putting. With its arcane notations (called algorithms) derived from linguistic theory (or semiotic theory, as it is called in England and the United States), it looks like hieroglyphics on the page. It positively reeks of abstruseness. Furthermore, the theory may seem like an excessively convoluted way to state the obvious—that meaning is contrived and subject to enormous variation. But poststructuralism does more than tell us what we may already suspect; it gives us an organized decoding system for exposing and picturing what we suspect. It provides a methodology for teasing out the algebra inside language. That algebra, when diagrammed, tracks the meandering trail of the meaning of words.

Specifically, poststructuralism (like its precursor structuralism) asserts that the link between a spoken or written word, such as "dog" (aka "the signifier"), and its concept, the mental picture of a four-legged animal (aka "the signified"), is arbitrary. There is not much about the sound of the word "dog" that connects it to "dogness." We could just as well call the concept a "*chien*" as the French do, a word equally disconnected from dogness. Hypothetically, we could assign the beast any name at all—with one big exception. We could not call a dog something that belongs in a mutually exclusive category—like "cat." In Western culture, ideas or things in mutually exclusive categories must bear mutually exclusive names. We define a dog as a dog and assign it a signifier (just as we do with all ideas and things) by its relation to the whole system of which it is a part; in this case, animal, or, more specifically, domesticated quadrupeds. Although both dogs and cats are domesticated quadrupeds, they are characterized by certain qualities that differentiate them from each other (and other domesticated quadrupeds), such as, for argument's sake, their vocalization: dogs bark; cats and other four-legged creatures do not. Barking is, hypothetically speaking, the distinguishing characteristic of dogs. It is difference—a quality that discriminates among things or ideas (here, barking)—that determines discrete categories, to which discrete words are assigned (here, dog). A category, hence a word, is what it is only because it differs from other categories, or words. So language is made up of a vast system of conventionally agreed-upon differences; and the meaning of words derive from their relationship to other words, not from any factors outside the system.

Thus far in this capsule explanation, poststructuralists and structuralists are in synch. Where they diverge concerns the link between the spoken word and a mental picture, that is, the connection between the signifier and signified. Both agree that the link is just a matter of convention, but they disagree about its sturdiness. Structuralists believe that the link is strong. According to them, the signifier and the signified are like two sides of the same coin. Poststructuralists, on the other hand, argue that the link perpetually breaks. Words (that is, signifiers) are promiscuous. They do not stick to concepts, but slide around freely.

Besides, poststructuralists argue, our mental pictures (our signifieds) may not represent actual things in the first place. Concepts are not anchored to reality. For example, there is no ready-made concept of "dog" before we assign a word to it. We probably would have a hard time describing "dogness" to a Martian, who, newly arriving on earth, might classify the universe of creatures it encounters according to their size. If, then, a particular dog were the same size as a cat, the Martian would be unable to distinguish between them. Similarly, if our inter-planetary visitor were to sort folks according to whether they preferred to have sex on top or on the bottom, or whether they had sex at night or during the day—as opposed to the presence or absence of a penis—the Martian would have a hard time distinguishing between males and females. Given the nebulousness of signifieds in conjunction with the free play of signifiers, it is no wonder that poststructuralists insist that ultimate Truth is impossible. Poststructuralism cannot prove that meaning is fluid, but, significantly, it lends that notion intellectual cachet. (Keep in mind that many of our most cosseted theories—bibli-cal, political, Freudian, etc.—cannot be proven per se.)

Fortunately, we do not have to follow the dense logic of poststructur-alism—which I, for one, happily leave to semioticians—in order to appreciate its usefulness. But, at the very least, we should realize that embedded in poststructural theory are the seeds of postmodern gender theory, for poststructural theory can convincingly demonstrate the arti-ficiality of the way we think and label things. Its methodology imparts a suggestion of seriousness and gravitas to a subject that is often dis-missed as merely prurient or trivial. In short, it provides us with a scien-tific-feeling justification for banishing the sex/gender binary.

Of course, taken to the extreme, poststructuralism would lead to *reductio ad absurdum*. There would be no consensus on the meaning of anything. It would foreclose human communication. But if ideas were to stand or fall on the basis of their logically possible consequences, we would have no ideas, because the ultimate conceivable consequence of every idea is an absurdity. Besides, most people don't take poststructur-alism that far, and the few that do are often subjected to mockery. Nev-ertheless, to do otherwise, to automatically petrify meaning (as in green = natural), to blindly succumb to the lures of advertising (as in valuing toothpaste because it is green), is also foolish. It would render us too credulous, too vulnerable to exploitation, too open to others' "takes" on reality, too subject to their domination—a bleak prospect for queers, and certainly for Martin the goat-lover. We would become irrevocable prisoners of mass-produced consciousness. Instead, I propose tactical usage of poststructural thinking.

Today we can't get away from postmodernism (generically speaking) for it has also seeped into the mainstream. It is part of our mental fur-niture. Its cool, blasé tone, its pastichy aesthetic, its cynicism and self-regarding irony saturate our media, which in turn saturates our lives. It is everywhere in our advertising, TV, humor, film, comics, and fiction. It is especially conspicuous in alternative music, cutting-edge architecture, MTV, and the Internet, all of which are routinely imbued with bursts of weirdly juxtaposed new and "borrowed" elements. The exposure to a PoMo sensibility starts early: consider the grab bag of short, colorful fragments and bits of information that are incorporated into computer toys and children's television. Curiously, shows such as *Sesame Street* also contain abundant ironic references, e.g., the Count's parody of Count Dracula—the meanings of which are probably only dimly understood by their toddler audience. Perhaps they are included to subliminally entertain the caretakers and thereby prevent them from changing the channel.

BUT MAYBE IT'S OVER

But, postmodern style may be so conspicuous a trend at the moment as to have lost its trendiness, at least according to the relentless hipsters who closely monitor such things. To them, PoMo is "way over," aesthetically impoverished, co-opted by the bourgeoisie. It is far too ubiquitous to cause much of a stir. When a movement attracts so many followers eager to be on the inside, the inside becomes indistinguishable from the outside. The allure of exclusivity is gone.

Postmodernism has lost its edge even in places where trends tend to cycle at less than warp speed, such as the sober environment of the university. Initially perceived there as a spicy fragrance, the theory began to smell fishy about fifteen years ago when the faculty began to notice the banal quality of the scholarship produced by their PoMo-inspired students. Instead of rigorous and creative analyses of subjects, young intellectuals were endlessly devising strategies for subverting the status quo. Unlike their parents, who took to the streets to rebel against the military-industrial complex, this generation of youths disengaged themselves from politics and, from the comfort of their armchairs, read Jacques Derrida and other French thinkers. Thrilling to the notion that language is coercive, they became linguistic revolutionaries, not activist ones. Young scholars began to search and destroy all the hidden, biased principles and structures that govern not only linguistics but all cultural forms, or "texts," such as film, fashion, striptease, boxing, political campaigns, religious rituals, gender, and even traffic signs. They proceeded in lockstep fashion to deconstruct everything they encountered. First hit in the '70s was the dead white male literary canon; then in the '80s there was patriarchy and colonialism; and in the '90s, compulsory heterosexuality.[6] Today, the subject of choice for deconstructors is gender identity.

Meanwhile, a backlash brewed among many academics and critics who regard this kind of student output as more hackwork than scholarship. Deconstruction, they argue, elevates cultural critique above the discipline students are supposed to be studying. It mistakenly subordinates reality to its interpretations. There are subtler, less mechanical ways to read texts than to perpetually search for coercive structures. Deconstruction, they contend, disrespects actual works of art. It is insultingly oblivious to beauty, fragile inner life, as well as human suffering. The cumulative effect of the old guards' *contra-coup* is that Science has regained the glamour spot in academia—Derrida is out, the laboratory is in. The pendulum in the seminar room has swung back from postmodernism to more classical ideology. What is fashionable in academe today mirrors what is fashionable in the world at large—neo-conservatism. Old-fashioned values, aesthetics, and politics are making a comeback.

This recent conceptual boomerang was helped along by various academic scandals. The most emotionally resonant of these was one instigated by a 1987 headline in *The New York Times* indicating that Paul de Man, the leading guru of American literary deconstruction, had written for a pro-Nazi publication in World War II. Deconstruction's association with the swastika did not disprove the validity of that sort of analysis, but it did not exactly win friends for postmodernism, either. More fuel was added to the fire with the revelation in 1996 of a wily hoax perpetrated by New York University physics professor Alan Sokal. As a ruse, the mischievous professor succeeded in publishing a purposefully nonsensical article (pretending to deconstruct quantum physics) in the prestigious American cultural studies journal *Social Text*.[7] He deliberately wrote the piece in a pedantic style, parodying the impenetrable lingo of contemporary theorists. Although crammed full of bad science, the parody was so good that it successfully withstood the scrutiny of the journal's referees, who failed to recognize the fatuity of the content. Widely publicized, the exposé of Sokal's deception made postmodernism and its adherents look ridiculous. And the seismic events of September 11th dealt another blow to the theory's already damaged reputation. After such a genuine calamity, many people felt that cynicism and detachment, the hallmarks of a PoMo sensibility, would be insensitive and self-indulgent.

ON THE OTHER HAND, MAYBE IT'S NOT OVER

Yet, reports of postmodernism's total demise are greatly exaggerated: it still has the power to provoke viewers in the art galleries of Chelsea and on stage at the Brooklyn Academy of Music. Debuting to rave reviews in the spring of 2003 at the Battersea Arts Center in England was *Jerry*

Springer: The Opera, a consummately postmodern occasion wherein trash TV met grand opera. Because of its success, it is scheduled to eventually cross the Atlantic. Postmodernism no longer may be quite so important, but it is not dead. And even as the theory is weakening its hold on the arts and humanities departments of academe, it is finally making inroads into the mindset of psychoanalytically oriented therapists, causing them to question their ideas about gender identity and sexual orientation. It's about time.

If American and British psychoanalytic clinicians had been more observant, they might have asked those questions decades sooner. As postmodernism penetrated field after field, genre after genre, it smashed the sex/gender binary at every turn. It radically uncoupled sex and the body. This widespread dismantling was not a result of a conspiracy among cultural theorists to promote polymorphous perversity. They did not put gender transgression into culture; they merely publicized it. Nor was the recurring eruption of gender-bending in numerous spheres purely coincidental. Rather, it had to do with subterranean rumblings in the Zeitgeist. Undoubtedly the gender categories were ripe for dismantling. That is what Anglo/American psychotherapists should have noticed....

QUEER ART

Take contemporary art. To the non-cognoscenti, it might look kinkier than porn—a veritable peep show, raw and visceral, with lots of flesh and other body-related detritus, much of it conveyed "up close and personal." As a postmodern aesthetic insinuated art circles (or maybe it was vice versa), the body became the new canvas. Experimenting with the body is now ground zero for artists. It's hard to think of an artist today who isn't referencing the body in some way—from hyperliteral representations, such as Robert Mapplethorpe's irresistibly elegant, classically composed photographs of erections (which insert homosexual desire and black bodies into the Western fine-arts traditions of the nude) to others, such as Rona Pondick, who refer to the body in more metaphoric terms. One of her sculptures, *Treats*, consists of hundreds of small pink balls that suggest detached breasts but have voracious, toothy mouths instead of nipples. These simple forms seem to compress male and female together, as well as sadism and play, infant and octogenarian, expressing a hunger bordering on lust. In another PoMo piece, the notorious *Piss Christ*, artist Andres Serrano placed a plastic Christ in a jar filled with urine. In formal terms, it was a beautiful composition, yet its title alerted the viewer to the nature of the amber fluid, thereby causing many to revile the work. But why, the artist seems to ask, must urine, a natural human product, be disgusting?[8] This is a very postmodern question.

Whether by magnifying it, disassembling or reassembling it, shrouding it, or defining it by its absence, artists are using the body (often their own) to expose the toll inflicted by centuries of disastrous ideologies. Popular targets are the binaries, the either/or system we use to classify and rank a body's characteristics—light skin/dark skin, normal/freak, beautiful/ugly, svelte/fat, smooth/wrinkled, contained/leaky, external/internal, and, especially, male/female, straight/gay. According to Derrida we have no access to reality except through conceptual pairs such as these, which are inevitably composed of so-called opposites wherein one member of the pair is always (but arbitrarily) deemed better than the other.[9] Although binaries are sometimes dismissed as trivial, or else are thought to be easily legislated away, they are covertly tyrannical, as any dark-skinned, ugly, freakish, female gay person with garments "stained" by her own body fluids will report. The artist's message: these divisions are false; the boundary within each pair is capricious, not written in stone. It's all about power: who gets to choose the binaries and ascribe the dividing lines.

These artists are putting PoMo theory into practice. Art is a perfect venue for conveying gender uncertainty in material form. Where, for instance, does "male" begin and "female" end? When Cindy Sherman photographs herself as a man, as a woman, or as various characters of indeterminate gender, she is literally "doing" queer theory, whose patron saint Judith Butler argues that all gender is drag. According to Butler, the outward appearance of gender, as communicated by dress and behavior, is always performed, consciously or unconsciously.[10] Similarly, when Robert Gober produces a wax torso that is half male, half female, he is not creating a "pervert" so much as he is saying that we are all basically the same, that too much can be made of male–female difference. That is also the message of the dance company Les Ballets Trockadero when it "queerly" puts tutu-clad men on pointe: male bodies are shown to be graceful and sensitive, ironically feminine. Conceptually in synch, though more deliberately artificial, are Matthew Barney's sexy, if ambiguously sexed, fairies with big biceps and Raggedy Ann–red hair but no reproductive organs. I dare the viewer not to look twice. These days queer art is getting more than respect. It is winning grants and awards and being shown at commercial galleries all over the world and in prestigious exhibitions such as the Whitney Biennial and the Venice Biennale.

This art did not materialize out of thin air. It comes at a moment when the issues of gender identity and sexual orientation encompass a thousand points of contention—and counting. Today's postmodern art seems to spring from today's postmodern sex. Or does it? So many contemporary artists in this era have studied queer theory in art school that it is hard to tell whether their art stems from a deep, personal, creative impulse, or whether it is, as some critics maintain, cookie-cutter conceptual regurgitation, this generation's form of ritual post-adolescent protest. Does this art imply anything about culture and humanity, or is it an academic exercise, art school homework? Does it resonate or merely shock? If there were no theory, would there be body art?

But the art is not entirely new. (Of course, neither is the sex. It's just more visible.) When the Dadaist Marcel Duchamp pencilled a moustache and a goatee on a reproduction of Mona Lisa in 1919 and titled the work "L.H.O.O.Q."—a French acronym for "she has a hot ass"—he put an entirely new spin on her mysterious smile and brilliantly presaged the current obsession with gender-bending. This theme was also visible in Duchamp's dramatic declaration of sexual ambiguity—the emergence of his female alter ego, Rose Selavy (Duchamp cross-dressed), whose visage was captured for eternity by photographer Man Ray.

Sharing Duchamp's prophetic mission, many other Dadaists, and especially their descendants, the Surrealists, also sought to disconnect anatomy from destiny. Consider Meret Oppenheim's fur-covered teacup, saucer, and spoon (evoking a domestic vagina crossed with a wild beast) or Hans Bellmer's freaky life-sized dolls with tumescent, flesh-colored bulges exploding all over their "bodies." Add to this Claude Cahun's multi-gendered photographic self-portraits, which are enjoying renewed popularity today, or Max Ernst's preposterously precise renderings of unreality, which literally represent the body as a battleground of irrational fantasies. These artists anticipated contemporary queer experiments in art by at least half a century. Like their future counterparts, they deliberately used the body to expose dark secrets, to unsettle conventional notions of sexuality, to tell hard truths, to uncover hidden pleasures. This was years before the invasion of French theory into art school and academic curricula.

Of course, new ideas often turn up in art before anywhere else. Perhaps that is what art is for. The time lapse between the original surfacing of queer art and the later formulation of queer theory suggests that the latter could not have conceptually flavored the former. Instead, both may derive from a common source: widespread subliminal discomfort with the sex/gender binary, a discomfort that has persisted over time and is becoming ever more apparent. To be sure, it is always difficult to map with any precision the complicated crosscurrents of ideas erupting in culture. It is a bit like trying to chart the movements of colliding ping-pong balls. The trajectory of influence is never simple or uni-directional. But the longevity of this discontent, and the high serious-ness with which artists then (before mid-century) and now convey it, lends it credibility. It is a discontent that refuses to die.

WHERE ARE THE FREUDIANS?

The Freudians were present at the origin of body art but remained only a short time. In the early part of the last century, artists and analysts were mining the same territory—uncensored desire—considered by both to be the authentic voice of the inner self (see Chapter 1). This was a wildly revolutionary idea in those decades. There existed between the two groups a mutually intoxicating commonality of purpose. Both excavated the anarchic contents of the unconscious, tapping into impulses that most people preferred to sweep under the rug. And instead of suppressing their findings, both brought them to the fore with an unvarnished frankness. Despite the fact that Freud personally found the Surrealists' interest in his work puzzling and was totally unresponsive to their art (which he considered crazy), the Surrealists did not return the disfavor. They openly drew inspiration from Freud's ideas. Their art could practically serve as illustrations for his writing. Painting after painting and piece after piece depict the enigmatic nature of passion, its slippery attachments to symbolic surrogates and part-objects (like shoes or eyeballs), and voracious, insatiable appetite. All were phenomena discussed by the founder of psychoanalysis.[11] It is hardly coincidental that the Surrealists' technique for delving into the unconscious, which they called "automatic" painting or writing, smacked of Freud's free association. Like psychoanalytic patients on the couch, they attempted to relinquish conscious control of their thoughts so as not to contaminate them by reason. But instead of reporting their unprocessed thoughts to a therapist for analysis, they converted them into art. They also took their dream life seriously, duly recording it and using it in their work.[12]

But over time, body art became more political, more in-your-face, queerer, such that in 1990 a French performance artist known as Orlan actually questioned the importance of the "natural" body altogether by undergoing a series of publicly telecast multiple cosmetic surgeries. Her televised performances were complete with costumes, make-up, inter-views, and camera crew. Whatever its value as art, this secular "reincar-nation"—a literal rebirth of the flesh—epitomizes the postmodern desire to erase the body as a biological category with built-in constraints such as size, shape, color, gender, and ornamental attributes. Reflecting the queer idea that raw flesh has no meaning until it is inscribed via language with a cultural identity, Orlan was quoted as saying: "I think that the body is obsolete."[13] By the time Orlan was flamboyantly re-fashioning her container (i.e., her body), the mutual fascination between analysts and visionary artists was long over. Re: the mind-body split—art was becoming more "mind," that is, more conceptual. Psychoanalysis was becoming more "body," that is, more biologically deterministic.

To be sure, Freud never advocated a fixed point of view that cemented anatomy to a specific sexual preference. His tentativeness may have facilitated the early body artists' interest in his theories. But after World War II, Freud's followers tilted the theory in the direction of essentialism, implying that there is an appropriate, inherent femininity and masculinity, and never the twain shall meet—except perhaps in the marital bed, with each other. They developed rigid requirements for the healthy male and healthy female. For example, Helene Deutsch, a prominent mid-century analyst, asserted that women were supposed to be passive, masochistic, bear a child and be happy about it, although apparently she did not meet her own standards for femininity since she hired babysitters. This kind of gender typecasting went on until feminists demanded rethinking in the '70s. Interestingly, there was at least one exception, the psychoanalyst Joan Riviere, who anticipated feminist revisionism as early as 1929. Unlike her colleagues, she maintained that the successful professional woman who flirts with men and masquerades around in ultrafeminine attire does so not because of her "real" intrinsic womanliness but to ward off anxiety from the perceived threat of retaliation from men for being too like them. Certainly she might have a difficult time finding a husband. This idea—that women must hide their intellectual powers behind a façade of self-demeaning femininity—is one that has launched a thousand women's magazines. Femininity is a social performance, and, by implication, may be learned.[14]

The Freudians did not pick up on this idea, although, as we have seen, contemporary artists did so with a vengeance. So Freudian psychoanalysts and the artistic community parted ideological company. The most recent flowering of body art has not surfaced on Freudian analysts' radar screens. They don't get it. While this kind of art is a "hot" subject for critical theorists, it is generally overlooked by the orthodox descendants of Freud. This is a noteworthy omission in that contemporary Freudians produce abundant critiques of highbrow art and literature from earlier periods. They routinely examine how authors' psyches are revealed in their work; for example, what *Hamlet* tells us about Shakespeare, or what "Oedipal" influences are operative between one writer and another another, like between poets Shelley and Yeats.

Yet they have remained a bit squeamish about tackling the recent avant-garde. Perhaps this is because many Freudians (with rare exceptions, such as Robert Stoller and Ethel Person) consider queer behavior to be inaccessible to psychoanalytic inquiry, and therefore regard queer art as prima facie inaccessible. Of course, psychoanalysts probably encounter few queers (if the term is defined narrowly to refer exclusively to transgenders). Very few seek psychoanalytic psychotherapy. This may be because they fear they will be misjudged. Or, more likely, as social outcasts, they are financially precluded from long-term intensive treatment. As a result, psychoanalytically inclined therapists have had little data on which to build a theory.

It took a Frenchman steeped in linguistic philosophy and expert in intellectual pyrotechnics to stem, or at least resist, the creeping tide of biological essentialism into American psychotherapists' thinking. French theory largely refutes the idea that anatomy is destiny, and therefore disputes its nefarious corollary, the idea (so eagerly embraced by American insurance companies) that neurosis should be relieved by medication rather than understood by analysis. The French psychoanalyst Jacques Lacan spiked psychoanalysis with poststructural ideas. His theories are highly complex and controversial and I cannot do justice to them here (but do slightly more so in Chapter 4). Suffice it to say, he emphasized the importance of language acquisition for developing a personal identity. In fact, he suggested that a baby's sense of self is more powerfully determined by language than by its social reality, like its body or the child-rearing practices of its parents. Without language, Lacan asserts, a baby cannot think or even "be" a self, that is, conceive of itself as a self differentiated from other selves. But, unfortunately (or fortunately, depending on your point of view), the instant a child assumes language it is limited by what language can communicate. Unlike latter-day Freudians, the followers of Lacan believe that it is language that thwarts human possibility, not anatomy.

While not exactly feminist or gay-positive in some of its incarnations, the insertion of postmodernism into psychoanalytic thinking has a number of virtues. At the very least it allows us to entertain the idea that genitals do not mean gender. This is because the acquisition of language—the mastery of the ability to think and use symbols, which is so important to Lacanians—is mostly a cerebral process. Lacan demotes the body. So we can use his theory to resuscitate Riviere's seductive thought that gender behavior may be little more than a masquerade.

Also, it enlarges our scope of critical inquiry. Theorists weaned on poststructuralism interpret everything in culture, not just the communications of patients on a couch. This is because they believe all phenomena—from PoMo art to hot dog stands, pornography, insane asylums, to the way we categorize sexual practices—have structures, and none are too small to escape being coercive. According to radical PoMo theorists, the embedded structures in these phenomena could (and may have) turn us into twitching drones, although their methods are subtle enough to conceal from almost everyone their quasi-fascistic influence. So it is an error, postmodernists argue, to confine psychoanalytical interpretation to the subliminal mechanisms of the mind. All cultural manifestations mask things (like power) and should be grist for the analytic mill.

Take the way traditional psychoanalytic theory deals with sexuality. It analyzes its development and unfolding but doesn't examine its linguistic construction, which it regards as a given. Yet a more comprehensive analysis of embedded structures would reveal that sexuality is, in fact, culturally invented. That is precisely the subject of the *History of Sexuality*, which is sometimes called the bible of queer theory. Its author, Michel Foucault, is to postmodern gender theory what Freud is to psychoanalysis.[15] Foucault's most striking claim is that sexuality, like most everything, is constructed, and he goes so far as to supply actual dates for some of its constructions. The homosexual, for example, was invented in 1870. (His assertions tend to be conversation stoppers.) What he meant was that it was only in the late nineteenth century that "the homosexual became a personage, a past, a case history, and a childhood, in addition to being a type of life."[16] Prior to that, same-sex sex was just a sex act in which some people engaged. The people who engaged in this act were regular folks, not a species. Henceforth, the word "homosexual" would be a noun indicating a kind of person as well as an adjective describing a sexual act (more about this in Chapter 4).

Thanks to the logic of theorists like Lacan and Foucault, we may now take seriously various lowbrow practices, such as drag shows, shopping, and advertising, that heretofore were foreclosed from scholarly consideration. These artifacts of popular culture contain important clues about the nature of gender and desire. By excluding them from analysis, we missed a rich opportunity for investigating sexuality. Postmodern culture may not be the royalist road to the unconscious, but it is a road nevertheless. Traversing that route gives us a way to plug the critical gap left by a theory of the unconscious that, until now, permitted only two ways to healthily manifest itself—male or female.

Postmodern theory can be used to make Freud more pertinent to the twenty-first century. It is a healthy provocation that I take up later.

Meanwhile, let's look at some of the things Freudians underplayed....

OTHER QUEER ERUPTIONS THE FREUDIANS MISSED

I worked for many years with "vile bodies"; that is, I counseled persons with disability. In calling these folks "vile" I am quoting a disfigured client of mine who facetiously described himself that way, probably in an attempt to preempt others' criticism. Sadly, it had the ring of truth. This young man was constantly rejected as a romantic partner. We may pretend that beauty is only skin deep, but misshapen bodies, spasms, and drool are not exactly sexual magnets. Many persons with whom I worked disclosed a paralyzing fear of never being loved.

It is not uncommon for cosmetically impaired individuals to withdraw into their homes. Some of this behavior may have to do with social and job discrimination, but much of it is fueled by an understandable wish not to be seen: to avoid scrutiny, the critical gaze of another person. They hide from public view in order to establish a domain in which to preserve their dignity. They needn't have read Jean-Paul Sartre to experience what he called the "shame of the eyes of the other."[17] If we were alone in the world, Sartre wisely pointed out, we would be utterly free to feel however we wished to feel about ourselves. Other people intrude on our solipsistic fantasies and have the audacity to see us from their own perspective. In effect, Sartre was describing the tyranny of our rigid social construction of beauty and sex appeal. This Darwinian ranking of sexual desirability functions even among people who have no visual cues about a partner's attractiveness. I recall treating a young blind man who used his sighted friend to scout out "babes" for him. What was operative for this young man was not actual beauty—which he could not visually perceive—but the power of the social construct of beauty.

Sartre was writing about the human condition, not the specific predicament of cosmetically impaired individuals, but he, himself, was notably odd looking—short, awkward, and wall-eyed. I mention this only because Sartre's ungainly appearance did not seem to hamper his womanizing. The positive sex value of his intellect seemed to neutralize the negative sex value of his demeanor. His situation illustrates an important point: The amorous appeal of an entity is not fixed. It is constructed and may be reconstructed. Advertising continually demonstrates this. The wizards of Madison Avenue can make even the curved flank of an automobile or the unfolding petals of lettuces have as strong an appeal to erotic desire as a peek of flesh of a human supermodel. Clearly, a lot of sexual magnetism derives from staging and lighting, smoke and mirrors, inference and innuendo, history and context. But if an inanimate object can be deliberately sexualized, why not body parts to which you might not ordinarily be attracted?

Perhaps they can. A century ago some Chinese men literally fornicated with the deformed cleft of an adult woman's size-three or three-and-a-half foot. It's not always explicable what attracts us and what doesn't. A recent example of this was recounted in a 2001 *New York Times Magazine* article that described Debbie's ten-year relationship with her partner Christina. The relationship had persisted even though two years earlier Christina had undergone a sex change, and thereafter referred to himself as Chris, a male. Following the procedures, Chris quietly delighted in his body's changes, but Debbie, a life-long lesbian, grieved the loss of her female partner—and with it, her own identity as a lesbian. Yet they remained a committed, loving couple planning to raise their second child, then on the way.[18] Apparently Debbie loved Chris emotionally and physically in spite of his new anatomy. It was the person that mattered to her, not the configuration of the shell that housed it. Her ability to eroticize Chris's altered shape acknowledges that lust is by nature wayward. There's no accounting for the imaginativeness of sexual fantasy and the permutations of sexual pleasure.

This is not exactly news. We often find ourselves perplexed by the erotic choices of another. Many of us claim to believe that beauty is in the eye of the beholder, that love is blind. We cling, for example, to the myth of redemptive inwardness, that your essence can trump your appearance. Even Freud noted that disgusting objects can and do become objects of desire.[19] Our unconscious can reinvent reality. Indeed, many of us who practice psychotherapy experience this reinvention firsthand when we are aesthetically upgraded in the mind's eye of our patients via their transference. But how powerful is this capacity to reinvent reality? And when does a person's perception become outright crazy?

In latter-day Freudian circles, the limit of reinvention is thought to be the body. Most therapists accept the corporeal binaries—male and female, vile and alluring, fat and thin, etc.—as self-evident. The body is bedrock. But while psychoanalytic theorists were looking the other way, pop culture, along with highbrow art, has been playing with these categories, revealing their artificiality. Cultural theorists might call these pop transgressors "postmodernists," but often the transgressors themselves are unaware of the PoMo label and couldn't care less.

Gender-benders are all over the place and are largely oblivious to queer ideology, despite the fact that they enact it.

Female bodybuilders are a case in point. Since the '70s bodybuilding has become popular among women, who now boast their own magazines and compete internationally. These are not the garden-variety women who go to chromed-up health clubs for keeping fit or body toning. They are the ones who go to hardcore gyms to seriously pump iron in order to build their muscles, and their numbers are increasing dramatically. But muscles are not neutral in our culture. They *mean* masculinity. So, how should we perceive women who deliberately bulk up their musculature? Are they feminist heroines who are smashing the gender stereotypes for masculinity and femininity by showing that women can be like men? Do they, like drag queens and other people who reside somewhere along the hypothetical sex/gender continuums, demonstrate the falsity of binary opposition? Or, are they self-loathing women who believe in the gender binary and who, consciously or unconsciously, wish to "be" the other one (i.e., men)? Does their oddness merely remind us of the binary poles, without which—if we stop to think about it—female bodybuilders would not seem odd? In other words, do they challenge the gender binary or affirm it?[20]

These questions come to a head during competitions, for there is much controversy over how women bodybuilders should be judged. The criteria for male bodybuilders are fairly straightforward, having to do with a participant's muscle size, mass, definition, and vascularity. But these same attributes may work against a female contender. The ideal woman bodybuilder's body must be heavily muscled but not "too extreme." When the crunch comes, the judges prefer the contestants to be feminine, even hyper-feminine, Barbie-like, with styled hair, big breasts, small waist, manicured nails, and a tan. This was dramatically illustrated in the film *Pumping Iron II: The Women* (1984): International Federation of Bodybuilding officials placed the audience's favorite (and brawnier) Bev Francis eighth, while awarding the title to a woman who "set the standard of femininity." Throughout, the film poses the question: Can a woman still be a woman if she looks like a man?[21]

The acquisition of a masculine attribute by a woman—in this case, big hard muscles—provokes anxiety, maybe even repulsion. Gender-bending is threatening to the onlooker, sometimes eliciting a strong visceral response. When female bodybuilders assume the trappings of cartoonish femininity, they are attempting, probably unwittingly, to reduce their disturbing effect on those who gaze at them. Their girlish embellishment serves to reassure the spectator that they are female after all. They may be muscle bound, but they are cute. We can relax:

ordinary gender arrangements are maintained. But ironically, women bodybuilders are caricaturing femininity even as they are caricaturing masculinity. It's all about artifice. They are not simulating real women or men, but hyper-real women and men.

Old-fashioned Freudians might interpret women's muscle building as propelled by penis envy. The subliminal cue that hardbodied women emit may be a shade subtler, perhaps, than that of Madonna's onstage squeezing of her crotch, but it demonstrates the same thing—the wish to have the male organ or, at least, to have what it represents. Muscles, in this view, are penis substitutes. But an alternative explanation is a postmodern one: that big muscles are slippery signifiers. They usually code male, but they don't have to. Robert Mapplethorpe's photographs of bodybuilder Lisa Lyon, for example, show that her excessively developed muscles do not make her mannish, but instead have been feminized to go with, not against, her flowered hat and lipstick.[22] Muscles are more like children's Transformer toys than airtight trademarks of gender. They may be detached from maleness. They have no natural meaning. Masculinity and femininity are examples of Baudrillard's simulacrums—exact copies of something that never existed in the first place. To the extent that we have defined gender by severable attributes—such as lipstick, blustery helplessness, hard muscles, guzzling beer—it can be replicated by anyone. Feminists have said that women have been impersonating females for years.

It is interesting to observe that some of the biggest muscles these days belong to gay men. Male homosexuals are not what they used to be. Far from being the limp-wristed, pinky-raising, swish dandies of Oscar Wilde's era, they are now often buffed and ripped. Today the gym body is a cultural marker of the gay man, both "to have" on one's body and "to hold" in one's arms. The forces that constitute the Chippendale hunk archetype as traditionally masculine are the same forces that make him so attractive to gay men. An unhappy by-product of this new subculture requirement is that more and more gay and bisexual men are trespassing into the formerly female territory of body-image dysfunction, eating disorders, plastic surgery—the Internet is littered with spam advertising penile augmentation—and exercise compulsion.

Other questionable outcomes include a continuation of, if not heightened, repudiation of "flaming" or "femme" gay men. The prejudice against effeminate homosexuals is operative not only among otherwise gay-positive straights, but also among gays themselves. Should you doubt this, peruse their personal ads. Almost invariably, gay males request "straight appearing, straight acting" traits in a partner and portray themselves as having such. (God forbid a man should act like a

woman! "Effeminophobia"—see Chapter 4—exceeds even homophobia in our culture.) And yet another consequence of the "cult of the
gym body" is a virulent brand of ageism that is reflected in gay humor;
for example: "I'm 40—that's 280 in dog years, dead and buried in gay
years." It's not easy being gay.

Despite this, straight men are following their lead with regard to
enhanced vanity, although they are probably clueless as to the source of
their new preoccupation.[23] Virtually every sentient male these days
aspires to the lean, fit body that was once the exclusive province of gay
male fantasy. There's even a newly coined name for these men—"metro-
sexuals." Consider the popularity of *Queer Eye for the Straight Guy*, a
hilarious reality show that premiered on cable channel Bravo in the
summer of 2003, in which five New York gay men make over a hapless,
style-impaired straight one in order to win the heart of his female love
interest. It's all about male bonding, with a significant subtext of gay affir-
mation. And advertising, ever the cultural Geiger counter, capitalizes on
this trend, liberally spicing its high-end campaigns with homoerotic
imagery. When Calvin Klein put a forty-foot Bruce Weber photograph
of Olympic pole-vaulter Tom Hintinauss in Times Square (with his large
penis discernible through his briefs), he found that his line of shorts
"flew off the shelves" in Bloomingdales.[24] Obviously, not all the custom-
ers were gay. Irony is piled on irony here. Not only are the top dogs
(straight men) aping the underdogs (gay men), but—women's lib notwithstanding—females are **not** worrying *less* about their bodies, while
males are worrying *more*. Apparently, some desires, like the culturally
propelled wish for physical beauty, easily trespass gender boundaries.

So has gay taste. Thirty-nine years after Susan Sontag described the
sensibility that put gays on the cultural map, that sensibility—
"camp"—infuses the mainstream. In her famous 1964 essay, Sontag
observed that there is good taste even in bad taste; hence, the ultimate
camp statement: "It's so good because it's awful."[25] In effect, camp is an
attitude that fetishizes bad taste—excessive theatricality, stylization of
manner and gesture, artifice, and exaggeration. But camp artifacts or
behaviors—like black velvet paintings, Carmen Miranda's tutti-fruity
hat, *Pee Wee's Playhouse* (a former Saturday morning kid's show), or
the high-flown dramatic displays of opera divas—are not taken at face
value by aficionados of camp. Instead, they are viewed ironically and
are used (with a knowing wink) to send up kitschy middle-class preten-
sions and naive bourgeois taste for the vulgar.

To be sure, male homosexuals did not invent this sensibility nor do
they universally embrace it. Nevertheless, since the '20s many gays have
had an affinity for camp. We see it in their ironic, sometimes (may I say it?)

bitchy humor, their passion for certain over-the-top movie stars, the practice of drag. Gays' attraction to camp is understandable. Until recently, homosexual men functioned in the straight world like double agents. Schooled by necessity to maintain a fastidious gap between public manner and private feeling, they may identify with camp's artifice. As longtime victims of snobbish derision, they may welcome the opportunity to turn the tables, to share a snobbish subcultural code. And because camp is often used to call attention to the spuriousness of our masculine and feminine norms, it allows gay men to disarm the very categories of sexuality and gender that marginalize them. It can be deployed as a subversive strategy, transforming the serious into the frivolous, rendering the pain of social prejudice into the smug satisfaction of barbed wit.

But that doesn't explain camp's insinuation into the ordinary straight mindset, especially that of Generations X to Z, where it also comfortably resides today. It cannot account for the popularity of, for example, Halloween, trashy television "reality" shows, John Water's movies featuring 300-pound transvestite Divine, all of which are so bad they're good. Perhaps this paradoxical "trickle up" in the status of camp from being the sensibility of choice for a stigmatized minority to the sensibility of choice for a much larger minority (alienated adolescents and cynics) has something to do with ordinary developmental rebelliousness. It's a safe way to be slightly naughty. Whatever its cause, it demonstrates that style and sense of humor are not biological "givens" peculiar to a subset of humans. Gays do not possess a camp gene. Aesthetic sensibility readily crosses sex/gender lines.

SOME RECENT GAY HISTORY: MORE EVIDENCE FOR QUEER REALITY

The evolution of the visual stereotype of the gay man—from pansy to he-man—suggests that over time he has given out so many conflicting signals about himself that there is no "essential" homosexual male, just as there is no "essential" heterosexual male or female. There is no "essential" lesbian, either. Around the same time that the gay male image was metamorphosing, a parallel evolution was occurring in lesbian circles wherein butch-femme roles went from being an erotic requirement to an erotic choice. In scarcely a quarter of a century, starting in the late '60s, the personae of the male and female homosexual seem to have changed their stripes. The love that once dared not to speak its name became a blaring Tower of Babel. Today, sexual nonconformity is characterized by diversity—by variation in the established formulas for conveying or provoking desire; in sex object choice; in rituals of courtship, seduction, self-presentation, gender identity; and even in sexual practices and their meaning.[26]

Sociologists note enormous differences among the three main queer cohorts active today. The first group consists of women and men who reached sexual maturity before the second wave of feminism and Stonewall—a bar in Greenwich Village that was the site of an infamous police raid in the summer of 1969 and a subsequent rebellion (including an impromptu transvestite chorus line performing a full kick routine), which marked the beginning of "gay liberation." The second group is composed of those who came out during the "liberated" '70s, and the third is made up of those who came out since the arrival of AIDS in the early '80s. These groups are divided even in the way they sometimes describe themselves—as "homosexual," "gay," "lesbian," or the disputed term, "queer."

Prior to Stonewall, most homosexuals and persons of alternative sexuality were in the closet, many leading a "double life." Re: males— think Rock Hudson, James Dean, and Liberace. The ultimate male gay sex symbols of the era were known as "trade," that is, sexually available but straight-identified men, usually young and working class. A man was thought to be a man only to the extent that he was not a woman; and anal or oral receptivity was considered womanish. Polarized gender play played a stronger role in gay sexual practices then than it does now, reflecting the sexist mores of '50s straight culture.[27] So trade inserted their penises into "queers" (a derogatory term at the time) while reserving their love for females. As penetrators, they were given social permission to preserve the fiction that they were the master of their own desire rather than the objects of another's. Only insertees were stigmatized; insertors were able to maintain their masculine status. (This macho bias persists in some Latin and Arab cultures, as well as in prison, where it is not a disgrace to sleep with another man, so long as one is *activo*, that is, a penetrator, not a penetratee. These biases date back at least to the ancient Greeks. See Chapter 3.)

Gender role-playing was, if anything, even more exaggerated in the lesbian world of the Eisenhower era than the male homosexual one, especially in working-class environments. A highly dichotomized butch-femme code of behavior was the modus operandi. The fact that these rules presided in certain circles does not disprove their artificiality. Far from coming naturally to all lesbians, they posed a hindrance for many who could (or would not) comply, like poet Audre Lord, who felt she was not "cute" enough for one role option, nor "tough" enough for the other.[28] Here's a snapshot of the period: the butch lesbian was expected to be active, the initiator. Regarding appearance, she sought to achieve the "hoodlum look" of Marlon Brando—white T-shirt, tight jeans, black leather jacket, slicked-back hair. In the prototypic sexual scenario, she "took" her femme, as a man "takes" a woman, and fought off attempts by others to poach her partner. But unlike the stereotypical sexist man of the period, the butch primarily "gave" pleasure in the sense of bringing her femme to orgasm, even as she semantically "took" her. The iconic butch was the "stone butch," who was unpenetrated and stood "stonily" by, cool and remote, as she pleased her femme sexually. Of course, the stone butch was not entirely altruistic in these encounters, as she undoubtedly enjoyed the secondary pleasures of controlling and satisfying her femme. Ironically, femme lesbians, unlike their heterosexual counterparts, were often the breadwinners in these arrangements, since they could pass more readily as straight and were therefore more employable.[29]

Then came the women's movement of the late '60s. Suddenly, within the dyke community butch-femme role-playing—"the silly, stupid, harmful games that men and women play"—was given a bad rep.[30] From a feminist perspective, such erotic scenarios parodied oppressive heterosexual norms, perpetuating the antiquated notion that gender roles are natural, eternal, and right. Butch/femme women found themselves ostracized—accused, in the jargon of the period, of internalizing and promoting misogyny, of caving in to the woman-oppressing institution of heterosexuality and patriarchal social conditioning. Femmes were regarded with especial horror, for they were seen as colluding with their own objectification and commodification. To be sure, some of this new ideology may have been class driven, in that the more politically minded lesbians tended to be white, educated, and middle class. But, on the whole, a newly idealized relationship emerged. It was egalitarian, mutually empathic, and relational (for which women presumably have a talent)—women loving women.

But an egalitarian relationship may be just another orthodoxy. I have treated a number of lesbians over the years and have not found them to be more naturally sensitive to each other than men are to women, or men are to men. Anger, aggression, competition, and conflict are not exclusive to men. The rigid imposition of a democratic relationship on dyke couples may be no less contaminated by social norms than "sexist" role-play. Although politically correct, egalitarian arrangements do not necessarily represent naive, pure, primitive desire any more so than the enactment of eroticized scenarios of difference. Indeed, not all lesbians welcomed the "liberation" from role-playing. Some revel in the *frisson* created by exaggerated masculinity and femininity. But with the maturity of a new generation of lesbians, who grew up in a more welcoming environment, butch-femme has come to be seen today as an acceptable erotic option, one among many. Identity is now a matter of personal choice rather than a political compulsion. There has been a rediscovery of, a celebration and even a commercialization of, butch-femme roles and identity. These are generalizations, of course, but now more than before, anything goes. Lipstick lesbians, biker dykes, vanilla dykes, androgyny, celibacy, S/M, porn, queer: it's all okay.

Stonewall was the equivalent of women's lib in the male gay world. It granted homosexual men dispensation. It was one of those moments when everything that was frozen—everything that seemed inevitable, unchangeable, oppressively and always just *there*—thawed. After years of camouflage, a lifetime in the closet, gay men started flaunting their sexuality. In the delirium of the post-Stonewall decade, "blatant was beautiful." Men began to proudly declare their homosexuality and to embrace a lifestyle that openly rejected such sacrosanct conventions as the nuclear family, monogamy, and marriage, norms they dismissed as outdated artifacts of straight culture. One of the most dramatic changes was a shift in sex symbols: instead of idealizing trade, gay men came to see *themselves* as the most attractive objects of desire. In sociological terms, they switched from pursuing exogamous relationships to endogamous ones; that is, they sought gay partners as opposed to straight ones. A widespread male homosexual style emerged that broadcast gays' sexual allure. All at once, in large metropolitan centers, gays began to resemble cowboys, construction workers, and tough guys. Dubbed the "clone look," it was characterized by a clipped mustache, flannel shirt, and tight, button-fly jeans, all ideally accentuated by well-developed muscles. The effect was hypermasculine. It branded gay men as a sexy, glamorous product, linking them with everything desirable. It radiated independence, toughness, and emotional imperviousness. Though obviously compensatory and conformist, gays' fashion preferences emphatically signaled that they were, above all, *men*, not pansies, a point that needed to be made at the time.[31]

As the '70s wore on, gay male sex, which in previous decades had often been quick and anonymous out of anxiety or necessity, was becoming quick and anonymous out of choice. Bathhouses, porn theaters, and "backroom" bars proliferated, along with disco bars (another aspect of gay life that became part of the larger culture). I suspect that this era-specific hedonism was a form of group-wide acting out; gay culture, in its twentieth-century incarnation, was in its adolescence, freed at last from the repressive strictures of its harsh parent, bourgeois society. Infidelity and promiscuity are probably no more natural to gay men than monogamy is to straight ones.[32] And, as we shall see, it faded somewhat, though the inaccurate association of gay men with lewd, wanton excess stubbornly persists.

With the insidious spread of AIDS in the '80s, the joyride ended. The bathhouses were closed. Bars and cruising areas declined in importance. New organizations arose to take their place: twelve-step groups, baseball teams, choruses, gay churches and synagogues, marching bands. A greater sense of social conservatism set in. Gays moved from urban ghettos into the suburbs. Some pushed for overt recognition of their sexual orientation in the military. Today most of the male gay patients I see in therapy are paired off or seek to be. Many are adopting children.

As male and female homosexuals were undergoing personae transformations, what happened to bisexuals? In a sense, they were ahead of the bell curve: they had been experiencing a category crisis all along. The very concept of bisexuality, by definition, calls into doubt any neat division between the genders. They are inherent gender-benders. Yet over time they have mostly been invisible. History is replete with examples of famous people who had lovers of both sexes—Caesar, Frida Kahlo, John Maynard Keynes, Edna St. Vincent Millay, Greta Garbo, Marlon Brando, John Cheever, Margaret Mead, and Susan Sontag, to name a few—who were rarely labeled bisexual. Usually they were described as changing sexual orientations: *first* they were straight and *then* they were gay—or vice versa.[33]

When not overlooked, bisexuals tended to get poor spin. Psychoanalysts have theorized that they harbor a grandiose wish "to have it all," that they have a false sense of omnipotence. Straight people often dismiss them as "going through a stage." Gays regard "bis" as wimps, as too afraid to come out homosexual. Lesbians view them as untrustworthy, possibly oversexed dabblers who are disloyal to women; and radical queers feel that the bisexual label is just another way of classifying people's sexual orientation according to whom they have sex with, rather than how they obtain sexual pleasure. From their perspective, the bisexual category is merely another way of regulating sexuality. On top of this, bisexual men in the '80s were demonized as double agents who might sneak AIDS into the marriage bed. Nevertheless, by the '90s there was a worldwide trend toward adding the "b" word to the names of queer organizations. Today, bisexuality tends to be acknowledged as a sexual orientation. There has been an explosion of new magazines— such as the one provocatively titled *Anything That Moves*—aimed at self-identified consumers. "Bisexual chic" is perennially recycled in fashion, a telling indicator of acceptable desire. And today's actresses who have had affairs with women—Drew Barrymore, Angelina Jolie, and Ally Sheedy, for example—are earning substantially more than their strictly heterosexual counterparts, according to a University of Maryland study.[34] Maybe it is the publicity dividend, but apparently in Hollywood it pays to be bisexual.

If, as we have seen, an individual's sexual attraction to a lover can accommodate variation in the shape of that person's genitals; if lust-producing objects vary across culture; if sexual practices can change from insertion to reception in a variety of orifices; if the norms for exclusiveness of attachment varies by decade; if an individual's gender identity may be time limited—then what is left of sexuality that is natural and stable? Clearly much of what we call sexual orientation and gender identity is socially constructed. Yet, for all its fluidity, it remains unruly, impervious to will. Sexuality cannot be truly altered by strength of conviction, conversion therapy, behavioral modification, or psychotherapy. You cannot make a homosexual into a heterosexual. These interventions simply do not work. Claims to the contrary have not been validated by empirical study.[35]

You also cannot make a male into a female, a fact tragically brought to public awareness by a front-page report in 1997 in the *New York Times* of a botched attempt to do just that.[36] The article revealed that the long-term outcome of a landmark case of gender reassignment, initially reported to have been a complete success, was, in fact, a failure. In 1967, after a bungled circumcision in which he lost his penis, David Reimer, then eight months of age, was further surgically altered and thereafter brought up as a girl. This was done at the behest of sex researcher John Money, who argued, as did many feminists at the time, that our sense of being male or female is primarily the result of how we are raised. In other words, our parents and culture shape our gender. But the "shaping" did not work for David. He always struggled against his imposed girlhood, and he eventually decided to live as a male. Sadly, even as a restructured male, he never achieved sustained happiness: he committed suicide in 2004.

We now know that mere social conditioning does not produce gender. Neither does mere biology, nor even a simple interaction of nurture and nature. This may be because sexual orientation and gender identity are radically socially constructed; that is, they are shaped not only by the person's body, socialization, media, and cultural arrangements but also by the most fundamental, taken-for-granted categories and linguistic devices we use to order the world. They are deeply socially constructed and not subject to weaker (relatively speaking) forms of social manipulation.

The power of "deep" social structuring is further illustrated by the infamous lesbian dildo controversy, which, to my mind, is a masterpiece of condensation of sex/gender issues.[37] The conflict concerns the visual appearance of the dildo. Some activist lesbians debunk the apparatus because it is most often deliberately manufactured to look like a penis or, perhaps, a superpenis. Why, they ask, would a woman-identified woman find a facsimile penis erotic? In an unsubtle attempt to break the association between a piece of silicon and men's bodies, these politically correct lesbians marketed a series of dildos that are shaped like dolphins, ears of corn, and even the Goddess. But interestingly, these "p.c." sex toys never caught on. In the end, lesbians with "uncooperative" sexual tastes still purchase dildos that are shaped like penises and named after macho superheroes.

The opposing faction argues that the appearance of a dildo is a non-issue. So what if it is made to look like a penis? It need not represent the male organ even when it resembles one. They contend that the gender of a dildo is not transparent but is subject to interpretation. It is possible for the dildo, as it were, to stand only for itself. In fact, it is nothing more than an androgynous sex toy, a device a person may use for the pleasure of penetration. Like big muscles, it need not always signify masculinity. So lesbians who use penis lookalikes for sexual gratification may not be betrayers of women after all.

Whether they know it or not, the "any-shaped-dildo-will-do" lesbians are making a case for queer theory. By arguing that dildos, irrespective of their appearance, are gender neutral, that their meaning is in the eye of the beholder, they are affirming the postmodern idea that meaning is unstable. By calling into question the gender quotient of even such an apparently straightforward item as a lifelike dildo, they are demonstrating the arbitrary and constructed nature of our own pleasure. The strange and wondrous ways our desires are sparked by someone or something are not always determined by its surface.

Lacan, as we shall see (in Chapter 4), took this idea further. Not only does a dildo not always symbolize a penis; neither does the portion of anatomy known as a penis. Lacan reserved the term "penis" for the actual biological genital, and the term "phallus" for the imaginary and symbolic functions of that organ (to which, feminists argue, he attached exaggerated importance). What matters, according to him, is not the physical reality of the penis, but the role it plays in fantasy, an idea implicit in Freud but not elaborated. Body parts are like Rorschach blots onto which we project our desires. They are analogous to texts, which are also variable by interpreter. Hence the famous postmodernist dictum that "the author is dead." The coiner of that phrase, Roland

Barthes, wasn't dumb enough to believe that there weren't live people writing their books, but that writers worked unconsciously, and that larger forces shaped them and their work.

Using this postmodern logic, bits of anatomy are not sexually exciting until the observer invests them with erotic value. Desire is stirred by the imagination, which does not distinguish between a thing *qua* thing and a thing *qua* fantasy, inside or outside, past or present. Because human sexuality is more a matter of imagination and fantasy than of biology, nothing pertaining to our sexuality is necessarily predetermined. So if a penis does not resonate "male" to some individuals, they need not be diagnosed as delusional, as long as they are aware, cognitively speaking, that a great majority of people in the world disagree with them. Gender-bending is not a valid or reliable indicator of pathology. Here we are in the realm of queer theory.

Let us see how a postmodern perspective may illuminate the understanding of a patient.

Charlie, a 32-year-old store clerk and self-described "ski bum," arrived on my office doorstep in desperate condition, stating he was "out of control." He was terrified that he might hurt himself or his former girlfriend, who had recently broken up with him. Charlie was not, to say the least, an obvious candidate for psychoanalytic psychotherapy, but in the course of trying (and failing for bureaucratic reasons) to hospitalize him that afternoon, I observed that my intervention seemed to calm him. So, after extracting a promise that he would do no harm, I set a second appointment, thinking I might use his transference to me to his advantage. But I was on guard, for Charlie was movie-star handsome, over six-foot-five, conspicuously charming, and I was in the throes of peri-menopause. Plus, I learned in that first session that he had been in jail for nine months a few years before—for exhibitionism. I was cautiously aware that I might be responding to the wiles of a seductive sociopath.

But the poignancy of his predicament as well as his persona intrigued me. It was replete with ironies. Why, I wondered, would someone so noticeably tall and attractive resort to exhibitionism when all he had to do was stand still? Even more ironic was the fact that Charlie hadn't been flashing a functioning penis at all, but a penile implant that he manually inflated. (The prosthesis and hydraulic pump were internal and therefore invisible to the onlooker.) As a result of an automobile accident fifteen years before, he had been forced to undergo the mutilation of the signature attribute of the male persona—his penis. In a sense, he had suffered "primal" humiliation. His life and perverse way of dealing with his catastrophic loss struck me as a cosmically dark comedy, a sick Freudian joke.

Charlie's girlfriend was quickly forgotten. It was the fixed tyrannical impulse to exhibit himself that drove him to therapy, though he was loath to admit it. Charlie was deeply ashamed, enraged, and depressed but thoroughly defended against any awareness of these feelings. His *modus operandi* was sensation seeking, not reflection. At the outset of treatment, he exhibited himself almost nightly. He was predatory: he sought women in isolated locations and would station himself under a lamppost (to spotlight his penis). He would quickly pump himself up, and, if there was time, use a penile ring to enlarge his erection. Then he would masturbate to orgasm. Charlie insisted that many women liked to look at him.

A prominent aspect of his behavioral pattern was a search for unknown women with outsize breasts to serve as his audience. To be sure, the attraction of large female breasts to straight men is far from unusual, but Charlie was obsessed and he actively pursued sightings day and night. In fact, his exhibitionism increased in the summer when women casually reveal more cleavage. Charlie jokingly told me that the fashion for push-up bras was a conspiracy designed to drive him crazy. His fantasy ideal consensual sex partner also had huge breasts, preferably surgically enlarged, which, he felt, would facilitate his continual attraction to her. They would serve as a perpetual, guaranteed fast-trigger sexual fix. In real life he had had sex with a number of well-endowed women, but he quickly lost interest in them.

Charlie grew up in a middle-class suburb, the middle child of five (four boys and a girl), and he blamed his ignominious position in the sibling birth order for his lifelong feeling of being "overlooked." He recalls once being forgotten in his crib while the rest of the family left to go out. He felt he was always a loner "living in his head," "an outsider looking in." His brothers were typical teen troublemakers; his father, a retired Naval officer, mildly alcoholic, cold, and uncommunicative; his mother and sister, unavailable. For the duration of therapy, Charlie described his family in monochromatic terms, careful to maintain distance. Had his family been outrageously awful, instead of merely neglectful and insensitive, Charlie might have had an easier time confronting his feelings about them. As it was, they were unaware of the real reason for his imprisonment, thinking that it was marijuana related, as all the siblings were users.

Just prior to entering college, he was in the aforementioned car accident, which he had caused. It initially left him paraplegic, but after a number of surgeries and difficult physical therapy, he was able to regain mobility and eventually to become an expert skier. Unfortunately, one of the surgeries destroyed his erectile and excretory capabilities; hence, the insertion of a penile implant. And so began a peripatetic decade of drifting, impulsiveness, shallow relationships, furtiveness, and exhibitionism.

Charlie got worse before he got better, and for a time he became a cocaine addict. Throughout his treatment, and especially during his major regression, he benefited from the assistance of a behavior therapist, a psychiatrist, a brief stint with Narcotics Anonymous, and the participation of two pro bono attorneys. His unfailing ability to enlist caretakers to work on his behalf is testimony to his considerable social skills. My once-weekly treatment of Charlie lasted three years, less the six months when he was actively abusing drugs. We terminated two years ago and he has remained symptom free with regard to exhibiting. He now works in a semiprofessional position in a social agency. Despite my early doubts, he has been able to display a great deal of genuine empathy for his clients.

Clearly, Charlie's irresistible impulse to display his erect genital was designed not for making love, but in a certain sense, for making hate. The enactment of his exhibitionism was so stereotypic for his diagnostic category that it sometimes felt to me that he had read a traditional psychoanalytic textbook to learn how to be one. When he forced the sight of his penis on a nonconsenting victim, like most exhibitionists he was giving vent to a primitive, vengeful aggression—in his case, a rage conceived in childhood as a result of empathic failure and escalated by the actual, horrific "unmanning" he underwent as a teen. The risky business of flashing enabled Charlie to triumph symbolically over his trauma. In its performance, Charlie was able to experience the thrill of defying the moral code, a kind of macho high. He bragged that he could make his penis nine inches long.

From being a victim, he became a victimizer. Put differently, his behavior enabled him to become the perpetrator of the victimization previously inflicted on him. Exhibitionism is a brazen antisocial act that invites punishment. Indeed, the threat of punishment was a vital ingredient in his ritual enactment. The potential of getting caught was far preferable to the terrible humiliation that might become conscious were he forced to acknowledge that he harbored murderous rage and had damaged genitals. It turned the spotlight (literally!) on a more manageable, "masculine" fear, that of incurring a penalty for a crime, rather than his feelings of annihilating shame and narcissistic injury.

Yet, at the same time, the act supplied masochistic gratification. It rendered him a "pervert," a cultural ranking so low that it is stigmatized even among the stigmatized. It is liable, for instance, to get one beaten up in prison. Ironically, this ignominious label served to relieve some of his unconscious guilt about his taboo impulses. Charlie's guilt, which he initially denied, was apparent in his repeated bids for external control, his self-sabotaging tendency to get caught, and his eventual pride in helping others. When deterred from exhibiting himself, he felt desperately anxious, panicky, agitated, crazy, even violent.

The acknowledgment of his rage was a sticky point in my treatment of Charlie, for he insisted that many women enjoyed his performances. He also felt strongly that women took sadistic pleasure in teasing men by dressing provocatively and then denying them sexual access. His reaction to sexily clad women, he reasoned, was involuntary. This line of thinking piqued my feminist sensibility. I firmly wanted, and believed, his thinking to be a rationalization, that is, defensive (an interpretation with which Charlie eventually came to agree), but I also recognized that viewing Charlie's explanations as mere wishful thinking bumped up against my queer political leanings. From a postmodern perspective, females should not be held responsible for males' sexual arousal. And women should be as attracted to men's exhibitionism as men are to women's.

But they aren't. The consumers of visual pornography today are overwhelmingly male—98.9% of the consumers of online porn are men.[38] Indeed, a number of research psychologists argue that the circuit from eyes to brain to genitals is a quicker trip for men than for women.[39] In other words, straight men seem to be more readily turned on by unclothed women than straight women are by unclothed men. Hence, the old chestnut that the equivalent of visual pornography for women is the romance novel. I suspect that this may be changing, but the important point here is that spectatorship, as it stands now, is lopsided: men look; women are looked at.[40] In reality, most women do not like flashers, and straight men like skin (and resent cock-teasers). In a utopian postmodern world, where signifiers float freely, these dynamics need not occur. Men and women might display themselves as they pleased. But Charlie lives in the present, where dress codes subliminally operate even when purposely defied.

In time, Charlie recognized his hostility toward women, especially when his feelings escalated to a wish to fondle the breasts of his victims. These feelings terrified him; he willingly submitted to external controls, and the impulses abated. He also learned about females' "looking" habits from a short-lived tenure as an online soft-core porn actor, in which he had "jokingly" participated for a few months as a way to "capitalize" on his problem. It turned out that the majority of paid "hits" to view him unclad were from men, not women. In the end, he was able to laugh about this. Indeed, Charlie continually displayed a good sense of humor, including an offer to pose nude for the cover of this book.

Charlie's obsession with breasts supplied a safe, "normal" expression of erotic desire but also allowed him to displace some of his anxiety upward. It was as if the egregious magnitude of a woman's breasts would compensate for the insignificant magnitude of his felt masculinity. His specific interest in surgically enhanced breasts had a fetishistic quality to it and perhaps involved an unconscious attempt to master his own surgical mutilation—or, maybe, as he said, it was because he had spent too much time in New Jersey. Perhaps his female bosom fixation also had to do with a wish for nurturing, a wish to get lost in a woman's warm fleshy body and fortified...to gratify his shameful longings to be dependent, vulnerable, submissive, emotionally fed, wishes that were not sufficiently gratified for him as a child.

What seemed to be most operative in my treatment of Charlie was my empathic stance, rather than insight per se, although he would tolerate interpretations now and then. He experienced my attempts to explore his unconscious dynamics mainly as humiliating. I was an idealized maternal figure for him, the Madonna (he was a lapsed Catholic), whom he still wishes to make proud: he has contacted me a few times since termination to "show off" his purchase of a new car, his progress in college, his buff appearance, and his job promotions. (Much of his interaction with me had a "look-see" quality to it.) As he mastered his exhibitionism and experienced other successes in his life, he was eager to terminate treatment and "do it on his own."

Thus far, my formulation of Charlie falls well within the bounds of routine psychoanalytic thinking. But his story is a rich source of postmodern interpretive opportunities. Looking at it through a queer lens, you could regard his behavior as consummately gender-bending. For example, he restored his wounded sense of masculinity by engaging in a practice that has long been associated with feminine seduction—displaying one's nude body. Charlie dreaded his powerful so-called feminine longings—his vulnerability, his passivity, his dependency wishes, his masochism—feelings that were magnified by his traumatic surgical emasculation. His solution—exhibitionism—enabled him to gratify his wishes for being passive (that is, to be the object of a woman's gaze) while simultaneously reassuring himself via a large erection that he was still a powerful and dominating male.

By flashing, Charlie was self-servingly playing with the power hierarchies of the gaze. As noted before, when we gaze at something, we are not "just looking." The gaze probes and regulates. It penetrates the body, critiques its flaws, and violates its privacy. Those with the power to look can devour others with their eyes. Historically controlled in Western culture by straight men, the asymmetrical dynamics of the gaze has long been reinforced by traditions in art and the media wherein women displayed themselves for male surveillance but not vice versa. Men's privileged access to unilateral viewing has served to objectify women, about which women have been vociferously rebelling since the second wave of the women's movement.

Today the visual playing field is a bit leveler, but not much better: Now everyone seems to be objectified. In Charlie's enactment of gaze dynamics, he oscillated between so-called male and female positions. First, he leered desirously at a woman's breasts. Then in fantasy, he gave up the object of desire (the woman's breasts) and invested his own penis with powerful visual appeal. In Freudian terms, he transformed *activity* (looking, which is coded male) into *passivity* (being looked at, which is coded female). But even as he fantasized being a *passive* object of desire, he simultaneously reassumed the male position by *actively* forcing the woman to watch. This switching of gender role behavior is, by definition, queer. In a truly queer world, as opposed to the sexist one in which we dwell, the discrete actions that comprised his exhibitionism would not be tagged male or female, active or passive, powerful or weak. Charlie's behavior would lose its transgressive punch. But then, in such an environment, he might not feel the need "to punch" anyone. In a world where there are no power hierarchies based on the presence of a working penis, his terror of being womanish would be moot.

Charlie's theatrical display might be seen as postmodern in another sense: he made himself "grotesque" (nine inches!). According to PoMo theorists, the grotesque body has a radical potential for being subversive. Because it is deemed repulsive, it can be slyly deployed to disturb the onlooker: like the surprise, outrage, and enormous guilt experienced by a former patient who was unwittingly fixed up for a blind date with a midget. Deviant bodies are inherent spectacles. Just by being displayed, they can turn the establishment topsy-turvy, as was ritualistically done by European common folk during the Renaissance in the shocking practices of their carnivals (a whiff of which is echoed in early Fellini films). Even the ecstasy-infused raves that exist today are said to pale in comparison to the parading freaks, crazed bingeing, gigantically featured masks, scatological references, and physical mutilation that characterized carnivals of the pre-Enlightenment past. Theorists, like Russian critic Mikhail Bakhtin, celebrate the transgressive qualities of those old carnivals.[41] As sanctioned extravaganzas of boundary violation with outrageous juxtapositions of kings and fools, disabled and able-bodied, filthy and clean, spiritual and material, young and old, male and female, ridiculous and sublime, carnivals were prototypes of postmodern possibility. They provided the grotesque a momentary place in the sun, an opportunity to exhibit themselves. By capitalizing on their ironic celebrity, people with stigmatized bodies could (and did) parody those in authority. Carnivals, in postmodern terms, were sites of resistance.

So Charlie's exhibitionism might be viewed as a throwback to the Renaissance carnival, a celebration and empowering of the oppressed. Here, the oppressed = Charlie himself. His situation recalls the feminist slogan: The personal is political. In other words, Charlie's personal pain could be construed as the fault of a political ideology that reinforces gender stereotyping; and his flashing could be construed as an understandable protest. For the unsuspecting victim of his protest, however, it may be small solace that twenty-first-century scholars would find cause for celebrating such a "site of resistance."

Charlie's body, a Duchampian assemblage of biological and engineered parts, is a postmodern theorist's dream. The implanting of a mechanical penile prosthesis into his mutilated genital rendered him akin to one of the central images of postmodernism—the cyborg, the hybrid of man and machine. Cyborgs have long been a provocative staple of science fiction but gained new prominence with the onset of cyberculture and the popularity of such cult films as *Blade Runner* (1982), *The Terminator* (1984), and *The Matrix* (1999). These movies convey the anxiety inherent in the concept of a hybrid artifact that is neither wholly natural nor artificial, human nor nonhuman. There is something chilling about a creature that cannot be categorized, whose technological possibilities could make it an instrument of destruction. Cyborgs have no genealogy, no nostalgia, and no stake in perpetuating humankind. They challenge our pride, our sense of human superiority over the nonhuman. In a cyborg, where does the person stop and the machine begin? As concoctions of real and fake body parts, they blur the boundary between natural and simulacra, ominously suggesting that there is not much difference. Is a cyborg only partially alive? Is the biotech part of a hybrid included in its concept of itself?

To be sure, a judge considered Charlie's implant to be a part of his self, in that he put the entire Charlie in jail. Charlie's behavior was deemed no less alarming because he had been flashing an inorganic, flesh-encased dildo rather than a functioning penis. Yet Charlie experienced his replacement penis as alien, deeply humiliating. It reminded him of his mutilation, his need for support, his lack of "wholeness." He could never experience his erection as his own. His response is consistent with the way many disabled folks first react to medical equipment and prostheses. When initially "confined" to a wheelchair, for example, many people become depressed, feeling that they are condemned to a life of pitiable status and relentless limitation. Yet, over time, many come to feel "liberated," because a wheelchair enables them to be mobile and independent. To a certain extent, then, their response is a matter of perspective. The reaction to medical apparatus is culturally constructed.

Prosthetic devices need not conjure up weakness, dependency, and despair. In a truly postmodern world, for example, even the most cold, inhospitable forms of technology can be given, of all things, an erotic edge—somehow, the libido finds a way. Orthopedic paraphernalia acquired an entirely new set of meanings, for example, when photographer Helmut Newton posed a Valkyrie-like model wearing sky-high stilettos in a red-velvet-lined wheelchair in the February 1995 issue of *Vogue.* Or, more accurately, he resurrected a buried meaning. As Freud noted, feelings of dread and sexual longing are not mutually exclusive in the unconscious.[42] Medical-looking appliances have long been used fetishistically, as is done in S/M. Newton, in another shot, equipped the model (still on stilettos) with a cane and shiny leg-brace. The apparatus was similar to the one worn by the actress Rosanna Arquette in the 1996 film *Crash.* The device concealed a car accident victim, in which the James Spader character later copulated.[43] Many viewers thought the outrageous sexual acts depicted in the film, which united ecstasy and repulsion, pain and pleasure, life and death, biology and technology, were postmodernism run amok. Others found the sexuality to be uncannily resonant. The portrayal certainly suggests that the meaning of a wound is not fixed. Mutilation may be just another signifier with slippery connotations. It turns out that many sites on the body, particularly those that are thresholds between the body's interior and exterior (such as a scar), are particularly susceptible to sexualization.[44]

Technologically altered humans—cyborgs—are rife with utopian postmodern potential.[45] An artificial body part need not be considered inferior, especially when it performs its function better than the original. Consider Charlie's implant. Arguably it is more reliable than the biological counterpart it replaced. It never inflated or deflated at its own bidding. Charlie's wish was its command. He will never need Viagra. In a sense, his prosthesis gave him a more ideally functioning body. But while he could experience hyper-real breasts on women as more exciting than the real thing, he could not experience his own implant as anything but pathetic—a feeling that had probably triggered his desperate exhibitionism. Even at the termination of therapy, he continued to feel reduced by his own prosthesis. To him it was just a sex release gadget, not a part of his Self. In an insufficiently queer world, how could he feel otherwise?

3

FACTS AND FACTOIDS

When I was in the third grade, a boy in my class asked me to shake hands. I complied, at which point he told me that he was a space alien and that his sex organs were in his hands. Sexual politics being what they were at the time, and because I was a very good girl, I feigned indignation. Surely no one could regard this interaction as anything but the most routine stirrings of very conventional sexuality. It could have been on *Leave It To Beaver*. Yet, in retrospect, it contained queer elements: On some level the boy and I knew very well that the significance of the handshake had changed when he assigned new language to it—that merely by labeling his hand a sexual organ, he had upped its erotic quotient. The interaction had not changed, but its connotation had. The meanings of things like behaviors or speech are constantly shifting. All acts may be construed as sexual and, therefore, queer. It's a matter of perspective.

I mention this because postmodern gender theorists have been accused of having an inordinate and maybe even prurient interest in the strange and mutant at the expense of the familiar. Indeed, some of the individuals I have described thus far may not be statistically average, though they are no less human than those who are. You do not have to travel to life at the margins in order to find the truth about gender. It's just easier to go there: The exotic so obviously exposes the artificiality of the conventional. The conventional, on the other hand, looks so natural that it masks its own constructedness (like the "naturalness" of eating three meals a day, as opposed to, let's say, five, or six, or however many). The truth is we all struggle with identity issues—Are we man enough? Too manly? Too feminine?—and it is when we look at those at the margin that we see this struggle writ large. But it is the same struggle.

Being out of touch with normality is only one accusation leveled against queer theory. Another is that it is shot through with politics. A theory that is concerned with the subordination of those who are sex/gender deviants is undoubtedly fueled at least somewhat by an ideological commitment to greater sex/gender equality. *Mea culpa.* Theories about humans, unlike most theories about nature, cannot easily be separated from their morality. Bigots aside, anyone who sits and listens closely to people cannot help but conclude that gender nonconformists are not automatically classifiable as repulsive, evil, or in the throes of mental decompensation.[1] Most sexual deviants work hard, are good citizens, are capable of love, and, contrary to their stereotype, do not have sex all the time. It becomes obvious that queers have suffered from defamation of character. But a bias in favor of sex/gender equality need not preclude tough-minded thinking about gender as long as the bias is taken into account. It may instigate the research, but, if researchers are careful, it need not contaminate the outcome. In a sense it is a bias against bias.

By normalizing sexual nonconformity I do not mean to categorically whitewash all gender nonconformists. Like their conformist counterparts, a percentage of them are, indeed, criminal and/or mentally ill. To be sure, some people specifically engage in unusual sexual practices because of personality flaws or for neurotic or psychotic reasons—they are without a conscience, for example, or they are unwittingly trying to master a trauma from the past or avoid intimacy. But it turns out that most human behaviors, even those that seem at first glance to be virtuous—washing your hands or martyrdom—may be used defensively to ward off anxiety or to unconsciously punish yourself or others. The neurotic possibility of even something like "virtue" is endless. The point is that the context and meaning of a behavioral act very much matter, as well as its compulsivity, effect on others, and, of course, who is doing the evaluating. Consider Wilt Chamberlain's claim that he had sex with close to twenty thousand women. Was he pathologically promiscuous, or heterosexually errant but not deviant, or the hapless victim of seductive "groupies" who follow teams around offering themselves up to vulnerable sports heroes?[2] Or was he, as many folks viewed him, heterosexually enviable? To tag a specific act as "sick" is a social act, not necessarily a medical one. In a queer world, an unusual sexual practice or gender identification would be neither necessary nor sufficient for an individual to be assigned a psychiatric diagnosis, though it need not preclude one.

Let me emphasize that I am not advocating orgies for everyone without moral constraint. The permutations of human sexual behavior verge on the infinite, including, in some instances, a penchant for brutality and bondage and a fascination with children. But not all sexual behaviors are okay—obviously unacceptable are those acts that are nonconsensual, exploitative, physically harmful, or socially destructive. I am strongly opposed, for example, to those members of a group in the mid-'90s called Sex Panic! who, supposedly in the service of queer theory, condoned unsafe sex regardless of the dangers of HIV transmission. Even if their political position had been a product of good rigorous theorizing, which it was not, it would have been unconscionable. My goal in exploring queer theory is to explain behavior, not to excuse it. There is an important difference.

The biggest objection to queer theory in university circles is that it is not "hard" science. In the academy's pecking order, cultural theory lurks somewhere near the bottom, far closer to astrology than to astrophysics. Cultural theorists, and other practitioners of interpretive disciplines such as psychoanalysts, suffer in prestige from the fact that they cannot form testable hypotheses, perform controlled experiments, and observe their results. They cannot invoke data to prove a point. Many psychiatrists and research psychologists, trained to privilege concrete evidence, dismiss cultural theory as mere speculation, not much better than a fairy tale. Their view touches on a complicated rift in philosophy between empiricists like themselves, who insist that Truth can be discovered only via the scientific method, and hermeneuticists, who argue that Truth can never quite be discovered, but we can further understanding by interpreting meaning. That, to my mind, is precisely what postmodern theory does for gender—it furthers understanding. It does not necessarily convey absolute Truth. Those who hawk it as a totalistic explanation of human life are guilty of disciplinary hubris. It is not the only key that can unlock the mystery of our sexuality.

Neither is biology or data-based psychology the only key. There is nothing inherently wrong with objective science: it is absolutely fundamental to good medical practice. But science prima facie deals with the observable, the measurable, and the rational. It stumbles when grappling with the raging, roiling contents of our inner life, fantasy, emotion, desire—the messy stuff that makes us human. It is not terribly helpful when called upon to explain things that cannot be neatly calibrated. But because something is not amenable to empirical investigation does not mean it is unimportant; it just means that it may be outside the scope of experimental science. So until investigators come up with a way of measuring the ineffable, scientific research into the causes of sex/gender will be unavoidably partial, lopsided, flattened. Good scientists keep that in mind. Yet a regrettable few have failed to recognize their limited perspective, like the characters in the film *Rashoman,* all of whom witnessed the same crime but came up with different self-serving explanations. In a number of instances, gender scientists have been spectacularly myopic; for example, those "hard" biological researchers who were convinced that sexual preference and gender identity would be explained by physiology alone, or those "softer" social scientists who insisted it was caused by environment alone (that was Dr. John Money's view—see Chapter 2). Both camps performed data-based research that looked respectable but did not withstand later scrutiny.[3] Objectivity may be in the eyes of the beholder.

Most biologists and research psychologists maintain that they are dispassionate scientists whose only priority is truth, and that their detractors are ideologically motivated. But despite their best intentions, they may be as mired in politics as cultural theorists are, and they too must be careful to note its insidious sway. A biological explanation for homosexuality, for example, may serve a left-leaning agenda. Many social liberals naively assume that proving that gayness is inborn will convince a hostile public that it should be accepted, just as it does freckles. If homosexuality is natural, it's not a homosexual's fault, they reason, so people will cease discriminating against them—in theory, but not in Realpolitik. Biological determinism does not seem to promote open-mindedness. The "born that way" argument has not been useful to persons of color who continue to be subjected to discrimination, despite the fact that their blackness was not learned or chosen. And feminists learned the hard way that being deemed "essentially" different generally resulted in women being precluded from certain tasks for which they were presumed not suited—such as voting. In the unlikely event that scientists' motivation for finding a physiological cause of deviance was a political strategy, they would not have chosen a very effective one. Then, too, if a "gay gene" were discovered it would enable people to abort fetuses that carried the offending DNA. Given humankind's history of eugenics, the discovery of a gene linked to sex/gender deviance could be explosive.

The environmentalist perspective, albeit scientific, is similarly vulnerable to political spin. It is the explanation of choice of conservatives who are hostile to sexual or gender nonconformity. Presumably, if you can prove that sexuality is responsive to behavioral shaping, you can develop a behavioral technology to shape it in any way you wish. The desire to convert homosexuals and other nonconformists into garden-variety heterosexuals is alive and well in the United States, a desire that may skew various research efforts.[4] My point is that political bias may taint science just as it may taint cultural theory. It is hypocritical for scientists to summarily discard interpretative thinking because it fails to meet a standard of objective purity that they also may, at times, fail to meet.

But because political bias may sully research does not mean that it has to. Politics is beside the point (as it should be) for the overwhelming majority of gender scientists laboring in the trenches outside the glare of the spotlight, whose findings, in any case, are not very useful for political sloganeering, as their research is far too complicated and subtle. Nor are these scientists guilty of disciplinary arrogance. They modestly propose that sex/gender is an intricately interwoven but unknown admixture of the "natural" (hormones, genetics, the brain, evolution, etc.) and the "cultural" (child-rearing practices, self-perceived gender assignment, societal shaping, happenstance, etc.). Biology, in their view, produces a faint signal in a child that somehow gets amplified. They make no dogmatic claims about which elements of biology produce the signal or how it gets amplified.[5] Despite its incompleteness, this is the preferred explanatory paradigm at present, and it is the one propounded in the most recent abnormal psychology textbooks.

It is a good explanation as far as it goes, but as we shall see, it does not go far enough. Unfortunately, the adherents of "empirical-only" Truth, including those who sensibly champion the "admixture" perspective, suffer from "dualism prejudice" that is inherent in language. That is, they tend to presume the duality of biological sex (and all its derivative dualities) and build that presumption into their methodology. So their research is designed to find something that is already assumed to exist whether it does or not. They are stuck inside their own cultural context. In that sense they may be no more value free than their flabbier counterparts, queer theorists.

But because scientific sex/gender research is imperfect does not mean we should jettison it entirely. That would be like throwing out the baby with the bathwater. Science today is full of promise, especially as we have now read the full sequence of the human genome, in which, it turns out, you may find food for most political thought. Ideology aside, we do not exist except in bodily form, so it would be foolish to pretend that biology plays no role in who we are. Let us review some of the more recent findings that have implications for the origin and development of gender identity, sexual orientation, and behavior.

BRAINS AND GENES

In the '90s a rash of neuroscience researchers made a stunning suggestion—that certain portions of the brain sculpted sexual orientation. In other words, gays and straights have different brains and this may be heritable. Reported in *Science*, a rigorous and respected journal, the research created a great hullabaloo, which persists today.[6] Similar kinds of findings had long been published about the differences between women and men—that men's brains are larger, run cooler, and, with age, shrink faster—but the differences are few, slight, and virtually uninterpretable with regard to their effect on behavior.[7] In other words, the jury is still out about the meaning of the physiological differences in men's and women's brains. Nevertheless, the fact that neuroscience has not resolved the male/female question has not lessened the clamor over its implications for the heterosexual/homosexual one.

In 1991, Simon LeVay, a biologist who now directs the Institute of Gay and Lesbian Education in Southern California, claimed to have discovered crucial facts about the brain.[8] Results of autopsies conducted on nineteen gay men, sixteen straight men, and six heterosexual women led LeVay to conclude that glands found in the hypothalamus (specifically, the interstitial nuclei of the anterior hypothalamus) of gay men and straight women were less than half the size of those in straight men. The report by LeVay made a big media splash: the *New York Times* gave it front page coverage on August 21st. LeVay appeared on *Donahue* and *Oprah*. Two years later, Dean Hamer of the National Cancer Institute, in what appeared to be a *coup de maitre*, found gay brothers to share a tip of genetic information at the end of the X chromosome, leading the popular media to hyperbolically announce the discovery of a "gay gene."[9] According to Hamer, homosexuality was more likely transmitted genetically through mothers rather than through fathers since males derive their single X chromosome from their mothers.

Both LeVay and Hamer touted the significance of the next "big" gene finding reported in *Science* in 1995 that revealed possibilities for a discovery of homosexuality's origins in the "gay" behavior of the lowly fruit fly.[10] Evidently, sexually mature male *Drosophila* aggressively court immature male *Drosophila*. The behavior deemed "gay" consists of male-to-male genital licking and touching partners with forelegs, and this behavior can be induced by techniques that abnormally activate a specific gene; hence, scientists implied, genes may analogously influence male sexual behavior in *Homo sapiens*.

These studies and the books they spawned—LeVay's 1993 *The Sexual Brain* and Hamer's (and David Copeland's) 1994 *The Science of*

Desire: The Search for the Gay Gene and the Biology of Behavior—
unleashed a storm of criticism, mostly about overinterpretation and
flaws in design, such as limited sample size and the fact that LeVay's
subjects were not controlled for AIDS. (All his gay cadavers had it, but
not all his nongay ones.) Their findings have not yet been independently confirmed and, in fact, have been disputed in a number of
instances, leading their rivals to disparagingly dub them "brain slicers"
and "New Age phrenologists." The insect researchers who made the
huge leap of extrapolating observations from fruit flies to humans
received their own drubbing.[11] In light of the criticisms and other conceptual problems I will describe later, we should interpret LeVay's,
Hamer's, and animal researchers' findings cautiously. There is
undoubtedly a case to be made for the view that neurological and
genetic influences have an important part in determining sexual preference among humans—there is no behavior that does not originate in
our having a brain—but the research thus far is hardly definitive.

EVOLUTION

It is a curious thing, but homosexuality runs in families, this despite
the fact that homosexual men and women reproduce less often than
their straight counterparts. If number of offspring is an indicator of
evolutionary success then homosexuality could be construed as evolutionarily maladaptive. You would think it would die out. Evolutionarily
speaking, we cannot account for its persistence. From the perspective of
population genetics, homosexuality occurs much too frequently and
consistently to be dismissed as a freak of nature: its rate of occurrence is
at least three to four times greater than the mutation rate leading to
genetic disease.[12] And far from heading toward extinction, the gay and
lesbian presence seems to be on the rise in the United States and else-
where, possibly because more people than ever before are now willing
to say they are homosexual, or allow others to make that inference.[13]

The proof that a proclivity for homosexuality is heritable is twin
studies. While older twin studies, like the oft-cited Kallman research
published in 1952, were beset with methodological problems, newer
research corrects some of the design flaws and comes to similar conclusions. In 1990, Michael Bailey and Richard Pillard assessed sexual
orientation in identical twin males, fraternal twin males, nontwin biological male siblings, and similarly aged unrelated adopted males.
If something genetic were going on, then identical twins should have the
highest rate of also being gay, followed by fraternal twins, with adoptive
siblings coming up the rear. That is precisely what they found: 52 percent

of identical twins as a whole, 24 percent of fraternal twins, and 11 percent of adoptive brothers were also gay.[14] Two years later, they found similar results for females. They concluded that genetic factors are important in determining individual differences in sexual orientation.

If sexual orientation were completely genetic, however, identical twins would always have the same sexual orientation. Obviously genes are not the whole story. The search for a single dominant gene—the "O-GOD" (one gene, one "disorder") hypothesis—that would influence a behavioral variant turns out to be whoppingly misguided. We now know that genes are highly dependent on each other as well as the environment. Far from being static blueprints that dictate our destiny, they can be turned on and off in different patterns and modified by experience and context. This is true even with simple physical characteristics that we've assumed were nailed down by genetics. There is no irrevocable rule in nature that XY has to make a man and XX has to make a woman. Birds do it the other way around. Many insects do not even have a Y chromosome. With regard to humans, scientists now believe height, for instance, is only 90 percent heritable. A person's gene might code for tallness, but poor nutrition might mask its development.[15] We're not entirely doomed to our supposedly imperial immutable DNA.

If the genetic precursors of a characteristic as straightforward as height are fraught with complication, then the genetic precursors for something as elusive, behaviorally convoluted, and time specific as becoming romantically infatuated, sexually aroused, and consummating sex are infinitely more so. Instead of an "O-GOD," it is far more likely that many, many different genes team up in an array of combinations that interact in unpredictable ways at various times with particular environmental factors to guide sexual orientation, all of which is mediated by the person's cultural/linguistic constructions and unconscious. This is hardly a precise or parsimonious explanation, but it is probably closer to the truth than a "gay gene."

Ironically, it is this very complexity that might explain why homosexuality and other nonheterosexual practices still exist when they apparently have little survival value in evolutionary terms. Because an exclusively gay sexual orientation is not reducible to one factor but may arise via multiple pathways, it may be more likely to persist over generations. Perhaps it silently piggybacks other traits (which, unlike itself, do have selective advantage) until the situation is ripe for its appearance. Alternatively, homosexuality may survive for the same reason that altruistic behavior survives, because it promotes the survival of its genetic material in its kin. In other words, gay uncles may be useful to a family, which passes on the uncle's DNA. Homosexuality—which is practiced by at least 63 vertebrates including monkeys, flamingoes, and male sheep—appears to play a social role in some species. Bonobos (pygmy chimpanzees), for example, will have sex with a same-sex partner to calm tensions after a squabble or to make sure that a large amount of food is shared.[16] (Interestingly, bonobos who engage in "gay" behavior are not thereafter shunned; indeed, homophobia is unknown in the animal world). Any gene that shapes an animal to help its relative may, with some probability, be favoring copies of that gene sitting inside those relatives. These are only speculations. Most scientists agree that homosexuality is an evolutionary mystery.

Not so gender behavior! Evolutionary psychologists (formerly known as sociobiologists) have razed forests writing about the evolution of male/female difference. These neo-Darwinists are obsessed with the deep and supposedly constitutive differences between men and women—differences that are allegedly hardwired by the machinery of natural selection.[17] Here's a capsule summary of the evolutionary psychology perspective: The object of mating behavior (unbeknownst to the participants) is the reproduction of genes. A man has a great statistical advantage over a woman because he is able to produce and deploy millions of gene-bearing sperm each day, versus her 400 eggs over a lifetime. Since he has so much reproductive capacity, he can get away with investing little in his offspring—minimally one dose of sperm and he can bolt. A woman, on the other hand, can have only a few children, so she has a much greater biological investment in the precious carrier of her genes. While he is out philandering, which is the genetically strategic thing for him to do, she must endure nine months of metabolic trauma and untold years of childcare. In contrast to the male, it is adaptive for her to choose quality over quantity with regard to a mate. Her genetic self-interest is served by finding a good father for her offspring, the kind of hominid who will provide status and stability, strength and devotion, not necessarily the one most willing to copulate (those are never in short supply!).

It follows from a "natural selection" standpoint that the most successful savanna-dwelling males were the ones who propagated their DNA most widely—so that is why men evolved to be more promiscuous than women. According to this calculus, men also evolved to have a stronger sex drive and to seek women with superior reproductive potential (read: young), which is advertised by such qualities as smooth skin, big eyes, full lips, a low waist-to-hip ratio (read: beautiful). The relative scarcity of eggs compared to sperm led men to compete with each other for women, which they did by looking flashy (the peacock strategy) or fighting other males (the deer strategy). The latter could account for men's larger body size and their aggression-promoting male hormones.

We all know men and women who resemble their evolutionary stereotypes. It makes great cocktail conversation. There is something very appealing about simple, linear, cause-and-effect explanations of things. The evolutionary psychology rationale was initially cited by my patient Charlie to account for his antisocial behavior. But the wanton use of this kind of logic can make everything look like an adaptation. Posttraumatic stress disorder, for example, might be adaptive because it can be emotionally paralyzing to its sufferers, causing them to curtail their activities, which may prevent them from encountering future trauma, which may prolong their life, which may, in turn, enhance their likelihood of reproducing. But that's a huge stretch. No one who actually works with people with PTSD would ever construe that affliction as adaptive.

When evolutionary psychology is used to explain behavioral differences between men and women, as opposed to mere physical differences, it can segue into Kiplingesque *Just-So* storytelling. As I mentioned in Chapter 1, biologist Randy Thornhill and anthropologist Craig Palmer recently argued in *A Natural History of Rape* that men rape women because nature programmed them that way.[18] Rape, they insist, is not an aggressive act, but a reproductive act—that is, one inserted by evolution into men's brains—to give sexually bereft men the chance to propagate their DNA. But many respected scientists consider Thornhill and Palmer's research to be bogus. University of Chicago biologist Jerry Coyne, for example, has pointed out that their conclusions (as well as those of many evolutionary psychologists) are lacking in the property known as falsifiability, the ability to be disproven by some conceivable observation.[19] They can never be shown to be wrong—which does not make them right, but does make them banal. The more the world is explained by evolutionary psychology, the less power evolutionary theory has to explain things, until the term "evolutionary psychology" becomes trivial. It doesn't tell us more than we already know. Besides, the theory soft-pedals cultural influences and totally disregards the importance of deep cultural and linguistic constructions for human behavior. Plus, it too easily gets us off the hook for our misbehavior, as it conveniently imputes our tendency to perform misdeeds to our remote ancestors.

But just because evolutionary theory may be construed as obvious or self-serving does not refute it. No sensible biologist would deny that the physical differences between men and women resulted from natural selection acting on our foreparents. Therefore, it would be foolish for us to deny a priori that evolution did not also produce some behavioral differences that evolved alongside the physical characteristics. Besides, evolutionary psychologists—like Steven Pinker in *The Blank Slate*—go to great pains to assure us that our genetic heritage does not doom us to sexism and violence.[20] As evolved humans, they insist, we can both recognize and condemn any dark biological side to humanity without necessarily repeating it. Women aren't sentenced to being nurturing and passive; men to being socially obtuse and aggressive; athletic males to being promiscuous; and lesbians to "lesbian bed death." We all know that there are extraordinarily empathic monogamous men and ferociously horny women who gallivant around. That fact alone should tell us that there's always some flexibility in even our most supposedly evolutionarily dominated traits.

Strict dichotomies—of nature versus nurture and feminism versus evolutionary psychology—lead us into the pitfall of reductive thinking, a profound shortcoming of any theory that seeks to exclude all others. The truth about eroticism is more likely a highly intricate "both/and" rather than a simple "either/or." Evolution is another key, one among many that may help unlock the mystery of our sexuality.

RAGING HORMONES

The short version is that it's not all about testosterone. But let's start with testosterone because it tends to make headlines. Both men's and women's brains have receptors for it, but beyond signaling a fetus to develop a male body, no one knows what testosterone does in the brain. It is unclear whether or not it affects gender identity and sexual orientation.

Here's what we know. We are unisex at the point of conception with proto-male and proto-female structures. About six weeks later, those fetuses with an XY chromosome start producing testosterone, which serves to develop the male structures and wither the female ones. Shortly thereafter, male external genitals start appearing. Females are the default sex (or the "original" sex if you prefer a more empowering adjective). Without prenatal testosterone the fledgling embryo takes on a female form, but it needs some estrogen to fully develop external genitals and any internal female genitalia at all (like ovaries and a uterus). We've known since the '50s that if you castrate a male rabbit fetus, choking off its testosterone, you produce a completely feminized rabbit.[21]

Obviously, we cannot construct experiments to assess this in humans but we can look at naturally occurring "experiments," those so-called accidents of nature in humans where a congenital abnormality does what a researcher is ethically obliged not to do—manipulate prenatal sex hormones. An excess of testosterone in utero (as in CAH, congenital adrenal hyperplasia) will produce an early puberty in a genetic boy and an enlarged clitoris in a genetic girl, though her internal genitals are usually normal. Not surprisingly, many of these girls grow up surrounded by gender researchers. The girls usually turn out to be heterosexual, in spite of their—often-severe—prenatal androgen exposure, though data are inconclusive.[22] As a group, CAH girls are tomboyish; they play hard and prefer trucks and pistols to dolls. But, of course, they were born with a boyish-looking genital, which undoubtedly affects their behavior and self-image.[23]

What about the opposite condition, an insufficiency of prenatal testosterone? In a syndrome called AIS (androgen insensitivity syndrome), in which there is a defect in a person's ability to process testosterone, a genetic boy will on the surface appear to be a girl. But internally, he has occult male testes. These "boys," not unexpectedly, are usually raised as girls, which is what they look like. They tend to grow breasts (in fact they tend to grow large breasts) and typically discover their abnormality only when they fail to menstruate. Obviously this startling information contradicts years of gender role development, and most of these individuals continue in their female gender role and most seek sexual relationships with men.[24] So, regarding the effect of prenatal hormones on sexual orientation…we do not yet know. All we can say for certain is that prenatal testosterone turns a neuter human fetus into a male one.

Theorizing about the importance of prenatal hormones for sexual orientation did not come out of thin air, but out of animal studies. It had been shown that depriving male rats of prenatal testosterone will make them act "gay" later on (if they're also given estrogen in adulthood); that is, they will exhibit "lordosis"—flex their backs up—which is what female rats do when they present themselves to males for penetration. Alternatively, when given testosterone very early in life, female rats will do what male rats do during copulation—mount. So, the boy rats act sexually like girls; and the girls act sexually like boys (at least with regard to their sex posture). Presumably, the sex hormones affect a hypothalamus-like part of their rat brains.[25] It was largely the results of animal work like this that led researchers such as LeVay to focus on the hypothalamus as the most promising area of the human brain to be causally related to sexual orientation. It was also the outcome of these studies that prompted more dire consequences—such as the German endocrinologist Gunter Dormer's proposal for assessing the sex hormone levels in the amniotic fluid of pregnant women as a "preventive" measure.[26] These animal findings are now vigorously disputed by Brown University biologist Anne Fausto-Sterling who points out that the research failed to consider the rats' environment, social interactions, and life cycle.[27]

Plus, there are major problems in extrapolating these findings to humans. Homosexuality and heterosexuality in humans have to do with the sex of the individual to whom the person is attracted, NOT the position the person takes during copulation. But animal studies have to do with positioning, NOT the sex of the mate. Male rats that display lordosis will do so not only when mounted by a male rat, but also when stroked by a human researcher (male or female). Lordosis and mounting are merely rat reflexes. In fact, a hormonally manipulated female rat will mount a hormonally manipulated male, which may at first seem to be mutually "gay" interaction, but, if you stop to think about it, is actually heterosexual. And in the real live world of *Homo sapiens*, homosexual men do not mount less frequently than heterosexual men, nor do lesbians engage in increased mounting behavior. Finally, even if there were a gene-to-hormone apparatus that organized the brain of humans in such a way that caused the individual to find the same sex desirable, it is not apparent how that would apply to actual gays and lesbians. Healthy homosexual men and women, as well as gender deviants, have hormonal profiles that are indistinguishable from so-called normal people, both before and after birth.[28] In short, gay men and male gender-benders have neither less testosterone, nor more estrogen, than straight men. Lesbians and female gender-benders have no more testosterone, nor less estrogen, than their straight counterparts.

The latest prenatal theory about the causation of sexual deviance has to do with the fact that the greater number of older brothers a male has, the more likely he is to be homosexual.[29] Evidently, male fetuses trigger an immune reaction in their mothers. If this reaction becomes stronger with each pregnancy, it might eventually affect the brains of younger children while they are in the womb, altering the sexual orientation of the males. This is all highly conjectural, and I suspect may fade from the literature, as was the fate of the theories about lesbians' so-called masculinized inner ear, which was presumably due to exposure to prenatal androgens.

Thus far, I have been talking about hormones and other aspects of life in the womb. Once born, a child's levels of circulating sex hormones are low but spike in puberty, resulting in all those things about which teens are embarrassed—like pubic hair, acne, facial hair and hairline recession (in boys), and breast development and menstruation (in girls). All grown-up males do not uniformly produce a single identifiable "masculine" cocktail of hormones, nor do all females produce a single identifiable "feminine" cocktail.[30] Instead, males and females produce the same kind of hormones, though usually in relatively different quantities. So even if men were from Mars and women were from Venus, here on Earth they're both on the same drugs. You cannot distinguish between men and women, or between gender-benders and straights, just by measuring hormones. It is true that without an upsurge in hormones at puberty people fail to develop much interest in sex of any kind, and with it they usually do. But hormones have no effect on the kind of sexual activity they wish to pursue.

This is not to say that hormones do not affect behavior. Testosterone makes people edgy and aggressive, and men average about ten times as much of it as women. However, it is not a very accurate predictor of violence. It cannot, for example, distinguish between criminal inmates and college students.[31] If you give it to gay men (who have a normal level in the first place), it doesn't make them straight—the Nazis tried that at Buchenwald.[32] If you give it to straight females, the women will develop male-pattern baldness and bigger muscles, but they won't turn into lesbians or become more combative. For all its celebrity, testosterone is an elusive factor in the complicated choreography of sexual desire, sexual orientation, and gender identity.

SEX/GENDER-LINKED BEHAVIOR...OR NOT

Now that young Palestinian women have begun to distinguish themselves as suicide bombers, and female American soldiers, along with their male colleagues, have been photographed enthusiastically abusing Iraqi detainees, you would think that we would finally give up the idea that women are the "gentler" sex. Yes, I know that men are overwhelmingly responsible for violent crime. They commit 90 percent of the murders, 80 percent of the muggings, nearly 100 percent of the rapes.[33] But women are equally hostile, just not so in-your-face physically aggressive. They become aggressors of a different kind, They taunt, rank, cocktease, exclude, name call, gossip. Hell hath no fury like a teenaged girl scorned by some clique. To believe that girls retreat into "niceness" around the age of puberty, as some feminists argue, is not to know girls. Psychoanalytic therapists who actually listen closely and attempt to analyze women's dreams and behavior, rather than take them at face value, seldom make the mistake of assigning them excess virtue.

There are plenty of bloodthirsty tyrants of both sexes, certainly enough women in that cohort to establish their credentials as equally reprehensible as men. Amid the apocalyptic atrocities in Rwanda in

1995, for example, one of the largest massacres of Tutsis was lead by Rwanda's female minister for women and family affairs, Pauline Nyiramasuhyko. The point is that a biological difference in aggression between the sexes may be more apparent than real. No matter how politically correct a person's family, male and female children are socialized very differently. Boys in general are prodded by various cultural cues to express their aggressiveness in one way—kicking butt, crunching beer cans, belching, pummeling people—while girls are steered into expressing their aggression in another way—by emotional manipulation, whining, and mean-spirited gossip.[34] This inevitably affects how they develop. In my psychotherapy practice, those patients who have the most violent fantasies are not necessarily male, but those who themselves had been victims of violence, such as the boys and girls swept into the Boston race riots and gang fights of the '70s. The warring factions were organized by race, not gender, resulting in equally rage-riddled men and women.

Regarding lust, men presumably have more. In his influential and occasionally mischievous book, *The Evolution of Human Sexuality*, evolutionary biologist Donald Symons wrote that "the sexually insatiable woman is to be found primarily, if not exclusively, in the ideology of feminism, the hopes of boys, and the fears of men."[35] Well, maybe. It's true, as I noted in Chapter 2, that men and women may "turn on" differently. Men are the major consumers of visual pornography. They are also the major consumers of prostitution. They have a far greater capacity for coercive sex, especially in times of war. They orgasm more readily—purportedly 90 percent of the time, versus 30 to 50 percent of the time for women—if you believe the sketchy data.[36] But with the decline of the infamous double standard, the popularity of TV's *Sex and the City*, the spirited search for the female Viagra, and the ascendance of "grrl power," I suspect the "lust gap" may be closing.

Lust is very complicated (an understatement!). Once again, any biological difference between the sexes may appear to be larger than it actually is. I have observed over the years that my male patients who engage in phone sex or cybersex or who go to prostitutes, in contrast to their evolutionary stereotype of irrepressible philandering, tend to prefer the **same** partner for their repeat encounters. Somehow, even in these anonymous commercial transactions, the quality of the relationship seems to matter to some men. My younger male patients who participate in the bar scene, which often unfolds under the watchful gaze of their buddies, complain of peer pressure to act promiscuously. This applies to young women as well. Contrary to the infamous female propensity to nest, many of my women patients do not seek sex exclusively in committed relationships, though they generally want sex with a skilled and considerate partner. The marital rate among young single women is plummeting in places like Japan and Italy, where there are housing shortages and marriage would result in a downscaling of their lifestyle. Their reluctance suggests that the desire to shop may trump the desire to wed. Of course, a cohort of Euro-Asian sophisticates and/or a cadre of East Coast, educated, therapy-seeking urbanites may not be representative of the population at large, though they tend to be a bellwether of what's to come. The bottom line is that there does not seem to be two utterly distinct sexualities based on the biology of the participants.

But that has not stopped folks like culture critic Camille Paglia from speculating that there are two distinct, essential sexualities—male and female—and, moreover, that gays and lesbians act out the extremes of their sex's innate sexual behavior.[37] Homosexual males are supposedly hyper-male with regard to their sexual propensities, and homosexual females, hyper-female. Hence, the oft repeated joke:

What does a lesbian bring on her second date?
A U-Haul.
And what does a gay bring on his second date?
What second date?

In other words, gays, being men, have a tendency to philander, and lesbians, being women, have a tendency to nest. Indeed, most of the same-sex couples who applied for marriage licenses in Massachusetts in May 2004 (when gay marriage was tentatively legalized) were biologically female. Lesbians also have a tendency to, figuratively speaking, "get headaches." Lesbian couples have less sex than heterosexual married couples, who, in turn, have less sex than gay couples.[38] (Evidently Gertrude Stein and Alice B. Toklas were unaware of lesbians' sedate sexual nature, for they happily wrote about their amorous activity in coded notes to each other.)[39]

These data may be accurate for late twentieth-century American couples, but it is important to understand that survey research such as this tends to define the term "sex" narrowly to exclude erotic behaviors like cuddling, touching, and hugging, which constitute sex for some people. In the real world, "having sex" is highly personal and variable; it may not even involve actual physical contact (as in peep shows and cybersex). Perhaps the outcome of this research would look different if the surveyors had asked about length of time of intimate encounters.

We also must be careful not to generalize a "lust gap" between the sexes to all people in all times. Just the briefest glance at Western literature reveals that women's libido used to be alive and well before the late nineteenth century. In the eighteenth century, for example, the fictional Fanny Hill was happily plying her trade and promiscuity was at an all-time high. In fact, until the Victorian period, women had been regarded as more sexually demanding than men, which may partially account for the virulent backlash against women in the form of early modern witch hunts. The writings of Chaucer, Boccacio, and Montaigne are filled with hapless men who cannot satisfy their wives, such as the bawdy Wife of Bath. Note that the ancient biblical *Song of Songs* has "his" and "hers" sections.[40] And those lustful pre-Christian goddesses were, well, pagan.

But female carnal desire came to an end in the nineteenth century, when respectable women were supposed to be as ignorant of sex as they were of business and politics, an idea revived in 1950s America. Sexual ardor became the exclusive province of men and lower-class women. How reproduction occurred is speculative. Presumably men snuck into a darkened room to perform their animal duty while their wives, purportedly like Queen Victoria, lay still and thought of the Empire or its equivalent. The proper pregnant woman stayed indoors so as not to reveal her bump to the public gaze, lest the world recognize that she had engaged in sex. Scarlett O'Hara, the heroine of *Gone With the Wind,* lost her reputation in postbellum Atlanta for trotting out. All of this goes to show how much ideology shapes thinking and feeling.

Ironically, while some people strongly believe in differing male and female desire as a way of accounting for the differing frequency in gay and lesbian sex, most scientists, and much of the public, think quite the opposite. Whether they know it or not, they are adhering to the quaint turn-of-the-century notion of gender inversion—that is, gay men are attracted to men, not because they are hyper-men, but because the are "like" women; lesbians are attracted to women, not because they are hyper-women, but because they are "like" men. That is what neuroanatomists and endocrinologists seem to assume, as they keep looking for analogous biological elements in lesbians and men, and, alternatively, in gay men and women.

A number of psychologists believe this as well, such as Cornell social psychologist Daryl Bem, who argues that sexual desire is directed at those who made you most uncomfortable at an early age. In the case of gays, that would be males; in the case of lesbians, females. This is because homosexual men, as youngsters, were presumably "gender nonconforming," preferring, for example, to dress G.I. Joe rather than engage him in combat. As nonconformists, they were ostracized by ordinary boys, who then became "exotic" to them. Bem's theory is called Exotic Becomes Erotic (EBE). Similarly, lesbians, as girls, are thought to have preferred fighting to playing house and were therefore shunned by other girls.[41]

Bem's theory depends on the fact that gay men were sissy boys and lesbian women were tomboys. This is a hot-button issue, very politically incorrect—perhaps because, if true, and parents were to recognize proto-gay behavior in their children, they might attempt to change it. Here are the facts: both the Kinsey Institute for Sex Research in the '70s and a meta-analysis of forty-eight separate studies by the aforementioned Michael Bailey and an associate in the mid-'90s found that homosexuals recall more gender atypical behavior in their childhood than heterosexuals do.[42] Such findings are buttressed by UCLA psychiatrist Richard Green's famed "sissy boy" study published in the '80s: out of sixty-six gender-nonconforming boys and fifty-six gender-conforming boys, an impressive 75 percent of the "sissies" turned out to be gay or bisexual, compared with only 4 percent of the conventionally gendered tykes. At his final interview, one of his "sissies" said he wanted to become a woman.[43] (No such studies have been performed on girls.)

The Kinsey and Bailey studies (which included females) were retrospective, asking people to remember how they were as children and so suffer from the bias of memory. Green's was prospective, though compared to more recent similar studies Green's results seem somewhat exaggerated. Like it or not, evidence suggests that gender nonconformity in childhood and homosexuality are correlated.

This is hardly surprising. The data merely affirm what many people already assume—that a percentage of gays are (and were as children) stereotypically effeminate and a percentage of lesbians are (and were) stereotypically masculine. It is not shocking to realize that behaviors have behavioral precursors. These studies also show that not all adult homosexuals come from the "sissy boy" category. Even strong advocates of the connection between childhood gender conformity and adult sexual orientation admit that only between a quarter to a third of all gender-atypical children become homosexual. Plus, the Kinsey study showed that half of straight women considered themselves tomboys in childhood. So, gender nonconformity in childhood cannot stand alone as an explanation of a same-sex sexual orientation. And, once again, we see that gender behavior and sexual orientation are not entirely collapsible categories.

Nevertheless, even if there were a perfect correlation between sissy boys and later homosexuality, why should this be disturbing? (Somehow, people are not so upset by tomboy behavior in girls.) Duke culture critic Eve Kosofsky Sedgwick argues that we suffer from culture-wide "effeminophobia" (see Chapter 2)—we absolutely hate effeminacy in boys and men. Apparently, the best thing to be in life, straight or gay, is a male. Even the most liberal psychologists are prepared to like only those homosexual men who are (a) already grown up and (b) act masculine.[44] But in a queer world, girlie boys and fruity men would not necessarily disgust us. We could take as a role model the mom in the charming 1997 French-language film *Ma Vie en Rose*, who loved and came to accept her cross-dressing little son without trying to change him.

In the end, there does appear to be a package of weakly linked sex/ gender characteristics, and some of these characteristics conform to sex/gender stereotypes. Straight men throw a ball better than straight women do; gays are about as "bad" as the straight women with regard to ball-throwing; and lesbians do better than both.[45] Also, gay guys are artier than straight guys (if the nature of the professions they enter is a fair indicator); lesbians have fewer squabbles with their mates over money than gay or straight couples; women read facial expressions better than men; men read maps better. How this came about is anyone's guess. There may be some biological predisposition to one thing or another. If that is true, we must make sure that we do not use science as a means of getting rid of deviant sex/gender, but to foster and protect an individual's right to be whomever he/she/it is.

THE ANTHROPOLOGICAL BUFFET

Just to emphasize how tricky all this sex/gender coding can get, let's catalogue some of the prevailing clichés across cultures and how they differ from our own. To be sexy and beautiful in Brazil if you're a woman, according to Holly Brubach, former style editor of the *New York Times Magazine*, is to have large hips, ample thighs, and what North Americans disparagingly call a "big butt," with, believe it or not, a small bustline.[46] In a country where plastic surgery figures in the press as a national industry, the most popular procedure is breast reduction—in stark contrast to the statistics in the United States. Ethnographically speaking, paradoxes like these abound. Here's another: though notoriously macho, Brazilians adore their drag queens.

So do the Japanese, where male drag queens may appeal both to businessmen whiling away the cocktail hour in the thrall of a transvestite geisha as well as to their wives. For many years running, an annual poll of Japanese women awarded the distinction of "sexiest male star" to a professional actor in Kabuki theater who portrayed women when on stage and dressed androgynously when off.[47] Japanese housewives and teenage girls also flock to the Takarazuka Young Girls Opera Company, where male roles are played by actresses, a few of whom have become major superstars with large groups of swooning female followers. Takarazuka actresses stage about seven performances a week at both of their 3,000-seat theaters. Packs of female fans wait breathlessly at the stage door for the moment when they can see, take photographs of, beg autographs from, give presents to, and maybe even touch their favorite male impersonator. There's a message of flexibility here about sexual desire.

Anthropologists came late to the study of sex and gender, viewing those areas as more pertinent to the realms of psychology and sociology. When they did field work, they tended to impute two sexes (and the "corresponding" dualities of gender identity, gender role, and sexual orientation) to the various cultural groups they studied. Unfortunately, anthropologists, like the rest of us, do not see with the naked eye but always through the lens of their own culture. Though maverick for their era, even Margaret Mead and Ruth Benedict, the anthropologists who pioneered studies of sexual development in non-Western cultures, who were one-time lovers and self-designated "misfits," never really questioned the preconception of there being but two sexes.

It took the second wave of the women's movement and Stonewall to propel anthropologists into thinking more about their internalized cultural assumptions about gender and sexual orientation to explain and do away with sex/gender oppression. Is oppression natural and universal? Do women, gays, lesbians, bisexuals, and transgenders always have to be the underdogs? In 1975, feminist anthropologist Gayle Rubin wrote a landmark essay, "The Traffic in Women," in which she pointed out the arbitrariness of our sex/gender arrangements and how ours, in particular, is both created by, and in turn, reifies, male (and implicitly, heterosexual) power.[48] Foreshadowing queer theorist Michel Foucault, her article suggested that any culture may organize biological raw material in its own way, thereby implying that our flesh has to be infused with beliefs and ideas before it becomes sexy. So, domination of one sex/gender by another is not inevitable, but rather a by-product of our beliefs and ideas. Do field data support this, or is this feminist wishful thinking?

Here again we encounter the "constructionist vs. essentialist" debate, this time couched in anthropological terms. It is at the heart of the sex/gender conundrum. Anthropologists are in an especially dicey position for grappling with this question because in order to make sense of things they must, as a matter of course, invent categories into which they can sort the information they collect. They are, by nature, systematizers. But in inventing those categories, they inevitably betray their own biases. For example, how they classify the sexual orientation of a biological male who has sex with a male transvestite will obviously affect their calculation of a base rate of homosexuality for a society. It is very difficult to operate outside of your conceptual system. A few anthropologists, like University of Chicago's Gilbert Herdt and unaffiliated scholar Will Roscoe, are valiantly attempting to purge taxonomies of "dualism prejudice" by suggesting that there may be three or four sexes and genders, which may transform into each other in the course of an individual's lifetime. This left-leaning contingent scrupulously avoids flattening a culture into the contours of their own and tends to dismiss the terms "gay," "bisexual," "lesbian," and "transgender" as meaningless oversimplifications, except when writing about modern time and culture.[49] Their anthropological inquiry segues into the cultural relativism of postmodernism, which is not surprising given the temper of our times.

For Roscoe, for instance, the Native American "two-spirit" people, formerly known as "berdache" (a non-Native term), are neither male, female, nor transgender, but instead embody a "third gender" (if biologically male) and a "fourth gender" (if biologically female). Male two-spirits have been observed in 133 North American societies and female two-spirits in about half that number.[50] Their behavior varies widely, but almost all cross-dress and have sex with "conventional" members of their own biological sex. (Their erotic partners, however, might also have sex with persons of the opposite sex.) Roscoe argues that two-spirits embody an identity beyond sex. The shining difference about two-spirits—the challenge as Roscoe sees it—is that native societies ascribe a superior status to these folks. Natives believe them to be honored by the gods and to possess supernatural power combining male and female. In many traditional societies there seems to be no hard-and-fast line between the role of shamans and two-spirits. A dream could be motive enough to change gender. There is no modern Western cultural equivalent.

Another so-called third gender, the Hijiras of northern India, Pakistan, and Bangladesh also assert a supernatural dimension. (They are sometimes called a "third sex" because the Western distinction between sex and gender is not a part of Indian discourse.) As with the two-spirits, their gender role purportedly arose, not from personal inclination, but was chosen for them by gods and spirits. Numbering several hundred thousand, Hijiras are biologically male, or, in rare cases, hermaphrodites. If the former, they are supposed to castrate themselves. The absence of a penis allows them to confer blessings (for reimbursement) on newborn sons and newlywed couples. While some Hijiras no doubt devote themselves to their ascetic sacred calling, many work as cross-dressing prostitutes, usually for a "conventional" male clientele.[51] Recently, Kimla Jaan, an illiterate and foul-mouthed Hijira, made world headlines, as she was unseated from her post as mayor of the city of Katni because she is biologically male and was functioning in a position reserved for women. Jaan's 1999 electoral triumph had previously sparked a spate of eunuch electoral victories. As one of Jaan's constituents put it at the time, "Most politicians turn out to be eunuchs, so we thought it was time to elect a real one."[52] This comment reveals the ambivalent status assigned to Hijira, who are both revered and reviled.

A few radical anthropologists actually view the concept of a third gender as too limiting because it operates within the confines of a dimorphic view of sex and gender. But most mainstream anthropologists are realists and therefore lean more to the right than the left in the essentialist vs. constructivist debate. In other words, they acknowledge their ethnocentrism, try to limit it, and plod on looking for human universals. Sociologist Stephen O. Murray, for example, agrees that the range of behaviors, subcategories, and meaning of same-sex sex are considerable, but argues in his encyclopedic book *Homosexualities* that there are, indeed, a few recurring patterns. His taxonomy is typical of many possible classification systems and I refer to it because it is recent, reasonably flexible, culturally sensitive, and comprehensive.[53] The patterns Murray discerns are largely though not entirely socially constructed and may or may not have to do with homosexual desire—how could an anthropologist know for sure?—but generally have to do with genital contact, or some proximate activity.

His first category, sanctioned *age-structured* homosexuality, occurs in a number of societies but is most famous for being the modus operandi of the classical Greeks. Here, a younger male has sex with an older male citizen. Boys were expected to resist the advances of the older men, relenting only after an involved courtship and then only to allow the older man "intracrural" (between the thighs) intercourse. In addition, the boy was not supposed to derive erotic pleasure from the interaction.[54] In New Guinea, boys spend years fellating and swallowing the semen of their elders, further years being fellated by juniors, and still wind up, as expected, married fathers. This puts an interesting spin on our response to pedophilia today.

In *gender-stratified* homosexuality, another of Murray's categories, the participants enact stereotyped "opposite" gender roles. In many Latin and Arab cultures, for example, being the male penetrator (the *activo*) is the defining act of masculinity, not having sex with a woman. To be *pasivo*, which is associated with femininity, is a disgrace. The *activos*, or *machistas*, do not consider themselves gay.[55] It's similar in prisons, too—a good indication of the power hierarchies involved. Murray includes Hijiras and two-spirits in the gender-stratified category.

The *egalitarian* type of homosexual relation, Murray's final category, is distinguished from the others by involving adults of approximately the same age and social status. This type of relationship is highly visible in our own society, although we do not know about its prevalence in the past. We do know of a few, such as the lesbian marriage resisters who worked in the silk factories in southern China.[56]

At the other end of the spectrum of anthropological inquiry are researchers such as University of Arizona sociologist Frederick Whitam, who use traditional Western ways of classifying sex/gender nonconformity.[57] They tend to take sexual practice at face value, making relatively little attempt to evaluate it from the perspective of the participants. Underlying their research is the assumption that there is a biological component to behavior that is universal. Go to any gay community in any society, Whitam insists, and you will find a subgroup of gay male transvestites and gay male transsexuals that resemble each other in great detail, though these individuals are members of communities that are separated by oceans and continents. He came to this conclusion after examining records from five societies—Brazil, Guatemala, the Philippines, Indonesia, Thailand, and the United States. These uncannily similar widespread clusters of characteristics include gestures, facial expressions, a tendency to theatricality, and a history of sissy behavior. Also, unlike their heterosexual transvestite and transsexual counterparts, gay transvestites and transsexuals do not cross-dress fetishistically (that is, to get aroused) nor do they seek gay male sexual partners, preferring straight ones. Ultimately, Whitam is arguing that sexual identities are transhistorical, essential categories that inhere in human beings and have remained the same in every culture or social construction. Of course, these data do not support a direct causal link between anatomy and sex/gender destiny. They do suggest a correlative relationship, at least for a subset of cross-dressing biological males who act in a similar manner cross-culturally and presumably do not consult with each other across continents as to how to behave. But we really do not know if these folks have the same neuroendocrinology, the same desires, or the same character formation as each other. We must interpret these data cautiously.

The jury is still out regarding the debate between essentialists and constructionists. But at the very least, anthropological studies demonstrate the multiplicity of sexual orientations and gender identities. Sex and gender are far more variable and fluid than we ever thought. Clearly, we live on a continuum of biological possibilities that can overlap and sustain many incarnations.

IS SEX NECESSARY? CRITIQUING SCIENCE

When humorist author James Thurber asked in 1929, "Is Sex Necessary?" he was surely thinking about his lack of access to sex and not of postmodern gender theory. Today his question has added resonance, for even biologists are questioning the necessity of neatly dividing people up into two sex categories. They are beginning to regard it as an impossible and intellectually misguided task, moreover, one that seriously comprised much scientific work of the past.

Anne Fausto-Sterling, a professor of biology and women's studies at Brown University, exploded the myth of two biological sexes in her 1993 article in *The Sciences*, "The Five Sexes: Why Male and Female Are Not Enough," which was reprinted in modified form in the *New York Times*. In place of the sexual binary, she suggested a five-sex system. In addition to males and females, she included "herms" (named after true hermaphrodites, people born with testes and an ovary); "merms" (male pseudohermaphrodites, who are born with testes and some aspect of female genitalia); and "ferms" (female hermaphrodites, born with ovaries and some aspect of male genitalia). Though tongue-in-cheek, Fausto-Sterling's article made a very serious point—that there are more than two types of human bodies walking the earth, and that these individuals are members of sexes just as viable as male and female, though they have been made invisible by the medical profession. Since the '60s, early surgical intervention on babies with ambiguous genitals (see Chris in Chapter 1, and David Reimer, Dr. John Money's patient, in Chapter 2) erased physical diversity. Surgeons, in Fausto-Sterling's view, inappropriately collapsed anatomical variety into just two configurations—male and female—because doctors, like most people, accepted the categories of male and female as self-evident. Her article caused an uproar.[58]

It shouldn't have. After all, the International Olympic Committee (IOC) also does not think a person's sex is self-evident, even in these days of spandex uniforms. Since the '60s it has been sex-testing women in female-only events, lest a male masquerading as a female infiltrate. This procedure is enormously controversial in part because it bears on the definition of biological sex. Are the sexes distinguishable on the basis of genetics (an X or Y chromosome); at the hormonal level (and if so, when in the course of a person's development from fetus to adult); at the anatomical level (and if so, which ones—internal genitalia or those viewed in the locker room)? Recently, the Olympic governing board has been using DNA to verify an athlete's sex, but, as we know, some externally anatomical women have male chromosomes. In fact, as much as 1 percent of humankind may not conform to the XX/XY pattern. Think of the distress that testing can inflict on an individual who may discover for the first time in her life that she is a "male," especially in the pressure-cooker atmosphere of the Olympic games. What kind of message is the Committee giving—that the Y chromosome indisputably signifies gender? But that's not quite true. Despite the near unanimity of opinion among scientists that sex testing is ill advised, the IOC remains wedded to the notion that it is necessary.[59]

Since the publication of her original article ten years ago, Fausto-Sterling has taken her theorizing even further: she now asserts that there are more than five sexes—in fact, that there are indeterminately many and these do not match up neatly with femininity and masculinity. What is becoming increasingly clear, she points out, is that you can find levels of masculinity and femininity in almost every combination of chromosomes, hormones, gonads, genitals, and so forth. Anatomy and gender behaviors are less like a paired ensemble than mix-and-match. With the revelation of cases of failed sexual reassignments and the emergence of intersex activism, the specialists involved in medical sexual attribution (pediatric endocrinologists, urologists, surgeons, etc.) are starting to listen. They are moving in the direction of person-centered treatment, of gender rights, including the right to decide one's own gender. In the case of infants, they are more willing to wait before assigning a gender and are insisting upon eventual full disclosure to the child.

At the same time, growing numbers of transgendered people, who in the '80s might have sought surgery to "untrap" the male inside their female body or the "female" inside their male one—such as surgically "corrected" University of Iowa economist Deirdre McCloskey (formerly Donald)—are now content to inhabit a more ambiguous zone. They might take as their model jazz musician Billy Tipton, who, unbeknownst to his five wives and adopted children, grew up as Dorothy. His "true" sex was discovered only after his death in 1989. Transgenders like Billy are choosing to live in the role of the "opposite" gender without benefit of the knife, though Billy himself, as a financially strapped product of his era, did not have the luxury of choice.[60] At the University of Minnesota's Program in Human Sexuality, one of the largest transgender centers in the United States, administrators now routinely admit patients who take only half the journey from one sex to another, choosing hormones without surgery, or surgery without hormones.

Fausto-Sterling takes for granted, as do most sensible scientists these days, the truth of the familiar feminist canard that gender behavior, like sexual anatomy, doesn't come in two flavors tied to the shape of a person's genitals.[61] Thanks to the women's movement, it is now generally accepted among enlightened people that gender behavior may vary across sexes and even within an individual over time. Some folks may not like women driving trucks or men working as "nannies," but their voices have diminishing resonance. Also, we now know that gender is not a zero-sum collection of male and female attributes. If you have a high degree of masculinity, you don't have to have a low degree of femininity. You can have traits of both. Masculinity and femininity are not opposite, as psychologist Sandra Bem convincing demonstrated in her early experimental research. Many folks are androgynous.[62]

But while many scientists now recognize that gender role polarization is artificial, they often fail to recognize the multidimensional nature of sexual orientation. Researchers persist in categorizing people as homosexual, bisexual, or heterosexual, as if those categories were distinct, mutually exclusive, and convey a great deal about the person's sexuality. In reality, the anatomical sex of an individual's sexual partner may be only a narrow part of that individual's sexual repertoire. After all, not all heterosexuals live their heterosexuality in the same way. Analogously, talking about homosexual or bisexuality as uniform phenomena is spurious. This is borne out by the sheer diversity of queer sexualities. Transsexual activist Kate Bornstein, a self-designated "gender outlaw," reported encountering an intricate handkerchief code that is used in certain circles for indicating one's sexual preferences. Just the briefest glance at the "hanky code" conveys the enormously complicated nature of desire. Colors mean "active" if worn on the left side and "passive" if worn on the right.[63] Note that the sex of the partner is not designated. I quote the code verbatim:

Left Side	Color	Right Side
Fist Fucker	Red	Fist Fuckee
Anal Sex, Top	Dark Blue	Anal Sex, Bottom
Oral Sex, Top	Light Blue	Oral Sex, Bottom
Light S/M, Top	Robin's Egg Blue	Light S/M, Bottom
Foot Fetish, Top	Mustard	Foot Fetish, Bottom
Anything Goes, Top	Orange	Anything Goes, Bottom
Gives Golden Showers	Yellow	Wants Golden Showers
Hustler, Selling	Green	Hustler, Buying
Uniforms/Military, Top	Olive Drab	Uniforms/Military, Bottom
Victorian Scenes	White Lace	Victorian Scenes, Bottom
Does Bondage	Grey	Wants to Be in Bondage
Shit Scenes, Top	Brown	Shit Scenes, Bottom

(continued)

(continued)

Left Side	Color	Right Side
Heavy S/M & Whipping, Top	Black	Heavy S/M & Whipping, Bottom
Piercer	Purple	Piercee
Likes Menstruating Women	Maroon	Is Menstruating
Group Sex, Top	Lavender	Group Sex, Bottom
Breast Fondler	Pink	Breast Fondlee

With this multiplicity in mind, the linearity of Alfred Kinsey's 1940's rating scale—with 0 being 100 percent heterosexual; 6 being 100 percent homosexual; and X designating no sexual desire at all—seems almost quaint. But while Kinsey's scale appears overly simplistic from a twenty-first century perspective, it was revolutionary for its time. Kinsey was a path breaker for not only "outing" the incidence of homosexuality in the so-called normal population but also for viewing sexual orientation as a continuum (as opposed to a binary). Today, gays still sometimes cite their Kinsey rating, though they tend to do so with a wink.

The scale per se is rarely used anymore in scientific studies. Yet some of its faulty reasoning persists. Researchers still make the mistake (implicit in the Kinsey system) of assuming that the degree of attraction to men varies inversely with the degree of attraction to women. Like the Kinsey researchers, today's scientists lump together people with very different sexual dispositions. (The scale cannot distinguish between bisexuals who, for instance, like sex a lot and those bisexuals who do not.) Also, in the real world, people can be sorted into all sorts of groups based on their sexual interests, but scientists, in the tradition of the Kinsey scale, tend to include only a limited range of features— namely, just the sex that a person is sexually attracted to—under the heading of sexual orientation.[64] In effect, they make the "sex to whom a person is attracted" a master category for defining a person's sexuality. But why focus on this one characteristic of sexual orientation? Why not include other dimensions—like the "hanky code?" To do otherwise, to collapse a person's complete life into a single scale, is to greatly flatten a highly complex phenomenon.

It is important to realize that with the very act of measuring, researchers can alter the social reality they set out to quantify. This review of data-based literature on the causality of sexuality suggests that our nomenclature and taxonomies of sex/gender—in biology, psychology, anthropology, medicine, etc.—are reductionistic. As scientists begin to recognize their oversimplifications and seek to correct by incorporating looser, more nuanced, multidimensional scales in their studies, they will inevitably be tilting in the direction of queer theory. It is interesting to note that just a few years before Fausto-Sterling demolished the myth of two sexes from a scientific perspective, postmodernist Thomas Laqueur did so from a cultural one.[65] In *Making Sex* he pointed out, on the basis of historical evidence, that prior to our two-sex model of the body, a one-sex model dominated Western thinking until the end of the seventeenth century. Women were said to have the same genitals as men, only inside rather than outside. If historically valid, Laquer's "back to the future" theory suggests that our understanding of even something as concrete as anatomy is situational. Whether scientists and cultural theorists know it or not, their viewpoints are converging: essentialism is meeting constructivism.

4

QUEER THEORY: A HISTORY OF AN IDEA

Consider the following headline-grabbing true story and decide which explanation makes the most sense.

In the predawn hours of July 5, 1999, an army private named Calvin Glover bludgeoned to death a fellow private named Barry Winchell while he slept in his bed. Glover, the near-alcoholic perpetrator, had recently lost a fight with Winchell, whom he thought of as gay. Glover was goaded into battering Winchell by Justin Fisher, the victim's roommate, who taunted Glover for getting "beat by a faggot." All three were part of the 101st Airborne Infantry, the "Screaming Eagles," stationed at Fort Campbell on the Tennessee–Kentucky border, whose tougher-than-thou machismo is legendary, even by U.S. Army standards.

The harassment against Winchell started when Fisher found out that Winchell was in love with Calpernia Addams, a preoperative transsexual nightclub performer to whom Fisher had introduced him. Fisher then instigated a four-month gay-bashing campaign against Winchell, which culminated in his brutal murder by Glover, who wielded the bat. At one point, the victim Winchell and his sergeant had gone to the Inspector General's office to complain about the ceaseless hostilities directed against him, but to no avail.

At the trial for Winchell's murder, a forensic psychiatrist revealed that Iago-like Fisher suffered from "transvestic fetishism," meaning that Fisher turned to wearing women's underwear for sexual arousal since the age of 14. He was known to be attracted to one of Addam's drag queen entertainer colleagues, Kim Mayfield. The murderer, Glover, was sentenced to life imprisonment; and in a plea bargain that effectively foreclosed further investigation of the incident, the instigator, Fisher, got 12½ years.[1]

How should we interpret these events?

a. Did Winchell die in a common fight; that is, did he die in what the base command labeled an ordinary "physical altercation"?

b. Or, did Winchell die as a result of a horrific gay-bashing incident? That is the liberal media's view. The left-leaning press also suggests that his death may be an unfortunate (though unintended) consequence of Congress's policy on gays in the military, known as "don't ask, don't tell, don't pursue, don't harass." The measure, signed into law in 1993 as a way of protecting lesbian and gay soldiers, has not eliminated homophobia but has ironically served to heighten its cover-up.

c. Or, did Winchell die, not as a result of a homophobic hate crime, but as a result of homosexual jealousy? According to the conservative press, Winchell was involved in a bizarre love triangle— involving a homosexual (himself), a transsexual (Addams), and a closeted drag queen (Fisher). Fisher hated Winchell because Fisher (as a repressed homosexual) wanted to claim Winchell for himself, and so prodded Glover to murder him. If Fisher couldn't have Winchell, no one could. The right-leaning media implied that homosexuality breeds crimes of passion, and, in the Winchell case, trumped homophobia as the motive for murder.[2]

d. Or, perhaps, Winchell's murder did not have to do with "real" sexuality at all. Indeed, Winchell may not have been homosexual, if the term implies an exclusive attraction to men. Although he was the victim of an antigay hate crime, there is no actual evidence that he was gay. Prior to Addams, he dated females, and he treated her as his girlfriend. In fact, none of the protagonists in the grisly drama may have been, strictly speaking, homosexual. As a male-to-female transsexual, Addams regards herself as a heterosexual woman. Before dating Winchell she had undergone a partial surgical resculpting of her body and, during their time together, she was undergoing hormonal treatment in service of her ongoing transition to biological female. The instigator Fisher may not be homosexual either, for most males who cross-dress privately for sexual arousal are heterosexual. Every element of the

Winchell case falls into the gray in-between of sex/gender. Ultimately, it mattered little whether Winchell was "really" gay or not. What mattered was that he was perceived to be gay.[3] His murder was a category mistake.

These interpretations of "truth" are not mutually exclusive. Nor are they nuanced or complete, even when taken together. But if you consider "d" to be a contender, then, whether you know it or not, you are leaning in the direction of queer theory where sex/gender is viewed as a gray, fluid in-between, rather than a mathematically precise black and white, where perception matters as much as reality. These days many people who have never even heard of queer theory resist superimposing a rigid grid of gender identity and sexual orientation on individuals, a view that seems especially apt in the case of Winchell, Fisher, and Addams, and maybe for a great many people. Within months of each other in 2003, two national cable TV stations broadcast major films that were sympathetic to gender-benders—HBO's *Normal* and Showtimes's *Soldier's Girl*—the latter about the Winchell case. In December of that year, there were so many actors brightening New York stages in opposite-sex roles and productions that the *Times* sponsored a talk entitled "Gender-Benders Onstage."[†] If these shows accurately reflect popular sentiment, then there is a growing climate of tolerance. But while more and more people may think that sex/gender deviance is okay, they have not arrived at their conclusion via a systematic, logically consistent theory. It is a gut feeling. Theory hasn't caught up with intuition.

Queer theory attempts to fill this conceptual gap. Queer theory is what happened in the early '90s when the highly contagious postmodern sensibility infiltrated the realm of gay/lesbian studies, an area of specialization itself very new in the academy, growing out of women's studies in the mid-'80s. Postmodernism, as we have seen, entails the thorough questioning of existing categories (hot/cold; art/schlock; flower/weed; beautiful/ugly, etc.) and even of the process of categorization itself. Hence, queer theory has no truck with fixed sex/gender identities. It transcends labels of male, female, homosexual, bisexual, heterosexual, transsexual, etc., opting instead to consider gender identity and sexual orientation as culturally invented, fluid, eternally unstable constructs that derive what meaning they have from their context. Smash the binaries! Instead of the shape of your genitals and whom

---

[†] These productions included *Lypsinka! As I Lay Lip-Synching, I Am My Own Wife, Matt & Ben, Hairspray,* and *Avenue Q.*

you have sex with, queer theorists are interested in how you obtain sexual pleasure. Only sex acts and practices matter, that is, bodies and pleasures, to paraphrase queer icon Michel Foucault, not gender identity or sexual orientation.[4]

The resulting theory was welcomed by a few academics but vociferously resisted by most, including many traditional gay/lesbian studies scholars. Its name alone raised hackles. The first time people hear the phrase "queer theory," they tend to think it's a joke because the word "queer" has very often been used as a homophobic slur. Then, when they learn that the derogatory term was deliberately employed because, according to writer Christopher Isherwood, "It makes heterosexuals wince," they think it's a bad joke.[5] How can people warm to a theory whose name was designed to affront their sensibility? But when they get to know it better and start gauging its impressive logic and radical potential for upgrading the lives of disempowered people who are subject to discrimination, harassment, and violence merely because of their identity, they may be more forgiving of its insolence. The word "queer" co-opts and subverts a term of oppression in the manner of "black is beautiful" and "crip is hip." It conveys a newfound sense of pride and self-assertion.

Queer theory emerged in the university at a propitious moment. The academy was reeling from the effects of three decades of left-wing social activism—civil rights, the student movement, the New Left, the anti-Vietnam movement, radical feminism, the Black Panthers, hippies, "yippies," gay liberation, the Lavender Menace—and was still, for a time, politically correct and earnestly permissive. Queer theory's seemingly liberationist potential gave it a modicum of leverage. These were the heady days of inclusiveness and multiculturalism, of "identity politics," collective movement-building based on the assertion of a common cause through shared characteristics. Groups of individuals—blacks, women, the disabled, gays—organized to protest their exclusion form the military-industrial complex, the bastions of power, prestige, and money. In a sense, queer theory seemed to up the ante, to expand the trajectory of liberation to include even such fringe "identities" as the "Norwegian moody artist type," who wrote into a Seattle newspaper personals column seeking "a relationship with anything or entity that has any orifice whatsoever."[6] The theory seemed to be a logical extension of a continuum of increasing acceptance of all people. It appealed to a liberal sensibility, though it was never accorded more than a marginal status and its institutional position remains highly tenuous today.

But queer theory is not exactly liberal. From a formal ivory-tower perspective, it does not expand the catalogue of acceptable identities, because, in fact, it aims to subvert the entire concept of identity. This idea may sound innocent enough until you realize that it has immense, antiliberal political consequences. How can there be women's liberation if there is no such identity as "woman"? How can there be gay liberation, if there is no category "gay"? Identity politics needs identities, which is precisely what queer theory subverts. Queer theory is far more radical than mere inclusiveness. It rejects all categories. Without categories, queer theorists assert, there can be no damaging hierarchies of respectability, and without hierarchies, liberation is beside the point. Everyone is liberated. There can be no snobbery, no exclusivity, no inequity, for there is no one to butt up against. In a postmodern theorist's view, "queer" is best understood as a nonidentity or antiidentity, an identity for people who don't believe in identities. To liberalism's offer to tolerate queers as just another minority, queer theory says "no thanks."

Nevertheless, few people actually construe "queer" in this "high concept" way. The average gay on the street, or anyone on the street, views "queer" as another label, albeit a hip, less restrictive one than "homosexual" or "lesbian." In popular culture it means an identity that is sexier, more transgressive, that signals a deliberate show of difference, that doesn't want to be assimilated or tolerated.[7] Folks who embrace this term do not necessarily reject the sex/gender binary; they just like the outrageousness of being branded "queer." To the dismay of queer theorists, the label has become contaminated by casual usage. As a result, feminist film critic Teresa de Lauretis, who had been credited with coining the term "queer theory" in an essay in 1991, abandoned it barely three years later. If "queer" were just another category, then instead of abolishing normative categories, it would depend on them for defining itself. Relegated to the status of being a mere identity, "queer" would be no better than the categories it replaced. The designation could be used as a basis for a new "identity politics," which would, by definition, exclude and restrict people, just like the old identity politics did. It would be like trading one straitjacket for another. In theorists' views, "queer" has been co-opted by those mainstream forces and institutions it was designed to resist.[8]

Today queer theory is probably best understood as an intellectual movement that is in the business of perpetually doubting the Grand Narratives of Sexuality, the ever-mutating cultural "operating instructions" for gender identity and sexual orientation. As such, it is forever indeterminate, a never-ending work-in-progress. Some argue that this indeterminacy is one of its constituent characteristics, that part of its clout depends on its resistance to definition.[9] Because queer theory is inherently oppositional, it cannot settle into a fixed system of abstract principles, lest it become that which it opposes—a comfortable set of hierarchies that brand some select people as good and healthy and others as bad and deviant. If it stopped opposing, it would evaporate: It pivots on transgression and permanent rebellion. Besides, as a step-child of postmodernism, queer theory cannot be captured and pinned down because reality—in this case, sex, gender, desire—cannot be captured and pinned down (think of Winchell and his murderers). That is precisely the point of queer theory: Gender identity and sexual orientation are never definite, finished, final, still. Perhaps the concept of "queer" works betters as a verb, as in "to queer," than as a noun. At bottom, queer theory may be more of a disciplinary stance than an actual discipline, one that exhorts scholars "to queer" ideas in any area of study, that is, to expose and critique underlying cultural structures for regulating sexual behavior in all disciplines.

Queer theorists dissect texts (usually literary works) like rabbinical scholars poring over the Kabbalah, but instead of searching for divine code they are trolling for gender slippage. They mostly carry out their project in academic settings, but, for a brief period, they spilled into the streets. In 1993, activist–political theorist Michael Warner put together an anthology that crystallized queer theory as a movement: *Fear of a Queer Planet*.[10] Queer theory, he insisted, yields a politics very different from that of gay and lesbian identity, which seeks only to legitimate their identity, not to question the whole concept of "identity politics." Queer activists like Warner oppose the popular attempt by more conciliatory deviants to clean up their image, to minimize the differences between themselves and straights in order to blend in to an imaginary mainstream. In contrast to assimilation-oriented gays, extremist queer activists position themselves against the dominant norms of society, refusing to "normalize" their sexual behavior just to win acceptance. They disparage, for instance, same-sex marriage, regarding it as an attempt to dragoon queers into "normality." If there is an ideal in this stance, it is perhaps sexual free will. Even in the wake of the AIDS epidemic, a number of radical queer groups like Sex Panic and Dangerous Bedfellows endorsed gay male promiscuity and almost any kind of nonstandard sexual behavior, including unsafe sex and intergenerational sex. A few extremists called the protection of children "erotic hysteria." This nutty, ethically dubious point of view was espoused in the service of ideological purity, obviously not common sense.[11] As a psychologist I am very aware that ideology may be used defensively to mask unconscious rage, even self-directed rage.

But to dismiss a theory on account of its lunatic fringe devotees would be a mistake. Queer theory invites us to think about ourselves, our patterns of desire and respectability. It forces us to ask the most basic questions about how society organizes itself. As a clinician working with actual people, some of whose pain is entirely attributable to their despised sex/gender identity, I find this invitation irresistible. Obviously, political activism and intellectual activities operate very much in tandem, but while direct social action is critically important, I will focus on the latter, as my interest in queer theory is in its conceptual usefulness for enabling ostracized people to live with themselves.

Queer theory is heavily indebted to feminist theory, gay/lesbian studies, and the scholars who reworked those disciplines through a French postmodern lens. In its latest incarnation, it is inflected with Freudian and Lacanian psychoanalytic theory. Let me connect the conceptual dots. In doing so, I am guided by accounts of queer theory from a number of historians' ideas.[12]

TILTING TOWARD CONSTRUCTIONISM

Feminist Studies

There could not have been queer theory in America without women's studies. Feminists were the first to intellectually disconnect gender from sex. To paraphrase French existentialist Simone de Beauvoir, women are made, not born.[13] In other words, women learn to be feminine; femininity is not congenital. This was a huge conceptual leap. But while feminists freed women from compulsory femininity, they did not consider freeing them from compulsory heterosexuality or compulsory female identity. In fact, for a while in the '70s, it was quite the opposite: the women's movement practically tore itself apart over sexuality and there was much bad feeling between lesbian and straight feminists.

Feminism has never been a tranquil, coherent, unified movement. For its entire 150-year history it has not been dependent on ideological purity. Today, four decades after the inception of the second wave of women's liberation, it is still plagued by civil wars over conflicting ideas.[14] To be sure, all feminists and most American women want political and economic equality. But, as an example of their many areas of dissonance, they differ about why women should be accorded this. So-called difference feminists foreground is the dissimilarity of men and women, embracing a kind of female chauvinism in which women are deemed morally superior—more empathic, nurturing, emotionally expressive, less warlike than men. These traits, which are seen as inherent, justify improving women's status. Difference feminism extends back to the nineteenth-century suffragettes, who argued that women should be given the right to vote so that they could bring their civilizing sensibility to bear on public matters. But "sameness feminists," who devalue male/female unlikeness, dismiss the idea of female moral superiority as sentimental hokum, mere feminine self-congratulation. They argue that an underlying belief in feminine virtue limits women to "female" roles. Women, in their view, should have equal access to mainstream social and political life, not because they are nicer (which they are not), but because it is fair.

Today, the standard-bearer for difference feminism and female virtue, particularly early adolescent female virtue, is Carol Gilligan, an educational psychologist at New York University, who, following the intellectual trend du jour, has recently expanded her initial interest in the sorry plight of girls to include the sorry plight of boys.[†] But in her early, more exclusively "girls-in-trouble" period during which she wrote her major work *In a Different Voice* (1982), she charged that there is male bias in the way we rank moral values. In the traditionally accepted pecking order of values, we rate individual responsibility as being better than collective responsibility. This hierarchy unwittingly betrays a masculine perspective. In the famous study that girds Gilligan's first book, she demonstrates that males seek autonomy and see ethical issues in terms of rules and rights, while females value relationships and respond more to others' needs.[15]

Neither orientation, Gilligan argues, is superior to the other. But even though Gilligan claims neutrality, she has been consistently misunderstood as favoring the female "care voice" over the male "justice voice," probably because she is such a strong proponent of primary female virtue. Her Arcadian image of adolescent girls conjures up Eve in the Garden before she partook of the apple. In *Making Connections*, for example, Gilligan contends that by the time they reach adolescence, girls' inherent kindness and self-confidence wilt into diffidence and low self-esteem. This happens, presumably, because of patriarchy.[16] These Rousseauistic ideas have been thoroughly refuted by objective studies indicating that there is no difference between boys' and girls' self-esteem.[17] But a gullible public cannot quite let go of the idea of natural feminine virtue—sugar and spice and everything nice—which is inevitably sabotaged by inherent male boorishness. It continues to support a veritable cottage industry in derivative books celebrating women's ways. Mary Pipher's *Reviving Ophelia*, a work heavily influenced

---

[†] Other high-profile "difference" feminists include law professor Catherine MacKinnon, linguist Deborah Tannen, theologian Mary Daly, and cultural critic Camille Paglia.

by Gilliganism, for example, spent nearly three years on the *New York Times* paperback bestseller list.

From an ideological perspective, difference feminism seems to segue into essentialism—the notion that women are different from men because they are born that way. It need not rest on a theory of innate difference, and many of its adherents explicitly say that they are talking about socialized characteristics, not inherent ones; but their accounts have a way of slipping into biological determinism.[18] In the same manner, sameness feminism has segued into constructionism, because it suggests that gender differences are constructed, not given. Sameness feminists, by the way, do not say that women and men are the same, merely that men and women differ unpredictably, as do women from each other.[19]

To be sure, this conceptual division among feminists is simplistic and overly schematic. The debate does not really reduce neatly into two camps. It is more a matter of whether feminists maximize or minimize male–female difference, and most writers are rather blurry about the cause of any difference. Nor is the controversy a "soft-minded" versus a "tough-minded" divide. Some of the most important contributors to rigorous feminist thinking, like sociologist/psychoanalyst Nancy Chodorow, have been lumped with in with difference feminists because she wrestled with the question of why women mother (and men generally do not), thereby seemingly emphasizing gender difference. But Chodorow does not suggest that this difference is inborn; rather, she speculates that it is based on widespread conventional family arrangements and the fact that the pattern is self-perpetuating.[20] Then, too, as we shall see, the French feminist reinterpreters of Jacques Lacan—Luce Iragaray, Julia Kristeva, and Helene Cixous—whose Gallic sophistication might suggest that they would deplore any "touchy-feely" idealization of women, in fact wax sentimental over mother's milk. You need a scorecard to discern feminists' ideological positions on the "sameness/difference" debate, because the issues are enormously complex and there are no consistent criteria for belonging to one group or the other. And no one really knows if, how, and why men and women differ. Nevertheless, most feminist scholars today lean in the direction of constructionism—a conceptual framework that sets the stage for queer theory.

Gay/Lesbian Studies

It was a relatively small step to go from separating gender role from anatomy to separating sexual orientation from anatomy. When feminist historians like Carroll Smith-Rosenberg began to investigate friendships among accomplished nineteenth-century white Western women, they were confronted head-on with provocative questions about women's identity and lesbian identity.[21] In letters to each other in those years, many of these respectable ladies were highly emotional and intense, bordering on the romantic (from a twenty-first-century perspective), but were they lesbians? Or was their overheated prose a matter of convention? We may never know whether these women had sex with each other. But their behavior certainly stirred thinking among feminists and about what constitutes "normal" sex and gender. In a famous 1984 essay entitled "Thinking Sex," anthropologist Gayle Rubin brought these historical questions into the present, arguing that the way we categorize sexual practices is not biologically preordained but is fundamentally political, similar to the way we categorize race and religion. It's about power and perspective, who gets to decide what is good and what is bad. French postmodern philosophy had not yet permeated feminism, but, apparently, feminists, unbeknownst to themselves, were thinking along the same lines as intellectuals across the Atlantic.[22]

By then there had been a gradual shift in generic sociological thinking as well as the specifically feminist sort. In 1968, British sociologist Mary McIntosh wrote that homosexuals should be seen as playing a social "role" rather than as having a condition. And at about the same time, American sociologists John Gagnon and William Simon reconceived homosexuality as a social construct regulated by "sexual scripts," thereby refuting the mainstream view of it as an instinctive drive controlled by inner psychic forces or hormonal fluctuation.[23] Meanwhile, historians of gay men were following the same trajectory. Digging deeper into the history of sexuality seemed to inevitably result in more and more historians concluding that sexual desire must be considered separately from gender: Historians simply had no vocabulary for explaining the sexual practices and attachments of the past. Jonathan Ned Katz, for example, whose pioneering 1976 work *Gay American History* was a fundamentally essentialist account of three decades of historical continuities in American homosexual life, later changed his mind about the existence of a continuous homosexual identity. After additional research and reflection, he became an outspoken adherent of the constructionist belief that successive generations can and do remake their sense of themselves and "their ways of loving," an idea he expanded upon in his 1995 *The Invention of Heterosexuality*.[24] In doing this, he joined the ranks of other avatars of constructionism such as historians Jeffrey Weeks, Martin Duberman, and George Chauncey, sociologist Ken Plummer, and literature professor David Halperin, among many others.

There were exceptions of course, such as philosopher Richard Mohr, literature professor Donald Morton, and, most notably, historian John Boswell, who made the startling (albeit disputed) discovery that homosexuality was tolerated in the Roman Catholic Church until the twelfth century. Boswell's essentialist subtext was that a gay identity back then and a gay identity now are equivalent. But social constructionism, not essentialism, became the dominant theoretical approach in the humanities. Most gender academics now pay homage to the French postmodern philosopher/critic Michel Foucault, whose *The History of Sexuality* appeared in Paris in 1976 and reached American shores in translation in 1978, and whose influence on subsequent cultural theory—with the exception of American psychoanalysis—cannot be underestimated.[25] Foucault was antagonistic toward psychotherapy, perhaps in part because as a university student he had gone to a psychiatrist who tried to "treat" his homosexuality. But Foucault would probably have denied that his antipsychiatry stance was influenced by his own experience in therapy, arguing instead that his conclusions were logical and necessary outcomes of his theories; that psychotherapy, like sex-segregated bathrooms, was just another tacit means of regulating the human body. Foucault's hostility toward psychoanalysis probably did little to enhance his prestige in psychoanalytic circles.

THE FRENCH INVASION

Foucault did not originate queer theory, nor was queer theory the destination of his thinking. But he was the man who ignited it. To be sure, his ideas entered the ears of Anglo-American scholars, who were by then poised to embrace them. But these scholars were not yet on the academic radar screen. It was Foucault who turned queer theory from a latent into a blatant discipline.[26]

His galvanizing influence may have something to do with the fact that he made irresistible copy. Foucault was the foremost intellectual in France, a country that takes its intellectuals seriously. While on the faculty at Berkeley in the mid-'70s, he openly participated in San Francisco's gay S&M and leather subculture, hardly an ordinary venue for college professors. He was also known to experiment with drugs such as LSD. Patently indifferent to propriety—a quality that endeared him to the young—Foucault was given to making shocking Delphic pronouncements that tended to turn received wisdom on its head, such as: "Sex is boring."[27] Or, when asked about the commonly pondered distinction between innate predisposition to homosexuality and social conditioning, his dismissive reply was, "On this question I have absolutely nothing to say. No comment," as if the question were so foolish as not to be worthy of a response.[28] At its starkest, his theory implied that nothing was what it seemed to be. When he died in 1984, it was front-page news in every French newspaper, though the cause of his death (AIDS) was not mentioned at the time. Youthful academics seized on his theory and ran with it, loading it with far more liberationist potential than Foucault probably had in mind.

Foucault, along with his countrymen—philosopher Jacques Derrida and psychoanalyst Jacques Lacan, among others—provoked a veritable paradigm shift in the way people think about sexuality: There is no particular "normal" form of sexuality. In keeping with the French postmodern tradition, they regard language as coercive, that it functions somewhat like a menu, restricting our sexual possibilities (like a menu does food), which, in a utopian world, would be endless. Given the menu of sexuality culturally available to us, we have no choice but to fashion our identity out of it. Actually, this menu, which Foucault calls a "discourse," consists not only of language, but also of a web of social customs, moral conventions, protocols, credentials, conceptual frameworks, and categories—anything that we communicate. French postmodernists argue that, unbeknownst to us, our discourse for sexuality contains complex codes, strict rules about what can and cannot be. Our sexual activities (or lack of them) can have no form of representation to ourselves or to those around us other than in the forms included in the discourse, and so we are inevitably forced to adopt one of these forms, such as "straight," "homosexual," "bisexual," "transgender," and so forth.[29] Each era develops its own discourse, but we are stuck with our particular one. Our discourses are so ubiquitous that, like air, we do not notice them. They feel natural. So people only think they are free, when in actuality they are victims of invisible societal forces. Discourse is a form of mind control.

It is good to keep in mind that this new philosophy was being formulated in a world that was reinventing itself after totalitarian insurgence, a world that had unaccountably complied with the appalling ideologies of the Third Reich and Stalin's Soviet Union. How did this happen? Why did ordinary, educated, otherwise good people blindly facilitate the obscenity of Auschwitz? Where was their moral compass, their critical capacity? Horrified, dumbstruck, obviously wishing to prevent a recurrence, intellectuals sought answers, bandying about such concepts as the "authoritarian personality," "propaganda," "brainwashing," and "the banality of evil." The classic film *The Manchurian Candidate*, made around that time, enacted those themes to great effect.

Reading between the lines of these postmodern theorists is the idea that individuals are little more than puppets operated by structures that they cannot see, the subjugating coercion of language. By this insistence on discourse as the source of all meaning, Foucault et al. have moved the center of gravity out of the individual person into the social realm.[30] This means that if we are looking for explanations for phenomena, we should look not inside individuals (like psychoanalytic therapists) but out into the linguistic space in which they move with other people. According to this thinking, humans are empty receptacles with no essential psychological characteristics, no "there" there, nothing to look into.

Taking this further—if the self is a product of language, it follows that the self will be constantly in flux, constantly depending upon the prevailing discourse to define it. Whether a self is pretty or ugly, healthy or sick, "in" or "out," or whatever, hangs on the way a particular language constructs those categories. Because language is slippery, so is identity. The fact that the meaning of words is perpetually evolving ensures a fragmented, shifting, temporary identity for us all. Herein we see the antiessentialism and antihumanism of postmodern French thinking. Humans do not have inherent qualities (by which they may be classified) nor do they have much potential for inventing themselves. People are passive; they have no "agency," no ability to exert power; they are helplessly programmed by their discourse. For example, in our own linguistic system (political correctness notwithstanding), "crip" does not signal hip; fat, beauty; transgender, normality. Though our discourse dooms us to a certain category (such as normal or abnormal), there is, theoretically speaking, a universe of possible discourses, and therefore the possibility for liberation. Abnormal individuals need not permanently suffer the barbs of abnormality because the significance of words, jargon, books, categories, humor, and so on varies radically over time. The abnormal just have to wait until the discourse changes; that is, until "normality" is redefined. In today's speeded-up world, particularly in hipster circles, "phat" is already good, as is "bad."

On the other hand, were we to rigidly employ this logic, we would have to conclude that the subjective feeling we have of personal coherence and continuity—the sense that we are the same person today as we were yesterday and will be tomorrow—is an illusion. A stable, unified sense of self is merely a spurious effect of communicating with others, a verbal handle we attach to a bunch of observations others make about us.[31] It is not something that actually exists in nature. And since language and social interactions cannot be fixed in time, it follows that our identities cannot be fixed in time. Our sense of ourselves, and others' perceptions of us, would be in ceaseless flux depending on whom we are with, when, in what circumstances, and to what end. Psychoanalysts would be forced to wonder which "person" was lying on the couch in any one particular session. This idea is utterly counterintuitive. If taken seriously, it would undermine all human behavior and interaction. Chaos would ensue. But we need not interpret postmodern gender theory so literally. It is possible to view French theory more flexibly, to pick and choose what is sensible. Let me start with Michel Foucault, the putative patriarch of queer theory (though he himself did not employ the term "queer" for his own politics).

Foucault

There are many excellent summaries of Foucault's thinking from which I borrow, as noted, as well as from the writings of the philosopher himself. Here I offer my own drastically selective capsule summary of his ideas that are most pertinent to queer theory.

Let me note at the outset that in tracing the antecedents of queer theory I am engaging in a most "un-Foucaultian" activity. Foucault challenged the traditional way of "doing" history, that is, of constructing a linear narrative connecting cause and effect. Traditional history, in his view, is just a dubious story written from the perspective of the present about the past. It is just one possible account of things. Despite their best efforts at objectivity, historians sift "facts" of their choosing, based on their interests at the moment, through the distorting lens of their own culture and psyche. They cannot help but project biased meaning onto historical events, creating a false sense of order, like the popular misconception that history is a story of progress. The result of historians' endeavors is inevitably contaminated.

Foucault, like philosopher Friedrich Nietzsche before him, speculated that the unfolding of history is far more irrational and accidental. There is no essential logic to history. So, rather than look for continuity in the past, Foucault jump-cut across history looking for discontinuities, calling his method "genealogy." In his view, systems of thought, which he called "regimes," could exist for a long period, and then change could happen quite suddenly and inexplicably. A prime example of such a discontinuity in Western history, described in *Madness and Civilization*, occurred in the eighteenth-century Enlightenment, when the Cult of Reason created supposedly rational standards of "normalcy."[32] Once "madness" was defined as abnormal, rather than simply eccentric, its victims were no longer allowed to wander but were segregated from the "sane" population into "retreats" (also used to keep lepers out of sight), where they were subject to observation, moral rule, and, eventually, intervention by psychiatric "experts."[33] Medicine, along with psychiatry, is implicated among the cultural forces that shape human behavior by virtue of what Foucault called the "clinical gaze," which transforms the body into an object of scientific scrutiny. For Foucault, the "knowledge" of experts gives them power over others, the power of defining them.

Foucault did not explain why these tectonic shifts in thinking about the insane or the sick occurred, for in true postmodernist fashion he rejected grand explanatory systems. Rather, he sought to document their points of origin, as he proceeded to do later with regard to other taken-for-granted matters. He turned away from analyzing "important" events, the usual province of historians, in favor of obscure and neglected phenomena and people that had been denied a history—the aforementioned mentally and physically ill, the criminal, and, most pertinent to the task at hand, the homosexual.[34] Arguably, the investigation of these marginalized people and topics is as legitimate for determining truth (or its approximation) as an investigation of the usual suspects—war, kings, the rich, and so forth.

The cornerstone of Foucault's thinking—and what was most revolutionary about it—was his insistence that power resides not only in armies, law, muscles, rulers, money, but also in our ordinary socializing practices that serve to "normalize" us. Power is not hierarchical, flowing from the top down, monolithic, and clearly visible. It is everywhere local—in our values; in the way we "do" sex; in our institutions such as the army, church, schools, madhouses, factories, corporations, and so on.[35] The prison is a case in point. In his brilliant book, *Discipline and Punish*, Foucault stunningly claimed that the modern prison system—presumably so enlightened compared to the public torture inflicted on criminals in the past—actually represented a more complete exercise of power than former methodologies of punishment.[36] Our penal system exerts discipline by the minute control of activities of inmates through rigid timetables and spatialization (the idea that each person has an appointed place), normalizing judgments, strict hierarchies, and repetitive tasks. This is a far more efficient regulatory system than the public display of pain, which was always haphazard and too costly in proportion to its results.

Prior to the eighteenth century, according to Foucault, rulers maintained discipline of the masses by staging ostentatious exhibitions of their authority, such as lavish royal processions, parades, and public executions, a precursor, no doubt, of modern politicians' "photo ops." These spectacles served to awe the viewer into submission. Foucault stressed that all forms of power rely on visual strategies to enforce the discourse. But in modern societies, power has become invisible, and therefore more insidious. Power today often relies on the all-seeing (but unseen) gaze, which functions like Orwell's Big Brother.[37] The Panopticon, an architectural configuration for a prison that Foucault derived from Utilitarian philosopher Jeremy Bentham, epitomizes the coercive force of surveillance. It is a mechanism of power reduced to its ideal form. In a Panopticon each inmate is confined to a small cell and may be observed at any time by a single person sitting in a central tower. No prisoner can be certain of not being watched, and so prisoners gradually begin to police their own behavior. They become critical surveyors of themselves. Freud and his followers call this process "internalization" but they did not assign it such paramount importance, as did Foucault.

Surveillance is an immeasurably more subtle and often more effective method of control than brute force. Anyone who has encountered individuals who have been incarcerated for long periods in mental hospitals or residences for the cognitively impaired (today's version of the Panopticon) will immediately recognize the deadening effect of being constantly surveyed and regimented. These "patients" have become institutionalized: There is an uncanny similarity to their behavior—extreme passivity, conformity, obesity, excessive smoking. They lack a social thermostat. In the Massachusetts area, folks hospitalized years ago in state facilities for "foreign insane pauperism" (code for drunken Irish) ended up decades later looking and behaving very much like those who were truly mentally ill. The same model is applicable to schools, hospitals, factories, and barracks—an excellent form of social engineering for creating "docile" bodies, wherein "each subject becomes his own jailer."[38]

The power that defines us constantly by gazing at our bodies resides not only in discreet institutions but is everywhere. It flows through our society as an invisible force insinuating our moral and religious rules, laws, sports, education, medicine, the workplace, and, especially, mass-produced images. Coercion need not involve someone literally watching us, for we have internalized the cultural gaze and continually "gaze" at ourselves, regimenting our behavior and even our flesh to conform to the dictates of culture. Cynically speaking, this body consciousness may be good for the psychotherapy business, which thrives on personal misery, but it is oppressive to those subject to its sway. It produces needless unhappiness. Feminists and minorities have been complaining for years about the tyranny of the impossible standards set by these cultural images and dictates.

But Foucault's point was not to praise or blame the power of the "gaze" but rather to recognize its impact in changing the ways in which we understand and experience our body. To the frustration of some political activists, he emphatically refused to protest the insidious images and ideas that, in effect, constitute contemporary brainwashing. To him, liberationist strategies were irrelevant. Foucault had little hope for a redeemed and perfected erotic world. He was opposed to championing one discourse over another because he believed that any discourse could be used to good or bad ends. Besides, outcomes were unpredictable. He observed that, historically, what looked like a change for the better often turned out to have undesirable consequences. In his view, we are prisoners of an all-enveloping structure of power, and real-life reform movements may end up serving power in new and treacherous ways. The practice of psychotherapy, for example, which sees itself as a helpful, freeing-up endeavor (in which "knowledge" about human beings is used to improve their lives), is actually just one more cog in the machine of social control. It establishes norms for "mental health" and seeks to transform people so they comply with those norms.[39] About the only tool that folks have for "doing" politics is to rework verbal categories, to poke fun at structures of power, to use words in an ironic, subversive way (such as defiantly embracing the term "nigger" for African American)—a fairly flimsy method in my view for producing actual large-scale social reform, although it does provide the harmless satisfaction of a coded smirk.

There is a kind of futility built into Foucault's thinking with regard to repression. Repression is inevitable. Wherever power operates, he argues, there will be prohibitions and restrictions. Yet wherever there is repression, there will also be resistance to it. Power and resistance are two sides of the same coin. Prevailing discourses, that is, "knowledge" or "common sense," are always under implicit threat from alternatives. The power of any one discourse is only apparent from the resistance implicit in another. If not for this resistance there would be no need to constantly reaffirm its truthfulness.[40] For example, if the notion of homosexuality as unnatural were really secure in its position as truth, there would be no need to keep asserting it. So, resistance coexists with repression. The only possible liberation is not liberation from repression, but liberation from discourse.

But Foucault adds that power is not always exercised in a repressive way. It is productive as well. It produces "knowledge"; that is, it puts its seal of approval on certain versions of reality and designates them as "true." Hence, Foucault's striking claim in *The History of Sexuality* that the homosexual and homosexuality were invented in the nineteenth century. Before that there were, of course, same-sex sexual acts. But the prevailing discourses prior to 1870, unlike the discourse today, did not define people who engaged in those acts as a separate species. Where before same-sex sex had been seen as a sin that, like theft, anyone could commit, it now became a symptom of a condition, "homosexuality," that characterized a type of individual, the "homosexual."[41] That there is a "homosexual" became a fact of "knowledge." Foucault's startling assertion served as a catalyst for the development of queer theory.

Foucault's main idea, implicit throughout *The History of Sexuality*, is that sexuality is a social artifice. He supported his hypothesis by dipping into various historical epochs and showing that sexual practices, thought by the participants to be a biological given, were actually constructed to shore up hierarchies of power (such as the adult male citizens of ancient Greece who were accorded the privilege of having sex with prepubescent boys). Sexuality, like insanity, criminality, and illness, reflects nothing that exists eternally in nature. Rather, it is derived from the language and customs of a specific time period and is transformed to grease the social wheels of that particular era. Queer theorists seized upon this idea with a vengeance and argued, moreover, that in a utopian world we can reinvent sexual orientation and gender identity as we like. They, like Foucault and unlike psychologists and scientists, are not interested in why any one person may engage in a certain practice, but in how sexuality is deployed in service of power. They couldn't care less about the causes of homosexuality or gender-bending.

Contrary to the long-established myth about Victorian sexual repression giving way to sexual liberation and enlightenment in the twentieth century—which Foucault called the "repressive hypothesis" —the Victorians were hardly more prudish than we are today. The seemingly overmodest sexual etiquette of that period may have ironically escalated (or at least preserved in coded form) the very desire it is thought to have repressed. In the first volume of his multipart study of sexuality (left unfinished at his death), he warned us that we should not take things—such as the practice of covering piano legs and censorship—at face value. Appearances may be deceiving. The fact that sex was not talked about in polite society does not alter the fact that it saturated people's mental lives. If sex were not an issue liable to erupt at the slightest provocation, then there would have been no need to demurely cover piano legs or censor certain literature. Evidence from the nineteenth century points not to a prohibition about speaking about sexuality but to an explosion in discourses aimed at scrutinizing, classifying, explaining, and ultimately controlling sexual behavior—in medicine, mental health, criminology, sociology, and sexology.[42] The Victorians constantly talked about sex—surreptitiously. The sum total of these discourses did not represent an actual increase in useful knowledge about sexuality, but a proliferation of classifications and divisions.

Foucault suggests that the Catholic confessional was actually the origin of the West's preoccupation with sex—a preoccupation that grew more and more (not less and less) intense throughout the Victorian and post-Victorian eras.[43] It was a place where penitents were encouraged to scrutinize and report their sexual behavior. The Church and Law had long been interested in regulating sexuality, but from the eighteenth century on, the interest accelerated. By then the state had become aware of the concept of "population" and the need for managing its growth, resulting in a new focus on the body and reproduction. Those in positions of authority took on the role of "inquisitors" and had the power to extort confessions about sexual practices from people under their supervision. It was at this point that the ideas of "sexual perversion," "unnatural practices," and "sexual immorality" became a possibility.[44] All of a sudden, the nature of sexual practices became very important—maybe too important: We came to see in sex the truth of who and what we are. The practice of extracting sexual confessions developed into a powerful form of social control as people began to internalize this inquisitorial process.[45] Today this is accomplished by modern inquisitors: social workers, cybersleuths, investigative reporters, prying guidance counselors, fetal ultrasound, security cameras, professionally nosy talk show hosts—and probing psychotherapists.

The modern "*scienta sexualis*" (sciences of sexuality) of the West, as Foucault called them, including psychoanalysis, are simply a continuation of a trajectory of increasing surveillance. Far from liberating human potential, these ritualistic confessional enactments—wherein a speaker produces a narrative about his or her sexuality that is interpreted by an expert—police it. Experts, such as psychotherapists, prod their patients to reveal their sexual fantasies and secrets, after which they inculcate in them a "true" identity (like homosexual) based on their confessions. Foucault's polemic strongly influenced the budding anti-psychiatry movement in France in the '60s.[†] Joining Foucault in his attempt to free desire from the hierarchical constructs of institutionalized

---

[†] This movement later spread to England and the United States, shaped by such maverick clinicians as Thomas Szasz and R. D. Laing, who questioned the very existence of madness.

psychoanalytic psychiatry were psychoanalyst Felix Guattari and philosopher Gilles Deleuze. Their *Anti-Oedipus: Capitalism and Schizophrenia* denounced the vertical tree-like thinking of psychoanalysis in which all ideas emanate out of a single trunk—the Oedipus complex—a method of analysis that they regarded as reductive, impoverished, and authoritarian. For Guattari and Deleuze, desire is created horizontally, by social interconnections, more like a stringer of crabgrass than a tree.[46] Like Foucault, they viewed psychoanalysis as another repressive watchdog of the modern state.

But Foucault also argued that top-down coercion is not always bad. Oppressors not only police their subjects; they also produce new vocabularies and "knowledge" that may be used by the oppressed to their own advantage. For example, the conception of homosexuality as a "species" (as opposed to a "temporary aberration") made strategically possible what Foucult called a "reverse discourse."[47,48] Using the very labels assigned to them by "experts," homosexuals could organize into a constituency and speak on their own behalf. With the shared diagnosis of "homosexual," they had a bona fide basis of solidarity. They now could unite to demand that their legitimacy be acknowledged.[49]

And, ironically, the various institutionalized methods of confession did not only serve to completely regulate desire. How foolish of us to have ever believed that talking about sex would make us less repressed —that open discussion and analysis would set us free! In fact, the examiner/examinee relationship—doctor/patient, teacher/student, priest/worshiper, and boss/worker—often lights more fires than it extinguishes—the "pleasure of analysis," that is, the pleasure of knowing the "truth," of confiding and exposing it, the delicious tension and erotic titillation of prying out and withholding secrets. The proof of this dynamic, in my view, is the fact that it sometimes inappropriately segues into actual sexual encounters. Our *scientia sexualis* may, in fact, function a bit like an *ars erotica* (Foucault's term for sexuality of the East). The *ars erotica* value multiplying pleasure, intensifying it, instead of, like the *scientia sexualis*, scrutinizing and classifying it.[50]

You can easily see how Foucault's writing provided an underpinning and maybe an impetus for queer theory. In it, the body and its pleasures are completely separated from sexual orientation and gender identity. Foucault pinpoints the invention of various sexual identities, thereby demonstrating that they are culturally malleable. There is no right or wrong sexual practice. Sexually speaking, anything goes. The idea that power doesn't come exclusively from above, but also "locally" from below—via opinions, habits, the discourse of the masses—is a compelling reversal of ideas (especially to those from below!). It suggests that there is a possibility for upward mobility. Adherence to the dictates of this or that god, or king, and/or the *New York Times* "Style Section" is not eternally mandatory. Our sexual practices depend as much or more on everyday "normalizing," brainwashing to which we are relentlessly exposed (via our media, educational system, churches, etc.) than brute force by a powerful elite. What we deem sexy varies in accordance with specific cultural formations, not necessarily in accordance with what the top dog says, and certainly not in accordance with so-called natural inclinations.

Foucault's ingenious, quirky theorizing exposed an important fault line in psychological theories to date—that they are culturally determined and historically specific; that sexual practices, for example, may be as much a consequence of the discourse du jour as Oedipal dynamics. It is important that psychological theorists take note of Foucault's ideas and that that they seriously purge their theories of deep-seated biases, including the sexist and "heterosexist" presuppositions of the language in which they think and write (e.g., having only two words for gender, or labeling a syndrome "homosexual panic"). Without a thorough ideological cleansing, traditional psychoanalytic theory is limited to explaining the development of a narrow group of individuals—Western white heterosexual males.

But Foucault's thinking is far from flawless. It has come under attack from many quarters. Historians dispute his chronology of events. Feminists deplore his neglect of women and the fact that he implies that the oppressed (read: women) are compliant in their own domination. Activists argue that his theory subverts the basis of identity politics (because, in Foucault's view, there is no such thing as a biologically ordained identity). Activists also dispute his "hip" cynicism about large-scale social change, pointing out that it is self-defeating. There are, they argue, mechanisms other than ironic wordplay available for producing actual improvement in the real world—bold, practical mechanisms with proven results—legal reform, economic intervention, and so forth. To rely exclusively on anemic symbolic gestures, like parody and transgressive talk, would naturally result in failure—thereby fulfilling Foucault's prophecy, but certainly not proving the futility of all social action.

Psychoanalytic practitioners rightly take offence to Foucault's highly cultivated air of disdain for their profession. But their strongest objection (with which I agree) is the fact that Foucault has next to nothing to say about individuals—actual people with real bodies and personal psyches. In Foucault's world there are only manipulators and the manipulated, conditioners and the conditioned, publicists and the public. People are like marionettes, with an invisible master pulling the strings. In a Foucaultian universe, there is no patient to treat, no "it" to study, no gays to fight the restrictions of straight society, no individual—just an empty space around which discourses frame an identity.

Derrida

From Foucault, queer theorists derived the idea that language constructs sexual orientation and gender identities. From Jacques Derrida, the preeminent French philosopher who died in 2004, they acquired a mechanism for dismantling language to expose its prejudices. Deconstruction, the name of that dismantling process (see Chapter 2), was his brainchild. With this rarified brand of surgical linguistic analysis, queer theorists can unveil the binary oppositions in our language with which dominant power groups maintain their grip and force us into the pigeonholes of male or female, gay or straight.

Unfortunately, the ordinary curious reader who does not happen to have a recent background in philosophy or the humanities usually finds Derrida's work impenetrable. It is dense with arcane language and obscure allusions to other theorists, presupposing prior knowledge. Of course, Foucault's work, though elegant, is also difficult, but at least he cited concrete historical events to support his arguments, whereas Derrida relies on an arcane, convoluted, highly abstract analysis of words and philosophical or literary texts (such as those of Hegel, Rousseau, and Genet). Derrida's writing, moreover, is glutted with typographical horseplay. A typical ploy of his (derived from Heidegger) is to print a word in cancelled form, with slash marks running through it, as though to include and exclude the word at the same time. The purpose of the maneuver is to indicate that that the cancelled word, though inadequate, is the best available. By putting words "under erasure" he metaphorically suggests that meaning is delusory, and that he, Derrida, refuses to be taken in; nor should you. It makes for daunting reading.

Nevertheless, inscrutability is not an indictment. Arguably there is something of substance behind the veil of difficult language that justifies the arduous task of puzzling out its meaning. Indeed, cultural theorists continually cite him, and maybe they're on to something. Derrida is the consummate smasher of binaries, which is the whole point of the queer enterprise, though the scope of his work transcends the mere deconstruction of sex/gender binaries. He deconstructs all binaries. Indeed, Derrida never seems to have come across a distinction he did not find inherently invidious and wish to break down. But here I limit my review of his thinking to those ideas that specifically pertain to laying the foundation for queer theory. As a carpetbagger to philosophy, I used secondary sources to aid me in deciphering Derrida's texts.[51,52]

Derrida is the foremost poststructuralist of our day. But before he became a poststructuralist, he was a structuralist (see Chapter 2). Recall that structuralism attempts to discover the universal underlying, but not consciously perceived, structures that organize and govern human activity (such as grammar, kinship systems, rituals of gift-giving, etc.). It found its first home in linguistics. Swiss linguist Ferdinand de Saussure, the putative originator of structuralism, argued that words (signifiers) are only arbitrarily attached to concepts (signifieds) but that signifiers and signifieds stick together. To reiterate the example I used previously: There is no natural connection between the sound of the noise "dog" and the concept of "dogness." But once the connection is established, it persists out of convention. The word "dog" (the signifier) is henceforth attached to the image of man's best friend (the signified). Taken together, the signifier and signified comprise a sign.

Saussure goes on to say that signs have no inherent meanings in themselves, but gain meaning from their relationship with other signs. In other words, the identity of something is determined by that which it is not, by its difference from other ideas or things. Whether something is regarded as "different" (or not) is governed by the system of rules built into language. As a result, difference determines meaning. A dog is a dog, for example, because English distinguishes a dog from a cat, a human, a bird, and so on. There is no ready-made idea of dog before the word "dog." A word can only be understood by locating it within the structure of language. People are born into a linguistic system that is already in place and they are trapped within it. We cannot view the world purely, that is, without the filter of language which silently directs how we think.

Seizing on the idea of underlying structures, social anthropologist Claude Levi-Strauss thought they might be useful for making sense of culture as well as language. Perhaps there are inborn propensities that lead people to categorize the world in the way they do. By analyzing phenomena such as tribal myths, rituals, kinship systems, and the circulation of women in a manner akin to Saussure's dissection of language, he searched for sets of rules governing behavior that might exist across societies. His findings suggested to him that, indeed, there are structural dispositions in the mind, and that these operate according to logic of binary oppositions, that is, the logic of "either/or"—that, for example, something is either raw or cooked, or natural or cultural, but never both. As humans, we relentlessly dichotomize. This binary thinking is common to all cultures. All meaning is constructed through these oppositions. The world's social systems, Levi-Strauss argued, have similar underlying structures. Hence, the inevitability of a sex/gender binary.

But in a lecture at Johns Hopkins University in 1966, Derrida unexpectedly parted company with the structuralists, coming out in the United States as a poststructuralist. His philosophy took American humanities (especially literature) departments by storm, turning much of their critical practice topsy-turvy. He wrestled with structuralism in a number of ways, and I shall describe just a few. First, he argued that the relationship between the word or symbol (the signifier) and its concept (the signified) is fragile: The pathways to meaning are a lot more slippery than structuralists allowed. Signifiers attach only fleetingly to different concepts, like an endless game of musical chairs with the chairs (the signifieds) sliding around, changing shape, appearing and disappearing, and turning into signifiers themselves. Words mean different things in different circumstances. Even within a single sentence, the meaning of a word can only be determined retrospectively, as later words form a context for it, most obviously in double entendres, haiku, many jokes, and so forth, but also in ordinary language. For example, consider the meaning of the title of Nietzsche's *The Gay Science* to a contemporary reader. I suspect it is not what Nietzsche had intended. This leads us to Derrida's concept of "differance," a term he coined to indicate that meaning may be derived from difference (as Saussure had suggested), but meaning is never fully present. Rather, it is deferred, postponed.[53] The term itself is a neologism combining "to differ" and "to defer" and is pronounced the same way as the French word "difference" (meaning difference), but intentionally misspelled. So "differance" cannot be distinguished from "difference" by speaking it, only when written. It is literally "unspeakable" (which, by the way, may be seen as applying to the condition of the repressed, invisible, voiceless, queer perspective). What Derrida means by "differance" is that we only understand words after the fact. Once language enters the public domain, the speaker or author loses control of it, as it is always open to new understandings and misunderstandings. Hence, as I mentioned in Chapter 2, the much-lauded "death" of the author and Derrida's dictum: "There is nothing outside of the text."

Also, words refer to other words. If you used a dictionary to obtain the meaning of the sound "dog," you would find only other words, other signifiers to be deciphered. Every potential meaning turns out to be just another signifier in an endless procession. You can never reach meaning—there is a perpetual chain of sounds, almost to infinity, or the zero degree of sense. Meaning is not present in the moment. Any meaning or identity (including our own) is provisional. Here, we can easily see Derrida's ideas dovetailing with Foucault's—the notion that identity (including gender) is contingent, not fixed.

Derrida agrees with the structuralists that Western thought has been founded upon the logic of binary oppositions—white/black, rational/ emotional, health/illness, male/female, and even speech/writing—but he critiques the tendency. Plus, he takes the idea further. He argues that we have a habit of privileging one term over the other. Regarding the aforementioned binaries, we tend to favor white over black, the rational over the emotional, health over illness, male over female, speech over writing, and so forth. This is because Western thought is based on the idea of a "center"—an Origin, a Truth, a Cause, a Transcendental Signifier, a God—that guarantees all meaning.[54] The idea of a "center" inevitably results in hierarchies. If, for example, you belong to a culture where Christ is the foremost icon, then Christians will be deemed central or natural in that culture and all non-Christians will be marginalized. When Freud pictured the vagina as a wound of castration, instead of picturing the penis as an enlarged clitoris, he was inadvertently using binary logic and privileging the male organ. In a binary classification system, the excluded become Other, and the Other's views are repressed. Also, "centers" tend to fix, or freeze, the play of binary opposites. Derrida identifies this condition as "logocentrism" and it is a condition from which postmodernists aim to escape via deconstruction. His method of deconstruction "decenters" or subverts hierarchies to reveal their falsity. It unmasks the problematic nature of all "centers" and encourages the free play of meaning.

A closely related idea is that when we give something an identity, it is necessary also to conceive what it is not. When we talk of heterosexuality, we implicitly also refer to what the heterosexual is not, what is absent from the heterosexual (in this case, homosexuality). Perhaps an example of this is my tendency to think about sex whenever I meet a Catholic priest. In a sense, Derrida argues, presence contains absence. We tend to forget these absences, to repress them. Yet they influence our thinking. Deconstruction reveals the way these absences function in texts, where they may betray a belief system of which the author is unaware (similar to Freudian slips). Like Freud, Derrida felt that the conscious self is influenced by traces of experience in the unconscious mind. He was not hostile to psychotherapy and, in fact, was long married to a psychotherapist, though I suspect he would frown upon a therapist who assumed a static, all-knowing perspective. A good psychotherapy session in his view would be a collaborative quest between therapist and patient for provisional insight. Multiple interpretations of feelings and behaviors would be held in tension, none automatically preferred over another.

In Derrida's writing, we can see the rudiments of queer theory. From it, we may conclude that straight/gay and male/female are crude, ultimately fictitious binaries, not natural facts. The human tendency to dichotomize everything is way too simplistic. In actuality, all sexual binary categories leak into each other. They are not mutually exclusive and, in fact, belong to the same conceptual network (that is, they are all manifestations of desire). Though they do not convey reality, binaries and "centers" (which breed them) are crutches that provide humans with a sense of order and a way to communicate. Without these crutches, identity would be more fluid, more contingent on circumstance. Derrida's deconstruction does away with these crutches. It grants more scope for sexuality and gender, more chance and creativity. The glaring drawback to this theory, of course, is Derrida's failure to explain how individual humans, with an ever-morphing sense of self, can possibly negotiate an ever-morphing world. His universe is a postmodern fantasy, utter chaos. It can never be realized, yet it offers a helpful corrective to the imprisonment of our classification systems.

Lacan et al.

A third French intellectual invader who might be seen as an inadvertent facilitator of queer theory is the flamboyant psychoanalyst Jacques Lacan (see Chapter 2), a reinterpreter of Freud, who became something of a cult figure with the publication of transcriptions of his weekly Parisian seminars for the training of psychoanalysts in 1966. He died in 1981. Unlike Freud, who never warmed to avant-garde art (much as he inadvertently influenced it), Lacan traveled in Surrealists' circles. Like Derrida, Lacan is renowned for being willfully provocative and maddeningly obscure. His dazzling but sometimes (sadistically!) incomprehensible prose is larded with allusions, puns, giddying flights of fancy. It has been said that Lacan wanted to be understood only by those who want to make the effort.[55] For him, clarity would misrepresent the nature of things. Even secondary sources about his work are difficult.

But he, too, may be worth deciphering, for embedded in his theory is an important idea for queer theory—that culture imposes meaning on (otherwise neutral) anatomical parts, that, for example, a penis does not automatically mean male; that a person's sense of self is more powerfully determined by language than by its body. And he has interesting things to say about the enigmatic nature of desire—that desire can never be satisfied regardless of our sexual practices. In his system, illusion—of satisfaction, of love, of wholeness—plays a big role in our lives, an idea that resonates with today's postmodern sensibility in which desire enacted on "reality" TV is taken at face value. (My patients often wonder about the legitimacy of what they feel because, somehow, their feelings do not seem to match the tidy portrayals of emotion in the media, which they construe as more real than their own.) The task of interpreting Lacan's formidable theorizing, which evolved and changed over his lifetime, is endless, and I make no pretense of presenting a complete or nuanced review, but merely wish to convey a few of his ideas that foreshadow queer theory. Once again, I made use of secondary sources as a roadmap for my intellectual journey.[56]

Lacan does not refute Freud. Rather, he can be seen as rescuing Freud from the parochialism of his heirs who, after 1926, tended to de-emphasize the power of the unconscious. Freud's descendants cited instead either the inadequacy of a person's emotional nurturing in childhood, or they turned back to biology for explanations of neuroses —perspectives that historically pathologized sexual deviance. Indeed, traditional viewpoints pathologized a lot of behavior we now deem benign, like ambition in women. But Lacan scrupulously kept psycho-analysis separate from simple social conditioning or biology. To be sure, there are many problems with Lacan's theorizing regarding its usefulness for queer theory, which I will address later, but it does have the potential virtue of making sexual orientation and gender identity independent of the shape of one's anatomy.

For almost two years I took part in a stimulating monthly seminar on Lacan led by sociologist/psychoanalyst Judith Feher-Gurewich at the Harvard Center for Literary and Cultural Studies and was immediately intrigued to note that I was one of very few therapists among the attendees. Most of the other participants were doctoral students or postdocs in literature, film, philosophy, or anthropology—folks who had never seen a patient and may never do so. Yet they took Lacan's psychoanalytic theory very seriously, assiduously parsing its meaning. But, unlike psychotherapists, who evaluate the worth of a psychological theory by assessing its empirical validity and clinical applicability, my philosophy-minded seminar mates tended to evaluate Lacan's theory by the quality of its logic. His popularity in cultural studies (vs. the clinic) may have to do with the fact that Lacan, though a practicing analyst, rarely wrote about his own patients but instead analyzed art (e.g., Bernini's *St. Teresa*); literature (e.g., Poe's "The Purloined Letter," Greek drama); philosophy (e.g., Hegel, Heidegger); newsworthy or criminal figures; or Freud's cases, as if he were carrying on an extended debate with Freud. It amused me to observe that many of today's humanities scholars' knowledge of Freud is filtered through Lacan's re-visioning of him. The Lacanian perspective emphasizes somewhat different works of Freud than those emphasized in American psychoanalytic training institutions; for example, Freud's sociological writing, such as *Totem and Taboo*, and his earlier essays and books, such as *The Interpretation of Dreams* and *The Psychopathology of Everyday Life*, in which the biological origins of our psyches are downplayed. To date, Lacanian thinking has not greatly influenced American psychotherapeutic practice, though it is operative in clinical settings in Europe and South America.

Lacan did to the mind what Saussure did to language and Levi-Strauss did to tribal cultures—he searched for underlying structures. Noting that Freud's dream analyses, and most of his analyses of the unconscious symbolism used by his patients, depend on word play—on puns, associations, etc., that are chiefly *verbal*, he famously pronounced: "The unconscious is structured like a language." By this he meant that the unconscious works with some of the same tools as language. Where Freud saw "symbolism," Lacan saw "metaphor." Where Freud saw "condensation" and "displacement," Lacan saw "metonymy." (Metaphor and metonymy are figures of speech, the former replaces one word with another, apparently unrelated word, e.g., "my love" for "red, red rose"; the latter strings associated words together, e.g., "rose," "thorn," and "Sleeping Beauty.") Both Freud and Lacan's mechanisms involve symbols, coding, and hidden meanings, but Lacan makes specific use of Saussure's structural linguistics. In effect, Lacan reconfigured Freud's psychical apparatuses into purely linguistic ones.

This has a number of implications. Whereas the manifest content of a dream reported in a Freudian psychoanalysis might produce a chain of associations, it is assumed that these associations relate to the latent content of the dream and that the dreamer is the author of the dream and the associations. But in Lacanian theory, authors are demoted. They are always at the mercy of the laws of language (such as the aforementioned metaphor and metonymy) that are preexisting. These mechanisms organize and connect the signifying chains of meaning and make the structure and cohesion of language possible. The same laws that govern language also govern the chains of associations reported by the patient in a therapy session. For Lacan, as opposed to Freud, a person (a conscious subject) comes to exist only after language is acquired. This may be a hard concept to wrap your head around. It may be helpful to think of the sound in a forest that occurs when a tree falls and there is no one to hear it. Does it exist? In a certain sense, it may not. Just as the sound may not have existence without a structure to make sense of it, our psyche may have no existence for us without the structure of language. We cannot really know the world or ourselves without the mediation of words and grammar, which organizes and prepackages all our experience. Hence, another of Lacan's famous pronouncements: "The subject is spoken rather than speaking."[57]

Note that the "self" in poststructuralist theory has become a "subject." This switch in jargon is significant. It accentuates the idea that human identity is shaped by language, by becoming a subject in language. It also highlights the fact that subjects are products of signs, or signifiers, which make up our ideas of identity. Selves are stable and essential; subjects are constructed; hence, provisional, shifting, changing, always able to be reconstructed. Selves, in this sense, are like signifiers in a rigid system, whose meanings are fixed; subjects, by contrast, are like signifiers in a system with more play, more multiplicity of meaning.[58]

Because we may know ourselves only through the medium of language, we have to adapt our fantasies and desires to the categories provided by our specific vocabulary and grammar. But these categories are always limited: They cannot fully express the contents of our mind. What cannot be expressed is repressed, pushed back beyond the level of consciousness. The repressed materials go to constitute the unconscious. This means that we are consciously aware of only some of what we want. That is our defining condition—the necessary absurdity of existence—that we long for what we want but do not know precisely what that is. So we are doomed to perpetual frustration. But buried desire sometimes pokes into consciousness in slips, gaps, silences, jokes, inadvertent comments or gestures as we attempt to articulate our feelings. These slips are what Lacanian analysts attempt to grasp, in a manner akin to Derridean critics who deconstruct texts. This process is not unlike Freudian analysis—except, as noted before, Freudians believe that there is an author producing the slips, and the slips have some order and meaning and may be understood and made manageable. Lacan, on the other hand, believes that the author is elusive and is constituted retroactively—after the slips, as it were—and that figuring out what the slips mean is ultimately impossible, though, with treatment, a patient may come to terms with this existential impasse. (Lacan's patients were mostly French, after all.)

Lacan, like Derrida, is a poststructuralist (though the two are by no means entirely in synch). But in the late '70s and '80s Lacan was viewed as a structuralist in America (as opposed to a poststructuralist) in that he was seen as uncovering linguistic "structures" in the psyche. Nevertheless, language, in Lacan's view, seems to be more like a flowing river (which is never the same from one moment to the next) than a frozen pond, an idea that assimilates more closely to the thinking of the poststructural camp than to that of its predecessor. Recall that Lacan states that the unconscious is structured like a language (the flowing river). Continuing with this analogy, the elements of the unconscious (the river)—wishes, desires, drives, images—all form signifiers (and they're usually expressed in verbal terms), and they perpetually stream about; that is, they slide, shift, and circulate along a signifying chain. (Note how Lacan translates the contents of Freud's unconscious into linguistic terms.) For Lacan, there are no signifieds; there is nothing that the signified ultimately refers to. So there is no anchor, nothing that ultimately gives meaning to the whole system. If there were, then the meaning of a particular signifier would be stable (and Lacan would be a structuralist, not a poststructuralist). In the Lacanian universe, meaning is eternally precarious.[59]

And since language constructs identity, identity is precarious, dispersed along a chain of signifiers—not coherent and stable, even though the ego works diligently to depict itself as fixed and in control, to stabilize itself as an "I." But stopping the chain of signifiers is an exercise in futility. Even anatomy cannot make one a man or a woman or a bisexual, or whatever. It cannot freeze-frame identity. The body is just like a Rorschach blot that takes on different meanings. Here we may see a likeness in Lacan's thinking to Foucault's and a gold mine of conceptual possibilities for queer theorists. For Lacan, as for other poststructuralists, there is no natural heterosexual or homosexual drive, or essential masculinity or femininity. These are only dubious categories in language. In Lacan's system the familiar classifications of sexual orientation make no sense, so he has no theory of homosexuality—or of heterosexuality for that matter. In fact, he once famously said, "There is no sexual relation," by which he meant that that there is no inborn desire in the unconscious (masculine or feminine, straight or gay) before the onset of language. Desire is unthinkable apart from words and symbols since it derives all its meaning and force the moment at which child acquires language—the all-important structuring instant. But, we are getting ahead of ourselves....

The origin of Lacan's thoughts on sexual difference lies in his account of the illusory nature of subjectivity. The infant, or what Lacan with characteristic wit labels the "hommelette" (its polymorphous desires moving in all directions like a raw egg being cooked into an omelet), is not yet a human subject.[60] It will only start to become one—that is, become an "I"—when, between six to eighteen months of age, it gingerly identifies with its reflection in its mother's eye, and later in a mirror. The baby falls in love with its tidy little image. Lacan calls this stage of child development the "mirror" phase. It marks the first time the baby sees itself as a separate coherent entity undifferentiated from its mother, that is, as a complete body with limbs that extend in space rather than a blob with an ill-assorted jumble of fleshy parts and disconnected sensations. Lacan here draws on Derrida's insight that identity arises only through difference—the child's difference from its mother.

But this image, though seductive, is a fiction, an ideal of integration. The baby's recognition of itself is actually a "mis-recognition." By taking the reflection to be its real body, the baby is entering the order of the "Imaginary," where seeing is believing. In actuality, the baby is not the coherent unit it looks like in the mirror. It is needy, dependent, uncoordinated, and not fully able to express itself. The reflection that the baby sees is a false image of wholeness. The child's identification with this deceptively sealed envelope gives the child an illusory sense of stability, but, at the same time, it takes the child away from itself. The mirror phase is not the beginning of a true self but of an inevitably constraining false self, a self that is distanced from the infant's inner fantasies and desires.[61] It is our fate as humans, according to Lacan, to be trapped in images fundamentally alien to us, outside us—the images reflected in the mirror or our parents' eyes. We learn what we are exclusively from the cues we receive from the outside.

Because Freud's Anglo-American heirs believe in an organized, stable, authentic identity—an autonomous ego, rather than an identity that is radically split between what we see in the mirror and who we really are—they are considered by Lacanians to be stuck in the deceptively comforting Imaginary order. The Freudian ego can do things—it can mediate between the id and the superego; it can adapt. It is at the center of the subject. The goal of Freudian therapy is to strengthen the ego, the conscious/rational identity, so it is more powerful than the unconscious. But for Lacan this is impossible. The Lacanian ego (the "I" that the baby becomes after it identifies with its reflection) is just a fantasy, a precarious object that has no agency. There's no "there" there that can initiate action or feeling or be strengthened. According to Lacan, the autonomy of the ego is merely another illusion. For Freud the tragedy of life is our ultimate inability to reconcile our nature with culture; but Lacan doesn't believe that we have a nature, or at least one that we can wholly conceive. The images we have of ourselves do not match our actual selves. So, for Lacan, the tragedy of life lies in the fact that we must endure a perpetual lack of wholeness.[62] Where Freud is interested in investigating how the child gets civilized, how it develops a conscience, Lacan is interested in how the child develops the illusion we refer to as the self.

More alienation follows when the child acquires language and enters what Lacan calls the "Symbolic" order—the world of culture, and in particular, the world of signifiers. It is the Symbolic order, not the ego, according to Lacan, that is autonomous. Prior to the assimilation of language, a child cannot really *know* what it wants. A crying baby does not understand its own needs. It is up to the caretakers to name the pain the child seems to be expressing (e.g., the baby is hungry). If a parent responds to its baby's crying with food, the discomfort will retroactively be determined to have "meant" hunger. This may or may not have been true, but constantly responding with food may transform all of the baby's discomforts into hunger. (You can see how this might lead to later eating disorders.) It is not the baby but others who determine the meaning of its cry, and they assign meaning on the basis of the language they speak. Language, then, is a foreign structure foisted onto the child, tainting its needs and wants, further alienating it from itself.[63]

Through the child's identification with the pseudo-fixed meaning of a word (like hunger), it can gain an apparently unified sense of self.[64] But this identification is yet another booby-trap, another misrecognition. Language is not only inadequate for conveying a child's inner life, but it is also, in and of itself, slippery. Words change meaning. Lacan warned analysts not to be fooled by a patient who says "I." The "I" of a person's speech might seem to refer to the speaker, but this is spurious. Unbeknownst even to the person doing the talking, the "I" he or she speaks veils a much more precarious inner "I," an impermanent "I" that cannot be fully represented in language. The fact that *both* identities formed by people during their development (the one produced in the preverbal Imaginary and the one produced in the Symbolic) are dubious and unstable lends Lacan's ideas their sophistication and complexity—and resonance for queer theory. The categories with which the child identifies are *constructed* categories, without any essence so, theoretically speaking, transgressing them is both possible and obvious, anyone's prerogative. Lacan's theory may actually provide space for those who cannot find exact words for themselves in our current vocabulary. Maybe "the love that dare not speak its name" may finally find a voice.

But all is not rosy. Lacan's Symbolic may not be the theoretical path to sex/gender liberation. It is a world of moral laws, prohibitions, and customs, all of which are delivered upon the child by its father—the Law of the Father. Here are some of the conceptual knots for queers. First of all, the child must position itself in language and may only do so by taking on a sexed identity. This is because Lacan (reflecting Derrida) assumed language to be founded on a system of binary oppositions, such as I/you and self/other. So when the child acquires language it must deem itself either a girl or a boy, feminine or masculine, based (infelicitously in my view) on the presence or absence of a phallus. Lacan designated the phallus as the ultimate mark of difference. It is a preordained privileged signifier, the defining term for both sexes. It puts an end to the eternal sliding of the signifier and thereby provides some stability to meaning, like, to borrow Lacan's image, an upholstery button does to a slipcover. To deny sexual difference would involve the denial of the Symbolic and would result in psychosis. This forced-choice predicament of the Symbolic puts women once again in the humiliating position of lacking something, and queers once again in the position of having no respectable category in which "to be." In that sense, the Lacanian system, though it had the potential to do otherwise, perpetuated and maybe even escalated Freud's phallocentrism.

A second and related bone of contention for queers is that chief among prohibitions imposed by the father is the incest taboo. Freud speculated in *Totem and Taboo* that the origin of this prohibition might be attributed to a mythic primal horde of males who kill their greedy, womanizing fathers to gain access to the women themselves. Then, feeling remorse, the sons proceed to forbid themselves the very thing for which they murdered their fathers—his women. They decide that henceforth their crime must never be repeated in future generations, and presumably this decision has remained operative in the form of the incest taboo. But this myth takes no account of female or same-sex desire. It is all about men's relations to their fathers. Nevertheless, Lacan adopted it wholesale.

According to Lacan, the incest taboo becomes operative for the child as it is acquiring language, that is, entering the Symbolic. The father-imposed incest taboo triggers the infamous unfolding family drama known as the Oedipus complex, a dynamic that was originally postulated by Freud but had lost some of its luster by the time Lacan took it up. Lacan put a different spin on Oedipal dynamics: what was for Freud a biological propensity, a naturally evolving desire of the child for the parent of the opposite sex, became for Lacan a linguistic transaction in which the child, whether male or female, always desires the mother. As '60s country singer Brenda Lee plaintively intoned, we all "want to be wanted." But the child not only desires to be desired by its mother, it also desires what the mother desires—here, presumably, a phallus (which she lacks). It follows then that the child, too, wants both to have a phallus and also to be the phallus, to fulfill its mother's desire.

This amounts to wanting a perfect union with the mother. Henceforth the child will feel a relentless but, as we shall see, impossible desire to return to that amorphous infant state before it became an "I" and became locked into a constant cycle of simultaneously both wanting what the "other" wants, as well as wanting to be what the "other" wants—the origin of all desire. This takes us to another of Lacan's famous one-liners: "Desire is the desire of the other."[65]

So all children want to be the apple of their mother's eye, but the father forbids mother–child union. The male child resolves his murderous Oedipal conflict with his father by renouncing his incestuous desire and by identifying with him, the father—he who, presumably from the dawn of history, lay down the law. In Lacanian terms, the male child assumes the "Name of the Father," which in French allows the pun—the No of the Father/the Name of the Father (*le non du pere/ le nom du pere*). The Name of the Father is a fundamental signifier that confers identity on the subject. The male child can assume it—and an identity—because he, like his dad, has a penis. The penis has this power even though it is a fragile organ, inflating and wilting according to its own whims, and vulnerable to castration (as evidenced by his mom's lack of a penis, which the child is presumed to think was cut off). The female child, having no part on her the body on which to construct a phallic signifier, is left in the ignominious position of missing something. Since a woman in the Lacanian system cannot assume the Name of the Father, she is incomplete, an empty signifier—a "lack." There is no positive term for her in the Symbolic order (never mind a signifier for gender-benders). At best, a woman may obtain a phallus by being one for her lover; that is, by being an object of desire for men, by masquerading femininity (recall Riviere, Chapter 2).

This is precisely the point that film theorist Laura Mulvey seized upon and amplified in a trailblazing feminist 1975 essay in which she argued that women in Hollywood cinema are positioned as passive objects of the male erotic gaze. Men look; women are looked at. Females are "fetishized" (her word) in film to keep at bay the threat they pose as reminders of castration.[66] If the entire movie-going audience consisted of straight men, her theory might be persuasive: A heterosexual man may understandably take pleasure in looking at a dishy dame whose performance allows him to feel himself to be the object of *her* desire. The glamorous woman gives him what he thinks he wants—which, in truth, is not far from the conventional wisdom about how to get a man. In Lacan-speak, attractive starlets are masquerading as the phallus to thwart the anxiety that the mother's castrated body originally provoked in him. When they wear top hats and high heels and wield canes (all phallic symbols), they are actually gilding the lily of the phallic replacement (themselves). But what about those movie-goers (straight women and sex/gender deviants) for whom women are not objects of desire? Why do they enjoy film? At best, Mulvey's theory is partial. Moreover, it presumes fixed sex/gender categories, a fatal flaw in queer theory circles. Her ideas have been heavily criticized down the years, and even Mulvey herself has revised her thinking about visual pleasure.

Given Lacan's glaringly phallocentric, heterosexist assumptions, it is no surprise to find both a gay and a feminine chorus aggressively repu-diating their collective repudiation. First, however, it is worth noting that there is a strong cohort of feminists—like Parveen Adams, Juliet Mitchell, and Ellie Ragland-Sullivan—who do not reject the Lacanian account, claiming that Lacan merely describes but does not participate in the subordination of women.[67-69] After all, mothers really **are** the primary caregivers of children and fathers really **do interfere** with the child's blissful union with its mother. And this **does occur** at about the time that the child is acquiring language and notices sexual differ-ence, all of which are lumped together in its head and presumably become necessary for sanity. Lacan did not create this scenario. He merely accepted it as a given and tried to explain it.

Then there are the male "anti-Oedipalists," such as the aforemen-tioned Gilles Deleuze and Felix Guattari, associates of Foucault. While they used Lacan's ideas and terminology in their work, they simulta-neously refused to uncritically embrace a theory of desire based on male organs. Their *Anti-Oedipus* idealized Lacan's concept of the Imaginary (the time before the acquisition of language) but regarded our entrance into the Symbolic (with the attendant phallus business) as tragic. This reprehensible situation may be rectified, in their view, only by a return to the Imaginary—to spontaneity, to primitive unmediated desire, to their romantic idea of schizophrenia and fused relationships.[70] Note that they were writing in France in the aftermath of the infamous Leftist stu-dent revolts of May 1968 when liberation was in the air. "Let yourself go" and "Do your own thing" were the slogans of the day. The French gay activist/theorist, novelist Guy Hocquenghem, following Deleuze and Guattari's radical anti-Oedipal trajectory, claimed that psycho-analysis arbitrarily glorifies the phallus while unfairly degrading the non-procreative anus, rendering it shameful, disgusting, necessarily hidden. Why not empower the anus? Hocquenghem advocated trans-forming the rectum into a "desiring machine." Presumably any part of one's anatomy may become an erogenous zone (and, indeed, the bodily areas of quadriplegics—above the point at which their spinal cord is damaged—sometimes demonstrably do). To him, casual, anonymous anal sex, wanton sex in which "organs look for each other and plug in…" was potentially revolutionary.[71] It certainly undermines the sex/gender binary. Clearly, these critics were stretching mainstream thinking beyond the banal (to, pardon my pun, the anal) and were paving the way for queer theory, though it took two more decades and a trip across the ocean for the term to be coined.

Finally, there are the feminists who radically modify Lacanian theory. Those most frequently cited are a triumvirate of Frenchwomen: the psychoanalyst Luce Irigaray, the author/critic Helen Cixous, and the psychoanalyst Julia Kristeva.[72-74] I cannot do justice to them here but do wish to convey the direction of their thinking. Each one attempts to celebrate femininity in her own way, to give it a signifier (to use Lacanian jargon), but none entirely throws out the baby (Lacan) with the bathwater. They do for women's genitals what Hocquenghem did for the rectum—rejoice in it. Irigaray fiercely objects to the female body being reduced to a "hole" and Lacan's marginalization of mothers. She stresses a female reading of culture, one giving the "maternal" equal status to the "paternal." She cleverly asks why it was a mirror that was deemed by Lacan to be the instrument of choice for producing a sense of identity. A flat mirror masks what is specific to women. Why not use a speculum? A vagina is not merely a cut, but a three-dimensional genital in its own right.

Helen Cixous seeks to undo women's ignominious equation with a "lack" by promoting an experimental form of writing (*ecriture feminine*) that stylistically affirms a woman's voice. This manner of writing does not rely on "imprisoning" binary logic and linear storytelling, which Cixous relegates to men. Rather, it attempts to convey the rhythms of a mother's body as perceived by the infant before language and is therefore characterized by disruptions, ambiguities, excess, fluidity, figurative phraseology, the free play of signifiers—all of which serve to destroy the closure of binary opposites. In effect, Cixous makes use of Derrida's deconstruction to disrupt patriarchal language and insert a repressed female one. Julia Kristeva also celebrates the early pre-Oedipal relationship between mother and child before the child acquires language, which she labels the "semiotic." Kristeva believes that the "semiotic" can be resurrected in the spoken word and used disruptively to undermine patriarchy. Although Anglo-American feminists applaud these Frenchwomen's goal, they sometimes dismiss them as essentialists—as dewy-eyed, milky, "difference" feminists, for their sentimental celebration of the female.

But Lacanians counter that Irigaray's, Cixous' and Kristeva's objections are beside the point because the phallus is NOT a penis. It is a symbol of the father's power, not a biological attribute. Either sex may have either a phallus or a "lack." An actual penis can never match up to the magical image of the phallus and thereby creates a sense of lack (castration) in men as well as women. To Lacan the phallus is a signifier, not an organ—it is the uber-signifier, the signifier of signifiers, the term around which all other signifiers revolve—but, importantly, it only *seems* to have power. Signifiers lack any value in themselves. So the phallus's power is bogus. And if the status of the phallus is false, then so are all the binary oppositions modeled on the binary meanings of phallus and "lack," masculinity and femininity, by which we structure our world.[75]

Despite these disclaimers, I suspect that Lacanian apologists protest too much. Their logic reminds me of the funny story Freud wrote about in *The Interpretation of Dreams*—a man was charged by one of his neighbors with having given him back a borrowed kettle in a damaged condition. The defendant asserted, first, that he had given it back undamaged; second, that the kettle had a hole in it when he borrowed it; and third, that he had never borrowed it at all. The Lacanians get similarly tangled up in their own explanations. First they would have us believe that the tie between the phallus and penis is not patently obvious.[76] Second, they insist that the phallus is not only not a penis, it is not even a male symbol, but rather a precarious, sex-blind emblem of power. Third—this is the most contradictory part—they state that the sex-neutral phallus (which is not to be confused with the visible penis) serves as the mark of difference between the sexes. It organizes sexuality. But, of course, if the phallus is invisible and entirely unrelated to anatomical genitals, how could a small child notice it (or its lack)? Conversely, if the penis is not the phallus, if it is just a piece of flesh without symbolic value, why is its presence or absence such a big deal? There seems to be no getting away from it; the phallus and penis are inextricably associated, both of which are cemented to images of power and agency. Any way you slice his theory, a person without a penis (that is, a girl) does not have what it takes to be an active, desiring, self-determining self in the world.

Indeed, Lacan has said, "Woman does not exist."[77] In his later writing Lacan did grant woman a form of desire specific to her—supplementary *jouissance* (unconditional, albeit, unbearable pleasure)—in which her "lack" was ascribed a libidinal value of its own. But this strikes me as an add-on, a theoretical stretch, like the Ptolemic theory of the universe, which, in an attempt to account for ever more complicated stellar movement, eventually succumbed to flabby inconsistency. In the end, Lacan freed the understanding of sexual difference from biological reductionism—a user-friendly idea to queers—only to imprison it in a not-so-user-friendly phallocentric, heterosexist Symbolic order.

FOUR AMERICANS AND A BRIT

But the theory-building juggernaut had been set in motion: The gay rights movement had provided the impetus and the French poststructuralist theorists had provided the mechanism and context for queer theory to emerge. Thanks to Foucault and company, people's identities could be seen as unstable, fluid, moving targets even to the people themselves, rather than something determined by their anatomy. And erotic desire could be viewed as constructed from the outside in, not from the body out. That is, vaginas did not necessarily seek penises, and vice versa. As these French writers were translated incrementally into English, the center of gravity of theory-building moved across the channel and ocean. While postmodern theory never caught on in mainstream psychotherapy circles, it gripped the imagination of Anglo-American cultural theorists and artists. Those theorists who focused specifically on viewing sex/gender through the lens of postmodernism became the pioneers of queer theory—our cultural "queerspotters."

Mostly arts and humanities professors, the architects of this new gender theory share certain traits. In general, they write about "texts" —literature, art, or cultural phenomena—not patients, which partially accounts for their invisibility in psychology circles and the great communication divide (see Chapter 1). Though they do not treat people, they do grapple with psychoanalytic theory and seem to read it more solemnly than actual psychoanalytic practitioners. Many engage in the paradoxical practice of using psychoanalytic methodology even as they are challenging it. They also carry on the annoying but venerable French tradition of using clotted prose to explain things in the most convoluted way possible. In addition, they analyze texts via Derrida's deconstruction, which, when practiced by them in particular, is sometimes called "queering." Queering quite literally "sexes up" an otherwise dry academic pursuit and undoubtedly served to make deconstruction the "hip" literary practice of the '80s.

Finally, and importantly, queer theorists (since they are poststructuralists) presume that language is not a neutral medium but one that contains hidden built-in biases against women and sex/gender nonconformists (phallocentrism, heterosexism, etc.). For this reason, Monique Wittig, a well-known theorist at the University of Arizona, for example, avers that she is not a woman. At first this claim seems patently absurd: It implies a denial of the concrete fact of her existence as a female. But her point is that "woman" is not an innocent self-evident label. Rather it is a concept that is irremediably imbued with deep-seated assumptions. What makes a woman is a specific social relation to a man—a personal, physical, economic, heterosexual obligation, from which even the label wo"man" is derived. Wittig rejects that obligation.[78] To theorists like Wittig, words are inadequate for conveying the queer experience, which is always perceived in terms of that which opposes the norm: their genital is a "lack," for example, or their desire is "perverse." So anyone other than straight males who attempt to express themselves in speaking or writing inevitably collides with their "silencing" within language, which results in conscious or unconscious slips, gaps, and contradictions (like the crypto-queers lurking in a macho Hemingway novel). Queer tacticians decode these slips, gaps, and contradictions.

Recall that deconstruction, the modus operandi of queer theory, works by exposing the central binary oppositions contained in works of art, philosophy, or culture. With regard to queer theory, the offending binaries are man/woman, male/female, homosexual/heterosexual, all of which are understood as expressive attributes of one's anatomy. The shape of one's genitals is the master mark of difference, the mark of difference that trumps all other marks of difference—race, class, lust level, preferred position for sex, etc.—as an organizer of reality. This is a mistake, according to queer theorists, as it serves to skew reality, a mistake they are trying to undo. What this means is that postmodern gender theorists deliberately "misread" literature and art by foregrounding its deviant sexual elements. They look for what is being said about sexuality, but also what is (perhaps only implicitly) being rejected, and from whose perspective. A hypothetical deconstructive analysis in PoMo-speak of the popular aforementioned TV show *Queer Eye for the Straight Guy* might be that it is a hyperbolic condensation of transgressive reinscription or gender sabotage in a condoned spectacle. The popular show both sends up and applauds stereotypic gay behavior. It oscillates between affirming a gay/straight binary (i.e., gays have good taste; straight men don't) and subverting it (i.e., both gays and straights are basically alike—lovable and better off using expensive hair products). The result: the viewer subliminally questions the binary.

Bersani

Let me cherry-pick among queer theorists and outline and connect the ideas of a few luminaries.[†] One of the foremost American "queerspotters"

[†] Other important French-inspired cultural critics include Emily Apter, Shoshana Felman, Jane Gallop, Alice Jardine, Nancy K. Miller, Jacqueline Rose, Naomi Schor, Kaja Silverman, and Gayatri Spivak.

is U.C. Berkeley theorist Leo Bersani, though he is ambivalent about the label "queer" for, radically interpreted, the label erases the specificity of gay sex. An obvious intellectual descendant of Foucault, he is, like his forefather, an advocate of sexual gymnastics and a confusion of orifices. He applauds, for example, the slightly wicked homoerotic images he finds hiding (in plain sight) in the Baroque artist Caravaggio's paintings. But perhaps Bersani is most well known for attacking one the most sacred of sacred cows of the sex act—the cultural valorization of thrusting over receptivity. He celebrates, instead, the pleasure of passivity—the appeal of being penetrated, powerlessness, the exuberant self-shattering that can occur for a man when he is a "bottom." In his infamous classic 1987 essay "Is the Rectum a Grave?" he esteems what homophobics disdain the most—so-called feminine sex, the "penetratee" sexual position.[79] This idea makes Bersani's thinking a bit difficult to classify. In his view, the phallocentrism of psychoanalysis is bad, not because it denies power to those who do not have or want a penis (the usual feminist/gay rights reason for condemning sexism), but because it denies the value of *powerlessness*.[80] There is something positive, he perversely argues, in being ravished, out of control: "the seductive and intolerable image of a grown man, legs high in the air, unable to refuse the suicidal ecstasy of being a woman."[81] At first glance, this comparison may be construed as insulting to both homosexuals and women; on the other hand, it need not be mutually pejorative. Might is not necessarily right. Why must we habitually value power and control (an especially operative sentiment in America) over playfulness and humility? Think of the pleasure some people obtain from surrendering to authority or chance—in Alcoholics Anonymous, in partying, in gambling, in extreme sports, in joining a cult, in "escaping from freedom," as the anti-Fascist critic Erich Fromm put it, or in joining a convent. These pleasures might be seen as okay, even expedient, if understood outside moralistic, religious, or medical frames of reference.

Dollimore

Another conceptual heir of Foucault, literary theorist Jonathan Dollimore (the "Brit" in the above subtitle), following the path of Bersani, argues that power and pleasure are not mutually exclusive but reinforce each other. But Dollimore has "purer" queer credentials than Bersani, if the open practice of sexual fluidity is a measure of purity: Dollimore left his male life partner for a woman with whom he had a child. By closely reading early modern literature, Dollimore makes the suggestive point that what is culturally peripheral often turns out to be symbolically central, for example, the role of the prostitute in Shakespeare's

Measure for Measure or membership in a racial minority in *Othello.* Analogously, he argues that the homosexual is also strangely integral to the very society that obsessively denounces him—"its cultural marginality in direct proportion to its cultural significance."[82] Dollimore's indebtedness to Foucault is obvious here (recall Foucault's ideas about the ironic high prevalence of stealth sex talk in Victorian society), but Dollimore calls attention to the fact that this idea has a more surprising ancestor—Sigmund Freud.

Freud, too, places the existence of perversion—which, like "inversion," Freud's sometime term for homosexuality, involves a turning away from what is "normal"—at the center of his account of sexuality. After all, it was Freud, not a contemporary queer theorist, who wrote that when "any one who has *become* a gross and manifest pervert, it would be more correct to say that he *remained* one."[83] In other words, children are born polymorphously perverse, and they are supposed to grow out of it. It is sexual perversion, not sexual "normality," that is the starting point of sexuality in human nature. Moreover, the conversion to so-called normality is a perilous process. And even when it succeeds, that is, when perverse desire is repressed, it may generate neurosis; hence, Freud's famous assertion that neurosis is the negative of perversion.[84] By this Freud meant that all of us harbor perverse desires in our unconscious that can never be totally repressed. They poke through indirectly in the form of neurotic symptoms, for example, as when a person with subliminal "unclean" thoughts becomes obsessively neat. In short, heterosexuality masks homosexuality. (Mind you, Freud came to precisely the opposite conclusion in the '30s when he speculated that homosexuality masks heterosexuality.[85] More about this later.)

Sedgwick

Dollimore's idea about the centrality of homosexuality to culture brings us to yet another heir of Foucault, literary critic Eve Kosofsky Sedgwick, currently Distinguished Professor at the Graduate Center of CUNY, whom *Rolling Stone* has called "the soft-spoken queen of gay studies."[86] She, along with the American feminist theorists Teresa de Lauretis and Judith Butler, set the agenda for queer theory. It is notable that they are female, and that Lauretis and Butler are lesbian. Up until then, both queer activism and theory had mostly been about gay men—once again illustrating the ignominious status of women in the scheme of things.[87] Sedgwick, who is long married to a man with whom she professes to have "vanilla" sex, designates herself "queer" in the elastic sense of the word. Her model of queer is about the need to reinvent for everyone—gays, straights, bisexuals, transgenders, whatever—more fluid, expansive self-definitions; it's about moving beyond conformity, beyond gender itself, to molding satisfactory selfhoods.

Sedgwick's "queerspotting" territory is nineteenth-century English literature. Like Dollimore, she reads between the lines of literary works to expose instances of "silent" sexual deviance, which she finds, metaphorically speaking, everywhere. "You can't understand relations between men and women," she told a *New York Times* interviewer in 1998, "until you understand relationships between people of the same gender, including the possibility of a sexual relationship between them."[88] Sedgwick trolls through literature traditionally seen as heterosexual to find and expose what she says are homoerotic themes. The Henry James short story "The Beast in the Jungle," for example, is usually read as a straight love story about John Marcher, who is too narcissistic to return the love of a woman, May Bartram, until too late. Only when the Bartram dies, the traditional reading goes, does Marcher realize the extent of his loss. At the story's conclusion, he hurls himself on her grave, looks up and sees in the distance another mourner, a man, and envies him his impassioned grief. It is an existential moment in which Marcher recognizes the emptiness of his life. But to Sedgwick, the story is about a man who is secretly gay but cannot acknowledge it. Bartram, Marcher's ostensibly thwarted female love interest, had actually been supportive of his true sexual orientation. The anonymous stranger in the cemetery, according to Sedgwick, was not so much grieving as cruising.[89]

Whether this sort of transgressive reading of a text is illuminative from a literary perspective is debatable. It certainly bypasses the aesthetics of art, which, in my view, is art's main point. But literature qua literature is not Sedgwick's concern. She aims not to explain literature but to call its bluff. Her deconstructive criticism, like that of Barsani and Dollimore, has led to some interesting psychological speculating. From Sedgwick's wide-ranging close reading of works by Proust, Tennyson, Melville, George Eliot, among others, she concludes that *all* men are prone to form intense homoerotic bonds with each other. Like Freud, she holds a "universalizing" view of homosexuality, that a tincture of gayness may be inherent in all people, as opposed to the "minoritizing" view held by gay political activists, that gayness, like race and ethnicity, defines a distinct group of people. According to Sedgwick, the dynamics that drive many plots in fiction—as in life—have to do with the "homosocial" (her word) relations between men (such as Marcher and the anonymous stranger) in which women (such as Bartram) are almost incidental. She traces this idea to Levi-Strauss, who, in *The Elementary Structures of Kinship*, suggests that men marry (or have sex with) women to repress their desire for each other. Women serve merely to sustain the homosocial relation among men, lest it burst into homosexuality and disrupt the social order. Women figure as only the object of exchange.[90] Presumably the most important love object for a man is a man.

Men must vigilantly guard against their homosocial preference segueing into outright homosexual desire. Maintaining a comfortable balance between permitted and taboo desire is a delicate matter, according to Sedgwick, making men prone to "homosexual panic," a concept she uses to explain homophobia. Some men are so fearful of their own potential for homosexual desire that they overshoot the mark in renouncing it and assign the contemptible inclination to others, whom they proceed to vehemently despise. Male bonding, for Sedgwick, is structured around a shared hostility to homosexuality.[91]

Freud used the logic of "homosexual panic" in his famous case report of the paranoid Dr. Schreber. Schreber's feeling that another man was persecuting him arose, according to Freud, from his hidden desire for that very man. As formulated in the Schreber case, a taboo unconscious wish ("I love him") is denied ("I do not love him, I hate him") but returns to consciousness as a projection ("he hates me and persecutes me"). This dynamic is so widely accepted as an explanation of prejudice against sexual deviants that it is almost a cliché. I include myself among others who tend to assume that those most eager to denounce homosexuality—like FBI head J. Edgar Hoover, lawyer Roy Cohn, literary scholar Allan Bloom—are frequently, like Schreber, secretly gay.

But the term "homosexual panic," as Sedgwick later pointed out, has become problematic and overemployed. It is used these days to defend perpetrators of hate crimes against gays, implying that those who commit these heinous acts couldn't help themselves. They presumably suffer from a pathological condition that diminishes their responsibility for their acts. Known as the "Homosexual Panic Defense," it is ironically turning the gay-affirmative politics of the term's former popularizers on its head. Also, it is a mistake to wholly attribute paranoid psychoses to this cause, which, if taken at face value, is mutually insulting (pairing two stigmatized conditions—homosexuality and mental illness), and, moreover, wrong. If Schreber's case exemplifies homosexual panic, the summer residents of Provincetown would all be hospitalized. "Homosexual panic" presumes rampant homophobia, lest people would not need to panic should they discover homoerotic feelings in themselves. It also presumes that gays internalize the homophobia around them. Happily the world is becoming more tolerant, and not all gays and deviants are self-hating. Today, most psychotherapists would attribute Schreber's condition to a combination of poor biology and sadistic fathering occurring in a sexually repressive environment.

Sedgwick carries her theories further by looking at the problem of "knowing," specifically the instances in fiction where one character is described as knowing something that is secret, often that another character is gay. She claims that the play of secrets and revelations that constitute the homosexual closet is an important metaphor for understanding Western culture. Willful ignorance, Sedgwick surprisingly asserts, may be as potent as knowledge, as in the "Don't ask, don't tell" ruling that allows homosexuals to remain in the military as long as the military is "ignorant" of their sexual orientation. When examined from a different angle, the circulation of "open secrets"—such as "coded knowledge," "the unsayable," "pseudo-innocence," "superior insight," "gossip," "innuendo," and "rumor" that Sedgwick compares with the choreography of "knowing/not knowing" characteristic of the homosexual closet—are actually mechanisms of domination. They're about power.[92] I suspect this dynamic may be operative when men justify sexually assaulting women who, they claim, dress provocatively. How "innocent" is sexy dressing? From whose point of view? My patient Charlie would claim that women "know" exactly what they are doing when they display cleavage. Feminists and legal experts might reply that "knowing" does not matter. But arguably, strategic "not knowing," playing innocent, gives women a certain power, albeit a rather pathetic version of it. Sedgwick is on to something.

Sedgwick created quite a scandal in 1989 with her notorious delivery to the MLA of an essay on the figurative use of masturbation in *Sense and Sensibility*. Naughtily titled "Jane Austen and the Masturbating Girl," the paper was regarded by many (who probably hadn't read the article or heard her speak) as proof that the humanities had at last decayed beyond repair.[93] How dare she desecrate every feminist's favorite heroine! I have to agree with those who find Sedgwick's implication that Austen's character Marianne Dashwood's psychological despair was caused, not by a romantic insult, but by masturbation, to be (pardon another pun) ham-handed. But despite a few excesses, Sedgwick offers many insights. To the extent that she domesticates deviancy by finding it coded in so many places in texts, some locations assuredly accurate, I applaud her endeavor.

Interestingly, in the past few years she has openly consorted with a bête noire of Foucault followers—a psychoanalyst. Considering the fact that Freud has been blamed for so much of the sexism and homophobia of the Western world and that Sedgwick is a self-professed queer, this was an open-minded and bold course of action. A recent book chronicles her helpful psychotherapy, in which she sought to put her emotional life back together after treatment for ongoing aggressive cancer.[94] In her psychotherapy she worked to accept the split in herself between her baroque sexual fantasies (the presence of which would be unremarkable in anyone and expectable in herself, given the nature of her literary theorizing) and her actual conventional sexual behavior. She also sought to reconcile the theoretical perspective and manner of her therapist with her own. Tolerating these splits in oneself and others is, of course, what queer theory aims toward, not necessarily the actual performance of X-rated sex, as some folks believe.

de Lauretis

As I mentioned before, the scholar who usually gets the nod for first using the phrase "queer theory" in print is U.C. Santa Cruz theorist Teresa de Lauretis, in a 1991 issue of the journal *differences*. At the time, lesbians were experiencing sexism in the male-dominated gay movement, and non-whites were experiencing racism in both the gay and lesbian communities. She had hoped that the term "queer" would repair such rifts. But only three years later, de Lauretis dismissed queer theory as a marketing ploy that had "quickly become a conceptually vacuous creature of the publishing industry."[95]

Apparently her goal in employing the term "queer" was never meant to wipe out the category of "lesbian," or any other category. She emphatically retains the classification "lesbian," which, moreover, she imbues with a "hot" multifarious sexiness. This makes her somewhat less than a radical queer among queers whose project is the erasure of all classifications and a somewhat problematic feminist among feminists whose "sisterhood" with lesbians has been fraught with sibling rivalry. But as a feminist myself in the trenches of actual psychotherapy practice, I agree with her grounded perspective and recognition of the fact that many people do have fixed identities and inclinations. Besides, compared to the world at large, and psychoanalysts in particular, she is still rather expansive in her conception of desire by acknowledging vastly different erotic "mappings."[96] She vehemently rejects the exclusive image of the lesbian as a repressive mother figure who sweeps lesbian sexuality under the rug of female friendship and mother-daughter bonding.[97]

Her starting point was film. Like many feminist film theorists after Mulvey, who had suggested that the camera functions like the lascivious "male gaze" poring over glamorous women's bodies, she sought to figure out why, if that were true, women like movies. What about a woman's desire? And what about a woman's desire for another woman?

Clearly it is too simplistic to argue that all images of women in film constitute phallic replacement. Her answer contains liberal doses of the neo-Lacanians Jean Laplanche and Jean-Bertrande Pontalis.[98] De Lauretis sensibly asserts that we need not perceive a scene in a film in a specific or stable way, as Mulvey had originally required us to do, but in a shifting manner, just like the child in Freud's famous essay "A Child is Beaten."[99] In Freud's account, the child fantasizes first ("My father is beating the child") and second ("I am being beaten by my father"). In other words, the child casts herself into more than one role in her fantasy. Analogously, the moviegoer may identify with numerous characters in a film and with multiple desires—active/passive, male/female, S/M, butch/femme, and so on.[100] So the viewer may "want" the glamorous actress in a film; or "be" the glamorous actress; or "want" the hero; or "be" the hero; or even "be" the voyeuristic camera; or all, or none, of the above. De Lauretis's use of Lacan's idea about the illusory nature of subjectivity is obvious here.

By now it is apparent that the current crop of "queerspotters," though heirs of the shrink-bashing followers of Foucault, routinely and unapologetically engage with psychoanalytic theory for explanations of sexuality and desire. If you were to scan recent queer theory texts, you would discover that, over time, the bulk of their content is more and more about revising psychoanalytic theory than about the literature, film, art, or philosophy they deconstruct. De Lauretis said this outright about her book *The Practice of Love.*[101] Many queer theorists now believe that postmodern gender theory alone is inadequate for understanding an individual's erotic inclinations. They admit that it is to early psychoanalysis, not queer theory, that they owe the insight that sexuality can never be reduced to mere biology. Sexual arousal is inevitably bound up with the construction of desire, which loops back to fantasy and the unconscious—ultimately psychoanalytic concepts. So psychoanalytic theory is ironically becoming the increasingly narrow target of interest of some queer scholars. To be sure, queers do not minimize the historical damage done in the name of psychoanalysis to those in their midst; they nonetheless believe the theory is salvageable.

Arguably, it takes a certain amount of "chutzpah" to revise a theory of human behavior without examining actual evidence from flesh-and-blood human beings. While psychoanalytically oriented therapists might dismiss critical theorists' work as empty because it is devoid of clinical data, I maintain that it is never a mistake to examine the work of others who are mining intellectual material similar to your own. It is an opportunity for genuine reflection. To do otherwise, to fall mindlessly back on the old ways and scorning those who are different, is to stagnate. Besides, psychoanalysts are not entirely without chutzpah themselves, sometimes failing to recognize that their theory is but one story of human functioning. As maverick analyst Adam Phillips suggests, "there are, and have been, many stories in this culture and in other cultures through which people examine, and do other things to, their lives."[102] Psychoanalysis is probably most valuable, he asserts, when removed from its "foolishly conventional knowingness," when placed alongside other narratives. Obviously, queer theory is one. But due to circumstances beyond both groups' control—disciplinary tunnel vision and the exigencies of journal publication—queer theorists tend mostly to converse with themselves. Their writing almost never appears in anything that clinicians read.

But two-way communication is in order. Psychoanalytic therapists should take a cue from queer theorists and actively engage in a bit of cross-disciplinary snooping. If clinicians are serious about breaking down the sex/gender binary, the place to look for inspiration is not mainstream psychoanalytic literature but in the topics it overlooks. To that end, let me recount a few provocative ideas of de Lauretis, though, of course, my account won't do justice to the supple byways of her thinking. De Lauretis's major project is to explain what women want, about which Freud had famously given up. She is specifically interested in lesbian desire, heretofore notable only for its absence in psychoanalytic theory. Neither Freud nor Lacan could consider the possible existence of an active and explicitly sexual female desire and, more particularly, the active and sexual female desire for another woman. After all, the love object of a homosexual woman doesn't have the necessary and sufficient tool for sexual allurement—a phallus. In the one case in which Freud describes his work with an outright lesbian, "The Psychogenesis of a Case of Female Homosexuality," he attributes the patient's lesbianism to a "masculinity complex." He reasoned that her so-called masculinity had its origins in Oedipal disappointment with her father, whom she had desired, which led to her subsequent identification with him and resulted in her repudiation of men.[103] Freud's problem, according to de Lauretis, is that he was determined to force his patient's story to fit his theory of the Oedipus complex. This reminds me of the old adage—when the only tool you have is a hammer, every problem starts to look like a nail. Not surprisingly, if the Oedipus complex is your exclusive explanation of sexuality, then all desire will be stretched and contorted into the appearance of heterosexuality, at least at the level of the unconscious. In Freud's system, there is no viable way for women to be sexual with one another without one of them having to occupy the masculine position. There is, for example, no explanation of the lipstick lesbian.

It was a theory limited to an explanation of straight men. Until recently, theorists deemed a positive resolution of Oedipus complex as compulsory for mental health. As we have seen, the Lacanians compounded the theoretical impasse. Sex and gender were irrevocably tied to the status of a person's castration (or not) experience (though in Lacan's case the penis is presumably symbolic, not biological). De Lauretis took a different tack. Her theoretical argument, proceeding from her analysis of Radclyffe Hall's novel *The Well of Loneliness* and Cherrie Moraga's *Giving Up the Closet*, does not replace or exclude the Oedipal framework, but expands the child's fantasies of vulnerable body parts. These losses include not only the usual fare—the penis and the mother's body—but the subject's own body. This can be resolved in fantasy, in sexual practice, "in and with" another woman.[104] Of course many clinicians now de-emphasize the importance of the "lost" penis. Where de Lauretis is unique is that she also de-emphasizes the importance of the "lost" mother. She argues that if the most painful loss to an individual is the mother's body (as some post-Freudians and post-Lacanians argue), it would confine that person to bland sex, to a vanilla erotica based on gooey nostalgia.

So, de Lauretis does not deny the notion of castration, for to do so is to foreclose the ability to symbolize sexual maturity. (You can see de Lauretis's reliance on Lacan here.) But she differs with others about the importance of *what* is castrated for a girl. In her view, it is her own lovable woman's body (desirable to her mother) that is the more profound loss. A girl's "loss" of a penis, that is, her recognition of a lack of one, merely rewrites this earlier, more thundering loss. Here is how the dynamic unfolds: As a girl develops, her feminine sexy body is symbolically cut off from her self and disavowed, covered over and displaced onto substitutes—"fetishes" (like a tattoo) that at once signal her desire and what her lover desires in her. She can lure other women in two ways: by assuming masculine trappings (one form of fetish), which conveys an active sexual attraction for the female body; or by becoming femme (another form of fetish), which, when offered to the butch, results in mutual pleasure. Both scenarios re-stage the loss and recovery of the female body.[105] (The appropriation by feminist theorists of psychoanalytic terms like "fetish" in their writing has been called "fetish envy" and "perversion theft."[106,107] But of course these feminists are being metaphoric and ironic, satirizing the fact that females do indeed have a lower incidence of DSM-defined fetishism than males, while at the same time rescuing the fetish from being understood exclusively in the classical way as a symbol of mother's missing penis.)

De Lauretis emphasizes that this model does not exclude others and that she herself experienced a positive Oedipus complex. She offers her theory as a "passionate fiction," one among many. But other queer theorists dismiss her reworking of psychoanalysis as a dead-end project that traps her in the discourse she attempts to decry. According to Elizabeth Grosz, her failure to sufficiently repudiate Oedipal dynamics leaves her vulnerable to that pet peeve of feminists and queers—the alignment of the penis with social power. Of course, Grosz adds, had de Lauretis abolished the Oedipus complex more thoroughly, her theory would cease to be psychoanalytic, which, Grosz also implies, would be a good thing.[108] I disagree. I regard de Lauretis's reconception of the Oedipus as an important attempt at preserving what is invaluable in psychoanalysis—fantasy, desire, the unconscious, symbolization—while reworking and de-emphasizing what is not—castration, the paternal phallus, the Name of the Father. Phallocentrism and heterosexism, in my view, are not necessary conditions of psychoanalytic theory.

Butler

In the academic family of queer theory, philosopher Judith Butler is the *capo di tutti capi*. Her ideas are the ones to contend with. Much of what I have been describing in this book thus far converges in Judith Butler's work, particularly in *Gender Trouble: Feminism and the Subversion of Identity*, published in 1990, and *Bodies That Matter: On the Discursive Limits of Sex*, published three years later.[109,110] These two books almost immediately became the foundational texts of queer theory. Currently a professor at U.C. Berkeley, Butler has been called one of the superstars of '90s academia. As such, she has been a lightning rod for criticism, much of it undeserved, though her opaque writing style is an irresistible target. In 1999 she was awarded the first prize in the fourth Bad Writing Contest sponsored by the journal *Philosophy and Literature*.

But buried within her turgid prose is a sweeping synthesis of the most radical theories about sex and gender. In *Gender Trouble*, Butler applies postmodern ideas to feminism, questioning the need for a fixed "female" category or, indeed, for any sex/gender category at all. Far from regarding gender as "natural," she defines it in Foucaultian terms as a "discourse" that is both constructed and maintained by society. Gender is not caused by the presence or absence of a penis. It is free-floating along with gender identity and the very concept of sexes itself. This makes her prima facie a queer theorist but, interestingly, in a 1993 interview for the journal *Radical Philosophy* she reported that she hadn't known about the existence of queer theory when she wrote *Gender Trouble*. She first found out about it some time later at a dinner party.[111]

In the same interview, Butler identified herself as being a feminist theorist, first and foremost, over a queer theorist or gay and lesbian theorist. Perhaps she felt the need to acknowledge her political sympathies outright because some feminists have leveled accusations of apostasy against her. Any theory, such as Butler's, that radically erases sexual identity poses a serious problem for sexual identity activists such as women, lesbians, gays, intersexuals, and transgenders. If there are no categories, how can there be constituencies to liberate? Viewing people solely as individuals as Butler does, rather than as groups, denies the common disadvantaged position of women and sexual deviants around the world. How can oppressed people, subordinated because of their sexuality, develop a sense of solidarity or act collectively if they cannot be identified by their sexuality? Queer theory does not exactly lend itself to the nuts-and-bolts of movement politics.

Yet Butler is in total sympathy with activists' goals, though she disagrees with their tactics. She argues that collapsing all people with vaginas into a single homogenous group separate from men—women's liberation for "women only"—is not only conceptually false but also detrimental to the feminist cause. It is crude and insensitive. It completely misses the insidious complexity of oppression, which cuts through differences of race, class, and sexual orientation regardless of gender identity. An African Moslem woman condemned to death by stoning for adultery would probably have a hard time relating to the grievances of, say, a Sylvia Plath heroine, typically a white Western woman trapped in a socially rigid golden cage. Where a Western woman might see a cage, an African might understandably see gold.

Moreover, a feminist politics based on the identity "woman" assumes and posits the very category that perpetuates injustice.[112] It inevitably, if inadvertently, sustains the binary. The lines should not be drawn, she implies, between men and women, but between those who are oppressors (especially around issues of sexuality) and those who are oppressed. Instead of anatomy, people might organize around a shared feeling of dissent. To do otherwise would lock us into the hierarchical man/woman system.

The overarching and most original claim of *Gender Trouble*, the claim that got the book into every gender theory syllabus, is that gender, and possibly even anatomy itself, is not an expression of who one is, rather a performance.[113] A person's gender is constituted retrospectively through a "stylized repetition of acts"—gesturing, dressing, speaking, etc.—that create the fiction that there is something inside of us called masculinity and femininity. A simplistic analogy might be that "if it walks like a duck and quacks like a duck, it is a duck." In her system, gender is a "fabrication" that is perpetuated by the inscription, over and over again, of gender-tagged behavior upon the surfaces of our bodies, which are otherwise neuter. (Terms like "inscription" and "surface" hail from French theory.)

Butler calls the repetition of acts that produce gender identity "performativity."[114] Turning conventional wisdom on its head, she argues that there is no core gender. Gender is produced after the fact, it is not originally present in an individual's body. It is a "sedimented" effect of behavior. A child "does" boy, for example, by playing with toy guns, or "does" girl by playing with dolls, and thereby becomes a boy or girl. The nature of a child's performance of gender is regulated by cultural norms, which at this moment in Western history happens to be based on the presence or absence of a penis. After all, if gender were a natural outcome of sex, Butler asks, why would Aretha Franklin sing, "You make me feel like a 'natural' woman"?[115] Obviously having a vagina was not enough for Ms. Franklin to feel like a woman. Butler, as the title of her book suggests, "troubles" gender.

Butler "out-Foucaults" Foucault with regard to social constructionism. Foucault had disconnected sexual orientation from the body but had presumed that there was a material body on which to inscribe a sexual disposition. Citing biologist Fausto-Sterling (see Chapter 3), Butler takes this further, to claim that even the way we perceive biological sex is socially constructed.[116] There is no incontrovertible reason to conceive of sex as a binary opposition between men and women. It follows that there is no incontrovertible reason to line up male anatomy with masculinity, a male identity, and an erotic desire for a woman; nor female anatomy with femininity, a female identity, and desire for a man.

Butler's way of thinking did not come out of thin air. She was trained as a philosopher and her work is part of a philosophical tradition arising from Hegel in which critics look for contradictions arising from the very terms of their argument, not from the outside (to the everlasting frustration of those folks whose feet are planted in the ground). Let me situate her in the poststructuralist pantheon. Like Foucault, she argues that sexuality is discursively produced, and she radically extends his critique to include gender identity and the body itself. As with Derrida, meaning for Butler is postponed: the gender of a baby's body is not originally present, but ascribed afterwards. Like Lacan, she uses the term "subject" to describe what Freudians call the ego or the self. Butler's subject, like Lacan's, is illusive—there is no fixed, stable "there" there. This formulation allows the subject to "do" any gender, despite what its body looks like. But, of course, she is critical of Lacan's phallocentrism. Her notion of performativity replaces Lacan's Law of the Father as the prime mover of gender identity. She critiques Irigaray and Kristeva for their positing a specifically feminine form of being, which taints them, she implies, with an essentialist, female chauvinist tinge. She also criticizes Wittig, who, you may recall, is "not a woman." But Wittig does identify as a lesbian, which she purports to be a third gender tied to sex (!), thereby rendering her also, according to Butler, too essentialist.

So "practice makes (almost) perfect" with regard to an illusive gender consolidation. Butler goes on to say that each gender defines itself, not randomly, but in fixed opposition to the other. Folks with convex genitals "perform" male, which is explicitly not female, and those with concave genitals "perform" female, which is explicitly not male. Each and every heterosexual performance sanctions and strengthens heterosexual cultural norms. These norms covertly legitimize heterosexual masculine power. Over time, the performances congeal and begin to seem natural and necessary, at once concealing their artificiality and masking their political stakes in preserving an oppressive straight male chauvinist status quo. With repetition, the artificial becomes indistinguishable from the real: airplane food is perceived by passengers to be actual food; the bachelorette on TV's *The Bachelor* is believed by the viewer to be "in love"; analogously, straight sex is good and right.

To keep gender in its place, heterosexuality is "compulsory." But if our desires were okay, we wouldn't need taboos, that is, compulsory heterosexuality (which in circular fashion makes our polymorphous desires "not okay" in the first place). A violator is deemed a "figure of abjection."[117] We are merely actors in a gender performance that is continually being scripted by social conventions and ideology.[118]

But, according to Butler, there are possibilities for resistance. These lie in certain "performativities," especially those that expose the trumped up nature of cultural gender norms and subvert them by parody. Her infamous example in *Gender Trouble* is drag. Butler's citation of drag got her into trouble with both the academic right and left, that is, with both traditional critics, who lamented the focus on trivia (especially sex) in the university, and feminists, who felt that female impersonators presume and strengthen stereotypic gender stereotypes rather than subvert them. But what Butler meant was that when we appropriate the signals and paraphernalia of masculinity and femininity and assign them to the wrong body, we reveal the artificial and arbitrary nature of gender itself. In the process of ostentatiously imitating a gender, drag makes us look at what is natural. Drag performers are impersonating an impersonation, an idealization of gender, not the real thing. It reminds us that there is no original gender.

Butler's ideas in *Gender Trouble* were taken by many to mean that gender is a kind of improvisational theater, that it is voluntary. Presumably a person may adopt different identities at will, like changing clothes. But in her subsequent work, *Bodies That Matter*, Butler took pains to distinguish between "performance," which is what a performer produces, and "performativity," which, instead, produces the performer. A performance presumes that there is a subject (a person doing the performance), but performativity, and performative speech in particular, questions the whole concept of the existence of a subject. Performative speech brings into being that which it names, which presumably wasn't there before its naming, as in the classic example of a justice of the peace uttering "I now pronounce you husband and wife," thereby creating a legal union where there had been none. So gender identity, for Butler, is an illusion retroactively created by our performativities. In her clarification of the distinction between performance and performativity, Butler added that a performance involves the simple repetition of acts, while performativity is a "reiteration" of acts under "constraint."[119] The latter is coerced into happening by pervasive mechanisms of surveillance, punishment, and discipline.[120] They invade, and knead and bully you into a gender. Gender is not freely chosen. "I never did think that gender was like clothes, or that clothes make the woman," Butler wrote in *Bodies That Matter*."[121]

Missing in Butler's theory, despite her many disclaimers, is a palpable person.[122] In her world, no one has a stable coherent sense of self or an individual thought. People are hollow—all surface, no depth. No one is a free agent, able to pick and choose how to behave. It's all about fixation points for Butler, all about the moment when the discourse stamps the subject into being.[123] This idea is deeply informed by Lacan's fictive ego that mistakenly takes itself to be unitary, fixed, and unconflicted. But, if it is only outside forces that form a person; that names and norms them; that gives them words and sets the conditions under which the word will be chosen, then there is nothing for psychoanalysts to uncover that they haven't already put there via their discourse.[124] At the center of a Butler human is a black hole containing a ghostly amalgam of circulating illusions. In her idiosyncratic cosmology, we are figments of our own imagination. But if this is true, isn't Butler's system just a new form of behaviorism, where there is no being, only a doing?

I am hardly the first person to note that Butler's idea of a person is hard to pin down. Elaborating on this, Harvard critic/psychoanalyst Lynne Layton points out that Butler actually offers two irreconcilable versions of the formation of the conscious subject in *Gender Trouble*.[125] The bulk of Butler's book puts forth the view I have thus far been describing, that gender exists only in the performative citing of norms, a view that, if taken at face value, would render all people a bit like Woody Allen's *Zelig*, a construction without a core, ectoplasmic fragments blowing in the winds of discourse. This is not a very psychoanalytic explanation. It is too mechanical; it is more like imprinting.

But, Layton points out, Butler also suggests another more psychoanalytic version of gender in the very same book, one in which the ego is more substantial. In a small section of *Gender Trouble*, Butler conjectures that heterosexual gender identity involves unresolved grieving. It is built from internalizations of lost same-sex love objects (resting on the theory of identification in Freud's 1917 essay "Mourning and Melancholia"). Straight sex, for Butler, contains the "melancholy" residue of tabooed homosexual love, which people are obliged to disavow (an idea that cleverly implies that rigidly "normal" sex is borne of grief, not happiness, thereby turning the notion that homosexuality is pathology upside down). Unlike other objects, the objects of homosexual love can never be properly mourned because they must be entirely effaced, deleted, as if they never existed in the first place. You can't mourn the loss of something you supposedly never had. Heterosexuality is based on a radical foreclosure of homosexual desire. This foreclosure is ritualized in the norms of culture.

It is notable that this branch of Butler's thinking starts with a solidly established subject that experiences a loss, which then modifies itself by installing the lost loved one into its head (i.e., its ego) via identification. It presumes that there is "something" in a person onto which identifications glom, and from which others are excluded, and, importantly, that there is "something" actively selecting (though not entirely freely) among the options. In this version of subject formation, a person is an "experiencing" self with an internal world of loved and lost objects. Here, a person has agency.[126]

The latter version of gender is the more useful to therapists because, at the very least, it provides them with patients rather than points in discourse, though practitioners, as far as I know, have not discerned actual clinical melancholy arising from gender "normality" in their clients. But ripe for employment in any upgraded theory is Butler's reworking of the Freudian ideas about the primary existence of incestuous and homosexual lust. She argues that gender is socially constructed through the specific prohibition of these desires, not via Oedipal dynamics. Once incest became taboo, children were obliged to divert their love for their mothers to others; once homosexuality became taboo, they were obliged to disavow their love for the same-sex parent. So, heterosexual desire came to be displaced onto one's age-appropriate lover, and homosexual desire came to be denied, made a part of a melancholic incorporation process.[127] In her Foucaultian way, Butler argues that the laws that regulate desire actually produce it. You are not born a gender, but become one.

Left to their own devices, psychoanalytic theorists might have lapsed into inertia regarding the sex/gender binary. Butler, along with her posse of postmodern gender theorists, should be given kudos for highlighting and reconfiguring some basic presumptions of Freud and Lacan. They remind clinicians that psychoanalytic theory is not an eternal truth, but just another grand narrative that privileges one particular story line about gender acquisition. Butler questions the veracity of the plot conjured up by psychoanalysts to explain gender, a story that involves a dubious archaic myth of origin in which a utopian primary bisexuality is rendered into heterosexuality through the inexorable force of the paternal law. This story artificially legitimates some sex/gender possibilities and excludes others, thereby conveying a false impression of a universal sex binary and gender stability. Why, Butler asks, do analysts insist on a paternal law, and not a maternal law, or a gender-free law? Is the incest taboo (which is the motor for the Oedipus complex) a cover for a prior homosexual taboo? She grapples with the idea that a person must "either" identify with a sex "or" desire it, never "both/and." Why, she wonders, must sex beget gender, which, in turn, begets sexual orientation? Why must there be a sequence, or even a connection? Does binary gender mask blurred gender? Butler also questions the necessity of the implicit timeline in Freudian theory in which certain identifications are deemed primary (that with mother) and occur first in forming a gendered self, while others (that with father or siblings) are secondary and occur later. Is this ordering preordained, universal, and eternal?[128] These are excellent questions, highly pertinent to sex/gender practices in the twenty-first century.

But critical theorists sometimes remind me of people who learn a language solely by perusing a dictionary: They are too literal. They may know the technical definition of words but don't "get" grammar, or idiom, the way words are understood by those who use them. PoMo critics' understanding of Freudian theory is similarly skewed. It is "book learning," not "street smarts." It is derived from the psychoanalytic literature (specifically, metapsychology), not from clinicians. Plus, unbeknownst to some of them, the version of psychoanalytic theory with which they wrestle is increasingly outdated. To a certain extent they are battling with a straw man. The theory that most psychoanalytic clinicians embrace today bears little resemblance to what its founder or mid-century descendants envisaged, the one which many queer theorists argue. Today's psychoanalytic therapists have long ago relegated some antiquities to the attic in favor of more up-to-date concepts. How many among us believe that women are constitutionally passive or that a fetish symbolizes the mother's lost penis? It is important that queer theory builders be careful about critiquing issues that psychoanalysts themselves have not already popularly revised.

A more profound criticism is the obvious fact that some people with unstable identities are anguished souls. Consider our colloquialisms for emotional misery: many imply feelings of pain accompanying states of instability and lack of cohesion—"becoming unglued," "cracking up," or "I'm losing my mind." The latter implies that one has a mind to lose. This sort of misery is why many people go to therapy. People seek treatment to "get it together," to have their head "shrunk" into a manageable, well-integrated entity, not to "fall apart." Butler does good philosophy (to my untrained eye) but somewhat doubtful psychoanalytic theorizing. She is refreshingly skeptical of some major psychoanalytical premises, and she makes sound deductions, but some of her tentative conclusions overshoot the mark. In her zeal to deconstruct rigid sex/gender pigeonholing, she bypasses the suffering individual. She puts too much stock in incoherence. She fetishizes fluidity.[129] In my experience, people want coherence, a sense that they are at least somewhat continuous with the person they were yesterday and will be tomorrow, some consistency, predictability.

Certainly, children need consistency in their parents—children want to put Humpty Dumpty together again, not have him shattered. It is very difficult to divest people of their wish for a modicum of control, safety, order, normality. Like Yeats we are not comfortable when things fall apart, when the center cannot hold. Slippery gender may be as mentally torturous as any binary. An unstable identity, fragmentation, and compulsory fluidity are as enslaving in their own way as compulsory conformity. A life of ceaseless change would be a nightmare.

Yet, even as I write about our wish for control, I am well aware that sexual pleasure—rooted as it is in childhood experience—is about letting go and losing control. There needs to be a balance.

5

MEN ARE FROM EARTH, WOMEN ARE FROM EARTH, AND SO ARE QUEERS

Valentine's Day, 2004. Something is happening in the queer community—gays are becoming more openly monogamous. On television I watch as hundreds of same-sex couples line up in the rain to receive marriage licenses from the spunky mayor of San Francisco. Back in Boston, the same thing had occurred at the State House. From a far-fetched argument propounded by a fanciful few, the reality of marriage is now being embraced by a great many, maybe a majority of, gays.[1] The silent types in homosexual culture are currently in the vanguard, demanding that marriage—institutionalized bourgeois fidelity (not hedonism!)—be open to them. Legalized same-sex marriage already exists in three Canadian provinces, the Netherlands, and Belgium and is emerging in Hawaii, Alaska, and Vermont.

Yet even as homosexuals are becoming more overtly monogamous, heterosexuals are becoming more promiscuous, at least in the sense of delaying marriage, dissolving marriage, and not marrying. People, despite their gender identity, sexual orientation, and body, are becoming more like each other; and their ways of being are multiplying. But as my foray into recent literature shows, no single theory explains why. No one theory fits all, or maybe any, sex/gender behavior in its entirety. All our theories collapse under the weight of scrutiny: the objective sciences, both hard and soft, are too reductionist. Traditional psychoanalytic theory is too value-laden, and postmodern gender theory, which is presumably value free, ultimately does away with the patient. The best we can do at the moment regarding an explanation of sex/ gender is "mix and match" theories—biological, social, psychoanalytic, linguistic, postmodern. Perhaps we should take a cue from our teens, many of whom today take this confusion in stride. They call themselves "gayish" or "heteroflexible" and leave it at that.[2] Whatever. Why bother to figure out why one might prefer convex or concave when it may change anyway? The only certainty is uncertainty.

While no theory alone can definitively account for gender-bending, a careful cross-pollination of queer and psychoanalytic theory may work in that direction. In effect it would subject Freudian theory to (in the jargon of the '60s) consciousness-raising, or (in that of the '80s) an attitude-readjustment. That is, it would purge psychoanalytic theory of its hidden biases. In turn, it would subject queer theory to a reality check. By eclectic interbreeding, we might preserve the best of both worlds.

Postmodern gender theorists, until very recently, positioned themselves in opposition to psychoanalysis. Dueling with Freudian concepts was practically a rite of passage for queers, though Freudians, formerly empowered, rarely deigned to duel back. Perhaps queers' ritualistic sparring was their attempt to dethrone the Oedipal father. But, if we look closely at the queer project, it is actually more like an impeachment than a dethronement. Their antagonism is more apparent than real. There is a visceral affinity between the two schools—an unusual respect for deep thinking, a rare inclination to ponder complexity, an irrepressible curiosity about hidden meanings, an infatuation with subtexts, a refusal to take all things at face value (though postmodern purists think that there is nothing beneath the surface, that there is only an ever-shifting surface). While queer theorists summarily discard the sex/gender binary, they also rework a number of Freud's and his followers' ideas. It turns out that the postmodern and Freudian perspectives are not mutually exclusive. There are important areas where they overlap.

Ironically, PoMo theorists provoke us to reread Freud—a nearly extinct activity in these days of insurance-driven psychotherapy—if only to figure out what they are responding to. Their wrestling with Freud reminds us that psychoanalytic theory is our most subtle tool for thinking about the mind and body. It is rich and nuanced, and, like the Bible, to which it is sometimes satirically compared, subject to multiple highly charged interpretations. Freudian theory was, and is, a work-in-progress. You can find justifications for many competing theoretical positions in the course of its long evolution, despite the fact that practitioners arrest from time to time into narrow-mindedness.

So before we relegate psychoanalysis to the dustbin of history, let us remember that it is the only psychotherapeutic regime that is centrally committed to probing the deepest areas of our inner selves. Though psychoanalysts got it wrong about sex/gender, they, unlike more medical or cognitive-behavioral clinicians, are highly respectful of our imagination, fantasies, and soul. Where else can you find textured concepts that explain our inherent self-centeredness to ourselves without moralizing? Where else can you find ideas that are resonant to art, creativity, paradox, metaphor, transgression, our dark side? Instead of bumper-sticker cliches and bromides, psychoanalytic theory supplies a profound, unsentimental, multilayered narrative to help us know our own minds. It recognizes the unruliness of our lust, the indignity of living in a disobedient body, the irreducible conflicts between the individual and society, the stuff of life. Because of its complexity and vitality, it is still the most hopeful site, despite its past failures, for formulating explanations of gender identity and sexual orientation.

In the following sections I sift Freudian theory through the filter of postmodern gender theory, which, as I have described, functions as a kind of Geiger counter for detecting subliminal biases, hidden agendas, and coercion.[3] I resuscitate some Freudian concepts that pass the litmus test of queer theory, dispose of some others, rebuild with the remains, and add a bit to its substance. I resurrect ideas both from the "earlier" and "later" Freud as well as from his revisionists, focusing on those concepts that postmodernists use as starting points. In doing this, I take for granted that our anatomy and urges operate in intangible ways, but that there is not a one-to-one relationship between body and mind. The power and way our flesh shapes our identity and desire is, as yet, undetermined. My synthesis of "deep" theories is necessarily schematic and idiosyncratic, merely a place of departure for future encounters. It is also a bit of a "heavy" read, but a necessary endeavor if we are to figure things out.

PSYCHOANALYTIC/QUEER THEORY COMPATIBILITY QUOTIENT

The Unconscious

While we cannot, here and now, establish the truth or otherwise of the unconscious, it has to be conceded that sex is not exactly a rational enterprise. Try to fall in love, or out of love, because it is sensible, and you will be engaging in an exercise in futility. Ask a shoe fetishist why a shoe is arousing, and he or she cannot tell you. Nor can an individual explain why he or she is straight or one gender identity rather than another. These are unconsciously, not consciously, propelled behaviors. Desire is the end product of processes of which we are not aware, let alone rationally able to change. In the modern age it was Freud who called attention to this hidden, wordless dimension of identity. Nowadays the idea of the unconscious is intrinsic to our view of *Eros*. Certainly since Descartes, most of us take for granted that "man" is divided within "himself." For Freud, we want what we cannot have—incest—and then repress our wish for it; for Foucault, we want it precisely because it is taboo; for Lacan, we have no words to say it; and for queer theorists, there is no such thing as knowledge anyway. None of these philosophical/psychological traditions forefront reason or view it as a powerful means of influencing gender identity or sexual orientation. None regard it as the exclusive pathway to Truth. They all maintain an affinity for the farside. They all share the view that there is something going on beneath the surface of consciousness.

Psychoanalytic/Queer Theory Compatibility: A

FLESH

Queer theory's Judith Butler's human is more like a hologram than a person. She seems to be arguing that a self is an object without a body. Her ideas are enormously important, but they are not elaborated psychoanalytic concepts and because of their political appeal they may be made to take on more weight than they can bear.[4] Her theory has been seen as epitomizing the queer project, one aim of which is to liberate people from "compulsory heterosexuality" and binary gender identity. But PoMo gender theory is hardly a settled doctrine. Rather, it is a lively and much-debated spectrum of hypotheses, with Butler residing at the radical end. In her worldview, genitals are completely disconnected from gender and sexual orientation.

Other queer theorists take the body more into account. If I am correct in my interpretation of the current drift in thinking, it is becoming more grounded, more, dare I say it, essentialist. Postmodern feminist critics like Elizabeth Grosz and Jane Gallop—following in the footsteps of Luce Irigaray, who, you may recall, is one of the French feminist revisionists of Lacan—are a bit more friendly to the idea of gender difference and gender subjectivity.[5,6] They are scarcely body fundamentalists, assigning a body part one, and only one, function and meaning, but they are not body atheists either: They allow that we have a physiology and that our flesh influences things. In the end, what renders these critics queer and distinguishes them from garden-variety critics is their conspicuously stronger belief in the symbolic malleability of body parts.

Unlike mainstream theorists, they do not assume that there is a strict limit in the number of erotic zones in the body or in the meanings we may impose on them. Nor do they believe in any foolproof way of predicting which erogenous zone, however unusual, will dominate a person's life. But unlike radical queers, they are not persuaded that the mind/body connection is entirely random and unfathomable. They are body minimizers.

Contrary to his billing, Freud is not entirely in disagreement. He is not consistently a body maximizer. Simply put, he oscillates. He is aware that brute flesh makes a mess of theory. Most of the time he does not assume a naturalness of the body; in his view, the biological body is rapidly overlaid with psychological and social significance. According to Freud, anatomy may be a given, but what is not given is what each individual makes of this anatomy. Anatomical difference shapes sexuality, not in itself, but through the meaning it takes on. In Freud's last paper devoted to femininity in *New Introductory Lectures*, he makes a clear case for women being made, not born.[7] He theorizes that girls develop into heterosexual women via a psychological process (not a biological one), after a homosexual phase, in the wake of disappointment.[8]

Yet Freud also asserts that "the ego is first and foremost a bodily ego."[9] By this he meant that we each have a sense of our self as a separate entity (a discrete unitary self with a boundary) that is derived from our own mental images of bodily sensations and/or from projections. His theory is larded with essentialist assumptions, especially in those portions dealing with female sexuality. In the same essay on femininity in which he hypothesized that female heterosexuality was made, not born, he also suggested that males are constitutionally active and females, passive.[10] Biology obviously has a central role in Freud's ideas about development. This is immediately apparent in Freud's description of the child's evolving sexuality, which is inextricably tied to its physicality and morphing appetites—oral, anal, and phallic—leading to castration anxiety or penis envy, culminating in the Oedipal drama and genitality. Presumably, a concrete body triggers the unfolding of these events.

In the end, there is an inherent, unresolvable tension between biology and psychology in Freudian theory.[11] Both conceptions of causality, however contradictory, coexist in psychoanalytic thinking, relating to each other like the side(s) of a Mobius strip. Later analysts (notably those writing in the '20s and '30s and then again in the '60s and '70s) opted for exclusively biological explanations of sexual orientation, gender behavior, and identity. (Lacan was an exception: he freed humans from the constraints of the body, though he entrapped them inescapably in phallic symbolism.) But Freud recognized the profound complexity of the mind/body issue. Sex is impossible to categorize because it lives on the threshold between the mental and the physical. Freud did not resolve the paradox of sex, but unlike some of his followers, he did not shirk from it. And he admitted up front that he could never figure out what women want.

Psychoanalytic/Queer Theory Compatibility: B-

LOVE OBJECTS

Queer theorists are famously democratic in their choice of "objects," the clunky psychoanalytic term used to refer to things (usually a person) that incite love and/or lust in a subject. Rather than limiting their object choice to a "whole" person of the opposite sex, they advocate erotic flexibility, fluidity of identity, diversity, and mobility—now a woman, now a man, now a mental image, now a butt, now a bit of underwear. In the tradition of early feminists, sexual deviants address Freud as their adversary, as he who pathologized their erotic choices. There is some truth to this idea, but the story is complicated.

Once again, Freud has been scapegoated for the nefarious consequences of the thinking of his followers. There is much that a card-carrying queer theorist might like in the "old" Freud. In his "Three Essays on the Theory of Sexuality," written in 1905 and revised repeatedly, Freud explosively claimed that sexuality was central to the life of infants, moreover, that the sexual drive and the object are merely loosely "soldered" together.[12] Girls are not born with a particular or exclusive proto-sexual appetite for boys and vice versa, a point that is perfectly obvious when we observe infants but was a radical insight at the time. As well as no pre-given object for the child, there is no pre-given "aim," that is, a specific erotic act it wishes to perform. Instead there is "polymorphous perversity," an openness regarding object choices and practices. Sexuality can move from object to object, and aim to aim, both passively and actively.[13] Noting the similarity of the blissful expression of a baby sated from nursing to that of an adult following orgasm, Freud suggested that the prototype for sexual pleasure is the breast, typically the mother's, the fantasy of which is later transferred to other objects, thereby suffusing them with eroticism. These sites become substitutes for the original. Hence, Freud's famous one-liner: "The finding of an object is actually a refinding of it."[14] Freud never entirely gave up the idea of the interchangeability of the things/persons to which we are sexually attracted. Near the end of his life, for example, he observed that sexual impulses are "extraordinarily plastic."[15]

But Freud contradicted himself. He also hypothesized that children gradually move from infantile sexual aimlessness to a purposeful adult sexuality, the aim of which is reproduction, ergo, heterosexuality. In doing so, he draws a troubling distinction among sexual orientations, prizing straight sex over gay sex. Nevertheless, he maintained that adult sexuality is always the result of the repression of the earlier polymorphous perversity of infancy and "is scarcely ever achieved with perfection."[16] Even when development appears to succeed, it is at the cost of happiness itself; there will always be an antagonism between our instincts and the demands of civilization. From this we may deduce that heterosexuality, like homosexuality, is a compromise formation. In other words, Freud believed that the achievement of heterosexuality was as problematic a phenomenon as the movement toward homosexuality. Both involve a drastic limitation on a person's choices of love objects.[17] Both involve inhibitions. Neither sexual orientation arrives in the infant full blown, like Athena from the head of Zeus. Both are the result of development—so both heterosexuality and homosexuality are in need of explanation.

What is most startling in Freud's early accounts of infantile sexuality, apart from his assertion of its existence, is that there is no gendered dimension to the numerous bodily sites and objects connected with the sexual drives. As feminist Lynne Segal pointed out in her incisive examination of sexuality in *Straight Sex*, Freud paid little heed to sexual difference for the first 30 years of his writing, and he only tried to provide a psychological model for it in the last years of his life. Ironically, the harder he tried to tackle the problem, the more the muddle and the greater the offense to anyone other than straight men who are comfortable in their own skin. The muddle and the offense were heightened by his heirs.[18]

Psychoanalytic/Queer Theory Compatibility: B-

BISEXUALITY

To the extent that "bisexuality" expands the sex/gender binary, you would think that queers might embrace the term. But many argue that it actually reaffirms a binary in the sense of implying a fuzzy middle region between two otherwise straightforwardly polarized sets of characteristics. Of course, there can be no label of which queers would approve, for they are inherently opposed to categorizing. But the term "bisexual" is problematic in everyday circles as well (see Chapter 2). Its indeterminacy seems to be a threat to many.

Bisexuality was also a fraught topic for Freud, who once again vacillated in his theorizing. He used the term to denote, alternately, biological facts and psychological facts, and even at the end of his life he had not satisfactorily decided whether it is one or the other. Early on, he presumed an innate bisexuality in humans, an idea he derived from the biological models of his time. But even as he suggested that we are originally bisexually constituted and that everyone is capable of a gay object choice—as he wrote in his 1910 essay on Leonardo—he also regarded the bisexual drive as something a child must outgrow.[19,20] An individual is supposed to repress "the attitude proper to the opposite sex," thereby forcing his or her body to conform to rigid gender guidelines based on his or her body's shape.[21] In Freud's calculus, conforming to gender rules offers us the best defense against neurosis. Given Freud's erstwhile insistence on the constitutional basis of bisexuality, you might have predicted otherwise. You might have expected him to make allowances for a spectrum of sexual practices and gender identities into adulthood. But as one writer pungently notes, the concept of bisexuality for Freud works better as a point of departure for the adventure of sexual development than as a destination.[22]

In his early writing, Freud thought that the sexual lives of little girls and little boys ran along similar pathways. Both boys and girls expressed active wishes toward their mothers and passive wishes for her care. In the child's first years there is only one type of sexuality, or libido, which Freud dubbed masculine, though he thought it to be the same for everyone. Sexual difference occurs later through the mediation of the Oedipus complex. Near the end of his life, Freud presumed that women remained more bisexual than men. Femininity, he felt, is not achieved without a struggle and is rarely complete. He attributed this to a female's initial "homosexual" attachment to her mother, which she must surrender in order to be "feminine." In Freud's model, the girl must give up her "active" desire for her mother (what Freud called her "masculine" aim) in favor of becoming a "passive" object of her father's affections (what Freud called her "feminine" aim).[23] A boy presumably has an easier developmental journey because he does not have to repudiate his active inclinations. These ideas were by no means rigorously or definitively worked out. Indeed, later theorists such as Nancy Chodorow and Fritz Morgenthaler argue precisely the opposite—that a boy has the more difficult journey because he has to "disidentify" with his mother.[24,25]

Recent developmental theorists such as Irene Fast imply that bisexuality involves "overinclusiveness," a kind of misguided arrogance, a failure to relinquish babyish notions of omnipotence and limitless possibility for sexuality.[26] In the course of development a person is supposed to commit to the so-called reality of gender limits and hence object choice. For Fast, girls are not propelled by a wish for a penis but a wish to identify with their mothers' childbearing capacity. So, from a queer perspective, she rescues people from phallocentrism only to supplant those constraints with another set of constraints based on the shape of their genitals, which determines the sex with whom they identify.

Though bisexuality is manifestly real, in that some people are sexually attracted to both men and women, it remains poorly understood across all explanatory and/or philosophical models. You could say that there is a convergence in the amount of misunderstanding of this topic, if not in the elements of that misunderstanding. However, the theories tend not to preclude each other.

Psychoanalytic/Queer Theory Compatibility: B+

SEXUAL ORIENTATIONS

Queer theorists advocate a postmodernist supermarket of erotic pleasures. Like the "early" Freud, they do not assume that the outcome of sexual development is a foregone conclusion, but that the sexual drive is, and remains, extraordinarily versatile in its aims and targets. But, as noted above, the "later" Freud contradicted his earlier theorizing by constructing a schema for libidinal development that culminates, when all goes well, in heterosexuality. The mechanism by which an opposite-sexed object choice is achieved is the Oedipus complex, the central phenomenon, according to Freudians, of early childhood.[27] (Initially Freud theorized that accompanying the "positive" Oedipus complex is a concurrent "negative" one in which the father is an object of desire as well as identification for the boy, but by the 1920s he downplayed this idea.) Resolving the positive Oedipus complex is an essential task for all human beings. It is the hallmark of gender identification and heterosexual love. True, this is an arduous, highly precarious, trauma-prone process (especially for girls), one that is continually undermined by the quirkiness of desire, but Freud insisted that the most appropriate resolution is a straight sexual orientation, which, he believed, is necessary for the survival of the species.

Here is where queers and Freudians radically part company. Queers emphatically deny that any sexual orientation is more appropriate than any other. They, along with generations of feminists, including feminist psychoanalysts, reject the universality and importance of the Oedipus complex with its renowned valorization of the penis. Why, they ask, should the male organ have such a decisive significance? They regard the assumption of the centrality and ubiquity of penis envy and/or castration anxiety as offensively male chauvinistic and arrogant. It is degrading of women, women's bodies, women's mothering, male-to-female transgenders, sissy boys, effeminate men, lipstick lesbians, and so forth. At best, Oedipal dynamics occur in the manner prescribed by classical Freudians in only some people.

Postmodernists do away altogether with the notion of a predictable sequence of sexual development, arguing that the moment we posit a predictable sequence of development we make choices about normality and deviance.[28] Implicit in developmental schema is the idea of a progression. It is generally assumed that if things unfold properly, later stages (typically deemed more "mature" than earlier ones) arise from the successful completion of former stages. But this "deeming" encodes a value judgement. Queers argue that the way we contrive a schema is contaminated by the limitations of language, cultural norms, and power politics, that is, by whom is doing the contriving.

To be sure, late in life Freud expressed reservations about the validity of his schema, pointing out that sexual stages may not be mutually exclusive; nor do stages necessarily unfold in a linear fashion.[29] These caveats notwithstanding, many of his followers, including his daughter Anna, devised additional developmental schema, so that today there are lines for object relations, ego development, sense of self, and gender identity. The inclination for establishing chronologies of development was probably nudged along by the newly popular science of "baby watching," which involved the direct observation of children, as opposed to relying on adult patients' reconstruction of their childhood from memories and dreams. From these proliferating studies, psychologists derived patterns of norms, which prompted an obsession with tracking and assessment that persists to this day. The specter of the "average" began to loom larger than ever. The middle of the twentieth century, when many of these timetables were being formulated, was a particularly low point for women and sexual deviants in the West, as I have noted before.

Despite Freud's late-onset conservative tilt, he was progressive for his time and at odds with contemporary prominent sexologists. The late nineteenth century was the age of self-appointed sex experts, who were then fastidiously cataloguing sexual practices and conjuring up theories for their causation. Unlike the German sexologist and jurist Karl Heinrich Ulrichs, the pioneering writer on homosexuality, Freud argued that homosexuality could not always be explained in terms of a male soul in a female body (which some neurobiologists still believe to be the case; see Chapter 3). Nor did homosexuals constitute a "third" or "intermediate" sex, as the German doctor Magnus Hirschfield believed (and which some anthropologists still believe; again, see Chapter 3). To Freud, homosexuality was a peculiarity of object choice, not an innately given perverse instinct.[30] It did not imply degeneracy, lunacy, or criminality. Nor was it a unitary phenomenon. Of course, even the "early" Freud could hardly be called "politically correct" from a twenty-first-century standpoint. While he did not regard homosexuality as a sickness, he did view it as a form of psychic blockage. His lifelong equivocation on this topic is reflected in his famous letter to an American mother of a gay young man, in which he managed to contradict himself within the same sentence. "Homosexuality is assuredly no advantage," he wrote, "but it is nothing to be ashamed of, it is not a vice, nor degradation, it is not an illness; we consider it to be a variation of the sexual function produced by a certain arrest of the sexual development."[31]

Had Freud stopped theorizing in 1905, he might now be considered more queer friendly. But Freud went on to elaborate at least four different theories of male homosexuality, all of which have been used to imply that gay men are damaged goods. In order to demonstrate how psychoanalytic thinking about sexual orientation and gender identity went astray, I shall trace the trajectory of Freud's metapsychology to that of his present-day followers in some detail. I extrapolate here from psychoanalyst Kenneth Lewes's masterful review of Freud's ideas about the etiology of male homosexuality:[32]

1. That the young boy's horrifying discovery of his beloved mother's castrated condition propels him into homosexuality. In the case study of "Little Hans" (1909) and in the essay on "Leonardo" (1910), each boy rejects his "mutilated" mother and seeks a substitute compromise figure in a fantasy "woman with a penis," personified in reality by an effeminate boy. In doing so, he magically avoids the whole issue of castration. He denies its very existence. (The fetishist is presumably driven by the same anxiety as the gay male but comes up with a different substitute—such as leather or fur—which unconsciously represents the mother's imagined penis. More about this later.)

2. A second theory, compatible with the first, is found in "Three Essays on the Theory of Sexuality" (1905). Here, male homosexuality is derived from the boy's refusal to relinquish his

first love object, the mother, and his subsequent unconscious identification with her and consequent search for lovers that resemble himself. In loving them he can reexperience the erotic bond that once united him with his mother. Both this explanation and the one preceding it involve "regression" because the boy "retreats back" into the anal stage, with its more primitive, self-centered, need-gratifying object relations rather than "true" object relations. According to Freud, this regression accounts for the importance of the anus in homosexual lovemaking.

3. Or, the mother's castration, as in the case study of the "Wolf Man" (1918), causes the shocked boy to relinquish his wish to actively penetrate his mother in favor of a wish to be penetrated by a father and thereby passively receive masculinity, everlasting love, and protection. (This is an example of one of the many instances in which Freud conflated stereotypic gender-related behavior, such as activity and passivity, with gender identity and the sex of the individual doing the behaving.) In this scenario, the negative Oedipus complex holds sway over the positive Oedipus complex. The boy unconsciously fantasizes using his anus like a vagina.

4. Finally, in his paper "Certain Neurotic Mechanisms in Jealousy, Paranoia, and Homosexuality" (1922), Freud suggested that male homosexuality might occur when an intense love for the mother is transformed into intense jealousy of siblings, and then into feelings of homosexual love through reaction formation. In effect, the boy is defending against his own aggression toward rivals.

All of these explanations of male homosexuality imply that something has gone awry in the boy's development. In Freud's scenarios, the boy is so horrified by the discovery of his mother's mutilation (and the possibility that he will suffer the same fate at the hands of a retaliating father) that he regresses to a "safer," more primitive stage of development. Henceforth he fears the vagina, so that, as an adult, he will be unable to have sex with anyone who does not have genitals like his own. In other words, he becomes overly narcissistic. Sexuality for him is not accompanied by true feelings of love and relatedness. Or, he renounces his love for his mother by identifying with her, much as mourners resolve their grief via introjection of the lost loved one. But in identifying with his mother, and failing to identify with his father (who represents law and order), he fails to internalize the norms and prohibitions of society. This results in a defective conscience and, as later analysts might argue, character disorder. Subsequent psychoanalysts of the so-called object relations school add that a boy's identification with his mother might also be a way of protecting her from his violent unconscious fantasies of revenge for her perceived inadequacies, or, to use object relations' jargon, oral aggression against a bad breast. Or the boy converts his love into hate, and vice versa, and thereafter contaminates his love with hate. While these speculations about the causes of male homosexuality are glaringly pejorative, they represent only one strand of Freud's theorizing. They must be understood in the context of his entire work on the subject. At times Freud thought that homosexuality was merely an alternative outcome of the Oedipus complex, as natural as a heterosexual outcome. But at times, as these explanations illustrate, he did not.

Some of Freud's descendants, in contrast, never accepted homosexuality as natural. Reflecting the bourgeois prejudices of mid-century America, they embraced his thinking selectively, developing those ideas that could be construed as implying that same-sex sex is maladaptive, while downplaying the rest. Since the late '20s, there had been a transition in psychoanalytic theory in the relative weight given to intrapsychic vs. interpersonal dynamics as determinants of behavior. The switch was effectively a shift "outward" from the internal mental processes of drive and defense inside the person to the arena of social interaction. Simply put: Reality mattered more. According to many psychoanalysts subsequent to Freud, psychopathology did not originate in the child but in what was done to the child and what the child did with what was done to it. This had the felicitous effect of upgrading the importance of early mothering in child development but the infelicitous effect of blaming the family (often the mother) for much of what went wrong. In the Eisenhower years, the pre-Oedipal reigned. For instance, in the early '60s psychoanalyst Irving Bieber published an immensely flawed but highly influential study of the origins of homosexuality (then considered pathological), which attributed male homosexuality to certain family constellations including "close-binding intimate mothers" and hostile, detached, and/or rejecting fathers.[33] The idea of a defective family, and especially of a "castrating mother," as causing male homosexuality infiltrated the public mindset. A corollary to this idea was the notion that homosexuality was "curable." No longer deemed constitutional, it was therefore considered reversible. Bieber claimed a success rate of 27 percent for converting gay men into straight ones.[34] Ironically, queer theorists agree with Bieber to the extent that he repudiated a biological component to sexual orientation, but they hardly view homosexuality as something in need of repair.

Another prominent trend in psychoanalytic thinking from around 1930 onwards, in line with the new emphasis on mothering, was the shift in interest away from Oedipal-level conflict toward those of the earlier, more primitive, oral stage.[35] The etiology of homosexuality began to be seen more and more as a failure to resolve the mother–child symbiosis of infancy and toddlerhood rather than a later conflict, which makes it akin to psychosis and borderline disorder— very serious, indeed! The most notorious proponent of this position was psychoanalyst Charles Socarides, who is still advocating this view as I write. Selectively interpreting Freud, he argued that a gay man can never be free of psychopathology because of his early fixation on his mother, whom he unconsciously both loves and hates (in that he perceives his mother as forcing a dreadful separation between them). So, he at once identifies with her to preserve the bond (and choose male sex objects, as she would) and feel dangerous aggressive impulses toward her.[36] This terrible ambivalence causes a split in his egos, which oscillates between idealizing his lovers and denigrating them after any perceived insult, the latter provoking a fear of retaliation. To lessen this anxiety, he becomes obsessed with sex, driven to have it. According to this logic, homosexuals cannot love unselfishly; their love is narcissistic, insensitive, entirely determined by their own needs and conflicts. Their egos remain forever primitive, pre-Oedipal. (Those gay men who do negotiate the Oedipus complex, according to Socarides, are actually "pseudo-homosexuals," not the real things.)

Despite the magnitude of true homosexuals' pathology, Socarides insists that they may respond to treatment. Like Bieber, he dismissed biological explanations of sexual orientation but, outdoing Bieber, Socarides claimed a 50 percent "cure" rate.[37] These findings were never independently validated or repeated. Both Bieber (who died in 1991) and Socarides campaigned vigorously against the deletion of homosexuality from the American Psychiatric Association's *Diagnostic Manual*. Despite their efforts, the diagnostic category was removed in 1973. Today many psychoanalysts regard Socarides as an embarrassing relic of a bygone era. But, as noted in Chapter 1, analysts' receptivity to out-of-the-closet homosexuals into their training institutes is a very recent phenomenon, perhaps a decade old, implying at best a longtime "benign neglect" of Socaride's views, if not an outright tolerance of them.

Let me supply some context. Until the '80s, even the less prosaic streams of psychoanalysis did little to undo the hostile tone towards sex/gender deviants. Lacan, as you may recall (see Chapter 4), did not have a theory of homosexuality, and in the well-known dictionary by Laplanche and Pontalis compiled in 1980, homosexuality is dealt with under the heading of "perversion."[38] In the wake of the second-wave women's movement, aided and abetted by the contributions of feminist psychoanalytic theorists like Nancy Chodorow and Jessica Benjamin, psychoanalysis started purging itself of its phallic-centeredness.[39,40] But, as Lewes insightfully points out, traditional psychoanalysts' sexist stance found refuge in their theories of homosexuality, which were dripping with antieffeminacy bias.[41] Because of gay men's real or perceived "feminine" traits, analysts persisted in viewing them as deficient males. This is a stealth form of homophobia. As I noted in Chapter 4, the proto-queer writings of the anti-Oedipalists (Gilles Deleuze, Felix Guattari, Guy Hocquenghem), the post-Lacanian feminists, and American constructionists provided an antidote to homophobia, but these had little effect on mainstream psychoanalysis.

By the late '80s many psychoanalysts recognized that the character formations of homosexuals were no different than those of anyone else. Psychoanalyst Richard Friedman, for example, saw the level of an individual's personality organization as independent from an individual's sexual orientation.[42] Yet at that point in his thinking he connected character pathology in homosexuals with a childhood history of marked gender nonconformity. In other words, "sicker" gay men were "sissies" as kids, an association that implies causality and ignores the confounding fact that effeminate boys are often the victims of virulent derision (if not outright persecution), which might account for their behavior. Interestingly, Friedman was a colleague of Richard Green, of "sissy boy syndrome" fame. As I discussed before (Chapter 3), these blithely offered connections make queer theorists' blood boil. Sedgwick, for example, using logic similar to that of Lewes, calls them "effeminophobic," arguing that they betray internalized hatred of "feminine"-acting males. While femininity was beginning to be respected in females, it was still mocked in males. She takes on Friedman in her essay "How to Bring Your Kids Up Gay: The War on Effeminate Boys," in which she argues that for all his gay-positivity, he is only prepared to like gay men who are masculine.[43]

Another problem with Friedman's theorizing in the '80s is that he implied that "once a homosexual, always a homosexual" (and the same thing goes for heterosexuals). In other words, he implied that he did not believe that there is unconscious heterosexuality beneath homosexuality or vice versa. This view has the virtue of sparing homosexuals from reparative therapy to release their inner heterosexuality, for, in Friedman's view, such "treatment" would be a futile endeavor; there is no inner heterosexuality to uncover. On the other hand, Friedman overlooked the fact that, for many folks, sexual orientation is complicated, multilayered, and slippery. He has subsequently modified some of his views.

Probably the four most important clinician/thinkers about male homosexuality remaining within the Freudian mould today are the aforementioned Kenneth Lewes, as well as Richard Isay, Ken Corbett and Jack Drescher.[44,45] They are attempting to open up Freud's developmental theory without jettisoning it entirely. Agreeing with Freud's early ideas about constitutional bisexuality, they, however, permit more variation in sexuality's unfolding. In effect, they add alternative maturational flowcharts to Freud's single Oedipally oriented one. The result is a blueprint for mental health that is less well ordered, more contingent. Their little boy might desire his father, not because he is retreating from Oedipal conflict, but just because he inherently desires his father—and that's okay. A "girly boy" might be considered just another acceptable form of masculine behavior, not a product of a mother who can't let go. In other words, there are multiple lines of development. This kind of thinking is very plausible, very democratic. But, of course, if we were to keep adding developmental lines for every individual sex/gender possibility we would undermine the explanatory and predictive power of developmental lines. Everyone would have his or her own personal timetable. Developmental lines would cease to have meaning. They would not tell us more than we already know.

There is a glaring omission in all this theorizing about homosexuality—lesbianism (by which I, of course, do not mean a phylum of illness, but a slippery point on the sexual orientation continuum). In 1998 a research team calculated that the entire psychoanalytic literature on female homosexuality reported on fewer than a hundred individuals.[46] This lack of psychoanalytic consideration probably mirrors the marginalization of lesbians at large, where gay women suffer the double ignominy of being both female and homosexual. Lesbianism is paradoxically everywhere and nowhere, for it often remains unnoticed when it is in plain sight. It is conspicuous by its absence even in the early work of second-wave feminist psychoanalysts like Juliet Mitchell, Nancy Chodorow, and Jessica Benjamin.[47–49]

Until recently, it was presumed in the psychoanalytic literature that any woman who loved another woman must wish to be a man. Women automatically suffer from penis envy; but men—even gay men—do not automatically have vagina envy. The sexism in that assumption is blatant. Also implicit is a belief in the sex/gender binary—that a person cannot both want *to be* a woman and want *to have* a woman. Genital shape is continually conflated with sexual orientation; vaginas exclusively seek penises and vice versa. Put differently, choosing a woman as a lover necessarily means repudiating men. (Using this logic, choosing chocolate ice cream over vanilla would imply a repudiation of vanilla, not merely a preference for chocolate over vanilla at that moment. But, of course, you can like both, in differing amounts, at differing times. Choosing an ice cream flavor is not a zero-sum game. Nor is sexual orientation.)

The idea that lesbians have a "masculinity complex" has held sway since Freud. Yet for all Freud's influence, he wrote specifically about lesbian desire in only two places: in the footnotes of the famous "Dora" case, "Fragment of Analysis of a Case of Hysteria" (1905), and in "The Psychogenesis of a Case of Homosexuality in a Woman" (1920) (discussed in Chapter 4).[50,51] Many critics note Freud's barely disguised distaste for both of these young women. While Dora has become something of a heroine to feminists for her resistance to Freud's Oedipal interpretation of her predicament, the patient in the latter case seems most well known for her lack of a pseudonym, which some lesbian writers regard as mildly insulting and dismissive. The Dora case has spawned a veritable cottage industry in commentary (including that of Lacan), much of it about Dora's alleged homosexuality, which Freud had speculated about almost as an afterthought. He regarded Dora primarily (and pejoratively) as a hysteric, which, in retrospect, was rather unsympathetic of Freud given the paucity of women's cultural options for behavior at the time. But, at least his formulation prompted future interest in Dora. On the other hand, the "Psychogenesis" piece, in which Freud grappled explicitly with female homosexuality, has been called his most overlooked case study.[52] Perhaps its explicitness about lesbianism worked against its popularity.

Like male homosexuality, female homosexuality, according to Freud, arises from a glitch in development. (Here Freud engaged in yet another inconsistency. As in the teen expression "they're the same, but different," at times he collapsed female and male homosexuality into one category to distinguish them from the category heterosexuality; at other times, he contrasted female and male homosexuality.) He explained the attraction of both of his young female patients to older women as a bitter unconscious revenge fantasy, a result of disappointed love for their fathers, whom they thereafter proceed to repudiate, along with all men. Put differently, these women retaliated against their fathers (and men) by attempting to beat them at their own game: They repressed their wounded femininity in favor of an aggressive identification with their masculinity.[53] Lesbianism was seen as a defense against straight sex.

Note that Freud perceived these young women's desire in male terms—as a failure to properly retreat from their primary active (code: masculine) desire for, first mother and, later, those with female genitals. He portrays their homosexuality as being more powerfully motivated by their inclination to renounce men than by their attraction to women. Freud did not conceive of a primary active female libido. This lopsided thinking was disputed late in his life by some of his colleagues—Karen Horney, Melanie Klein, and Ernest Jones—who argued that femininity was constitutional, not acquired.[54] A girl's anatomy, they argued, is known to her in a positive way rather than just experienced as a lack. These ideas represented a return to biological explanations of femininity and masculinity. But even though the early revisionists allotted women feelings of femaleness from birth, the lesbian was still seen as one who regressed in a way that made her masculine—mostly as someone who was fleeing from the Oedipal complex via male identification and/or, in later theory, as someone with an exaggerated mother fixation. As I noted before, the psychoanalysts of the late '20s recognized the importance of the pre-Oedipal mother, and much pathology was attributed to interaction (or lack of interaction) with her. Though these early revisionists of Freud supply the girl with a primary femininity, they still assume that, if all goes well, her inborn femininity will blossom eventually into erotic desire for a man. They still conflated anatomy, gender identity, and sexual orientation. In their view, lesbianism remained a negative outcome: it was either heterosexual imitation or pre-Oedipal immaturity.[55] Pick your etiological poison.

This dispute between Freud's revisionists and Freud came to be known as the Freud–Jones debate, and it has persisted in one form or another into the present.[56] It metamorphosed, broadly speaking, into the recent overlapping "difference/sameness" feminist controversy; the "essentialist/constructivist" controversy; the "unified self/multiple 'subjectivities'" controversy; and the "agency/no agency" controversy. To be sure, these disputes are not mutually exclusive, and, indeed, they segue into each other. But here's a crib sheet: the "difference," "essentialist," "unified self," and "agency" camps tend to cluster together. So do the "sameness," "constructivist," "multiple 'subjectivities'," and "no agency" camps. In other words, folks, like Jones, who tend to believe that men and women are fundamentally different, tend to think that they are born that way, that their selves are fixed and have discrete boundaries, and that they have some control over their fate. The other camp—the queers—like early Freud, tend to think that men and women are fundamentally the same. Later on, they also came to believe that sex/gender categories are constructed by subliminal, ever-changing linguistic rules, that identity is fluid, and that individuals are ultimately victims of outside forces that they cannot control by reason alone.

The heiress, broadly speaking, of "difference" feminism (the Jones side of the debate), who insists, however, that she is not an essentialist, is the French post-Lacanian analyst Luce Irigaray (see Chapter 4). In *This Sex Which Is Not One* (1985) she effuses about the fluidity of women's sexuality, the multiplicity of their erogenous zones, implying that "a woman needs a man like a fish needs a bicycle," though she conveys this sentiment in far more poetic terms.[57] (The fish quote, by the way, has been commonly misattributed to Gloria Steinem but actually was coined by Australian feminist Irina Dunn in 1970.) Why should males' single visible sex organ trump women's numerous, more hidden zones in the collective imagination? Why should the paternal trump the maternal as provocateur of development? Why should the male, more visual means of "turning on" be the dominant erotic model rather than women's so-called preference for tactile stimulation? (I am reminded here of the Greek mythological dispute between Zeus and Hera about whether the pleasures of love are better enjoyed by men or women. When the transsexual Tiresias answered "women," Hera blinded him/her, but Zeus gave Tiresias the power of a seer.)

Irigaray was obviously contesting Freud and Lacan's phallocentrism, but she was also surfacing the idea that women may desire women without anyone "having" or "being" a penis or a symbol thereof. Lesbians might now have an innate or psychically constructed (based on their bodies) respectable desire of their own. With the current popularity of the comedic play by Eve Ensler, *The Vagina Monologues*, which sends up peoples' squeamishness about the female sexual organ, I suspect these genital pleasure wars may be running their course.

In France, the clinical and philosophical realms leak into each other. So it is not surprising that Irigaray's theorizing foreshadowed American queer theory, which derives in part from French philosophy while it has had little effect on the American clinic. As we have seen (in Chapter 4), theorist de Lauretis, in the manner of Irigaray, extols primary lesbian pleasure, though she deplores the tendency of recent psychoanalysts to explain lesbian desire in terms of the desexualized mother–baby bond. In that model, she complains, "hot" ruthless sexual pleasure seems to fade out of the picture in favor of milky, immature fusion. Queer theorist Butler, citing Irigaray, also opposes the male-centeredness of psychoanalysis and its failure to represent all sexualities. If you were to plot the trajectory of these folks' thinking, the two sides of the Freud/ Jones end up intersecting on this point (recall that Butler is a conceptual descendant of the "early" Freud, and Irigaray of Jones). But Butler vehemently disagrees with the idea that there is a particularly female sexuality. As a radical queer, she is opposed to all categorization. She would prefer to think of lesbianism as a "performance" of sexuality, a strategy, rather than a specific "other" sexuality. In that sense, male sexuality and female sexuality are more alike than different. Of course this is all very academic, rather like taking sides on the question of whether a glass is half empty or half full. Whatever their theoretical genealogy, these lesbian queer theorists put lesbian theory on the critical map. Still missing was the voice of the American working clinician.

Those few clinicians of psychoanalytic persuasion who grappled with lesbianism after Freud, like those who analyzed male homosexuality, drew on his later, less politically correct theorizing. Rewind to the late '20s. By then, the subtlety of Freud's positions was lost. Homosexuality was deemed sick.[58] Gone was Freud's elastic position on bisexuality. Mother asserted herself in the mindset of psychoanalysts. According to Jeanne Lampl-de Groot, for example, a lesbian is suffering from an extreme form of the masculinity complex involving either a denial of sexual anatomical difference and/or regression to her first love relation, that is, her mother.[59] She toxified Freud's early benign idea of a negative Oedipus complex by explicitly shifting it, should it persist into adulthood, out of the realm of normality into the category of pathology. Women could not love women without being male "wannabes." Even Freud's loyal disciple Helen Deutsch went from penning sensitive psychoanalytic descriptions of lesbian eroticism to writing censorious accounts.[60]

For a few decades starting from the mid-'30s, interest in female sexuality generally took a backseat, perhaps as a response to the horrors of the world wars and a wish for peaceful-seeming soothing "normality." The second wave of the women's movement revived interest, but when theory about female desire reemerged, it was largely unreconstructed. Psychoanalysts (even female analysts) still took for granted that women suffered from penis envy. True, they tended to presume that femininity did not result from the Oedipus complex; they nevertheless presumed that there is a universal Oedipus complex that must be resolved. They remained unrepentant straight-only male chauvinists, oblivious to actual life outside their narrow circles. France's Janine Chasseguet-Smirgel, for example, argued that females are aware of their femininity from the beginning (the Jones side of the debate), yet they still wished for a penis (albeit defensively) to protect them from a devouring mother.[61] A boy is lucky to have a penis but fears losing it; a girl may obtain one only through intercourse. I am oversimplifying, of course, but in general femininity remained "un-queerly" grounded in biology. Heterosexuality was still compulsory.

The Socarides of the lesbian community, in the sense of being vilified, is French psychoanalyst Joyce McDougall (though, importantly, she, unlike Socarides, revised her views). Regarding McDougall's negative press—for example, one therapist, herself lesbian, wrote about the pain she felt listening to McDougall in psychoanalytic meetings "declaring on the basis of her experience with six lesbian patients...that all lesbians—in contrast to heterosexual women—deny death, sexual difference, and separation from mother; that lesbianism is a last-ditch defense against psychosis."[62] Female homosexuality, in McDougall's view, is a desperate effort at avoiding psychic disintegration involving projected paranoid rage, fantasies of murder and being murdered, and depersonalization. Lesbians, for McDougall, also suffer from impaired gender identity.[63] In writing this I am aware that I am not doing justice to the nuance of her thinking, but I cannot help but wonder that, had McDougall treated six straight women who functioned at a borderline level, whether she would have attributed their straight sexual orientation to desperation. Her most recent book, *The Many Faces of Eros: A Psychoanalytic Exploration*, published in 1995, is less pathologizing.[64]

Just as a critical mass of feminists in psychoanalytic institutes instigated new ways of theorizing about women, so may a critical mass of uncloseted lesbians and other deviants stimulate new ways of thinking about lesbians and deviants. As they become more conspicuous as therapists and patients, so will their mental health, which is undoubtedly indistinguishable from that of nonlesbians and nondeviants. There is already a small but discernible lesbian voice in psychoanalytic literature.[65] Their thinking has influenced a number of prominent feminist analysts of undesignated sexual orientation. Benjamin, for example, now suggests that a person does not necessarily have a unitary sex/gender identity but must balance a multiplicity of identifications and desires. Chodorow, resurrecting an early Freudian idea, recently averred that straight sex may be no less a product of conflict and trauma as gay sex.[66] Hopefully, the mainstream will follow suit.

Meanwhile, only a handful of generic psychoanalysts—mostly of the "relational" school (to be discussed later)—are grappling with queer sexuality. It is interesting to observe that the idea of "polymorphous diversity," a term coined by queer critic Judith Roof, seems to be somewhat more readily embraced in the lesbian community than in the gay male one.[67] For example, Kenneth Lewes (the most thorough and thoughtful chronicler of psychoanalytic ideas about male homosexuality) is more resistant to queer thinking than Noreen O'Connor and Joanna Ryan (the most thorough and thoughtful chroniclers of psychoanalytic ideas about lesbians).[68,69] Perhaps this has to do with lesbians' historical—albeit ambivalent—ties to feminism. It makes sense that left-leaning women, having long critiqued gender roles to which they were assigned, may be more open than men to critique gender itself.

Psychoanalytic/Queer Theory Compatibility: D

KINKS

There are a few buzzwords in the queer/psychoanalytic communities that trigger instant anxiety and controversy, reflecting, no doubt, the anxiety and controversy swirling around these topics in the world at large. These fraught terms mostly concern kinky sex—"perversion," "fetish," "S/M," "transvestite," and "transgender." Let me disentangle some of the thinking about them and the related concept of "core gender identity."

In books prior to the '70s, quipped reluctant sex guru Alex Comfort, perversion "meant quite simply, any sexual behavior that the writer himself did not enjoy."[70] His *Joy of Sex*, published in 1972, at the height of the sexual revolution, became the best-selling sex manual of all time. It was a period of transition. In those free-wheeling years, behaviors formerly known as perversions—pornography, oral sex, symbolic aggressive play, cross-dressing, etc.—abandoned the margins and began conquering the mainstream. They were assigned a new, ostensibly more neutral label—the "paraphilias."

Thirty years later this open-mindedness about sexuality has become more complicated as various sex rebels, wielding scholarly and/or political justifications, test the limits. No one seems quite sure what a perversion is anymore, not even a self-proclaimed pervert. Yesterday's sleazeball Larry Flynt now claims to be a defender of cherished constitutional values. Many therapists, myself included, deem all sexuality acceptable if it occurs among consenting adults and does not result in physical, psychological, or social harm. But this view raises thorny clinical problems. What constitutes "consent"? What constitutes "harm"? And what constitutes an "adult"? I saw a patient once whose girlfriend frequently masturbated with their dog, about which she (my patient) was repelled. But, I wondered, what about the dog? True, their pet was an "adult" dog, but did it consent? Was it "harmed"? Does the girlfriend's distasteful, albeit trivial (to my mind), proclivity qualify as a paraphilia? What if her interest was not bestiality, but autoerotic strangulation or necrophilia? What's an aspiring-to-be-broad-minded therapist supposed to think?

Pondering these dilemmas, I read with interest queer-positive psychoanalyst Muriel Dimen's recent reaction to gay activist/journalist Michael

Bronski's detailed account of his erotic behavior.[71,72] His sexual practices involved allegedly tenderhearted cutting and blood sports with consenting adult male partners, performed in the context of loving relationships (and sometimes drugs). Bronski describes his use of razors, scalpels, and Exacto blades during lovemaking as the most potent stimulation he has ever encountered. Dimen valiantly attempts to avoid pathologizing Bronski's behavior but ultimately sees his inclination to mutilate and be mutilated as representing, unsurprisingly, a mutilation—a disturbance of the self and relatedness. "What wounds of yours were healed by those scalpels?" Dimen asks Bronski.[73] Though Bronski disputes her speculations, it is notable that she does not damn him to the ranks of the seriously character disordered or the psychotic, as a previous generation of psychoanalysts would undoubtedly have done. She seems, instead, to assign him to the ranks of the ordinary defensive neurotic (without using that word)—not much of an insult. He is, she conjectures, someone who has been injured, someone who dissociates during sex. She even goes on to leaven the mild sting of that description by adding that ordinary sexuality also involves dissociation. But her analysis begs the question of whether these inclinations and practices may occur among folks who had happier childhoods. The veritable *samizdat* of alternative sex sites online these days suggests that practices such as cutting, scarification, intense stimulation via pain, etc. may not be limited to the emotionally wounded. We simply do not know.

The textbook definition of a perversion is based on statistical norms—it refers to an irresistible, habitual sexual aberration that manifests itself through sexual arousal by unusual or bizarre objects (such as feet, leather, or by Freud's patient's certain "shine on the nose") or by unusual and bizarre practices (such as masochism or exhibitionism). To qualify as an official perversion—a "paraphilia" as the latest label has it—it must get in the way of an affectionate relationship with another consenting human being. Until the '70s, of course, homosexuality was considered a perversion but, interestingly, Freud did not systematically classify it that way. He frequently (but not exclusively) described homosexuality as an "inversion" rather than a "perversion," in that it involved a variation in the sexual object, not a variation in the sexual aim. But later theorists did not maintain a distinction between the two, and the term "inversion" has become obsolete. Most insisted on classifying homosexuals as perverts.

Today's standard definition of perversion—aka paraphilia—and other labels based on cultural norms, mainline queer outrage. They are precisely the concepts against which Foucault railed, the stuff that postmodernism refutes. Queers are cultural relativists. As we have seen, they are in the business of protesting norms, not clarifying or explaining them. The official definition also poses problems to "sameness" feminists. It turns out that when the definition is narrowly interpreted, almost all perverts, including fetishists—folks who prefer nonliving objects or body parts above whole human beings for sexual stimulation—are biologically male. There is one exception, sadomasochists, but even among members of that cohort, the ratio is strikingly skewed toward men—approximately twenty males to one female.[74] Sadists are far rarer than masochists. Within the S/M community, it is often said that "a good top is hard to find," and female sadists are so highly prized that masochists will travel hundreds of miles to meet them.[75] This conspicuous imbalance in the incidence of perversion would hardly seem to be an issue for feminist quibbling, especially as it could be used in some circles as evidence of the moral superiority of females, were it not for the fact that it panders to the essentialist point of view.

No sooner are these data cited than an array of "sameness" feminist responses is marshaled to refute them. Psychoanalyst author Louise Kaplan has summarized some of the stock rebuttals. A number of objectors, she says, dispute the accuracy of the data by citing the obtuseness of doctors and the world at large for not recognizing female perversions that are right there before their very eyes. Perversity is inherent in the way women are programmed to behave, in their exhibitionism (obsessions with fashion and weight), in their masochism (subjectivity to men's abuse, eating disorders, self-mutilation), and so forth. As I mentioned in the previous chapter, this attempt at appropriating perversions for women has been jokingly referred to by feminists as "perversion theft" and "fetish envy," by which they mean that it might (oh, my god!) represent another form of penis envy. In other words, it may be another instance of women supposedly envying what men have, which, of course, is precisely what feminists wish to refute. (Yes, some feminists are able to laugh at themselves, especially when they have an opportunity for irony and clever wordplay.) Other objectors suggest that women act out their aberrant sexual desires on their children. Still others argue that women would be as perverse as men if they were granted greater sexual freedom.[76]

Kaplan herself sidesteps the issue. While the incidence of perversion, technically speaking, varies between males and females, the "perverse strategy," she argues, operates in the same overall way for males and females.[77] According to her, a perverse strategy is one that uses the performance of gender caricatures to deceive the onlooker. In men, it involves a compulsive demonstration of sexual excitement and performance, hypermasculinity. In women, it involves an impersonation of a feminine gender ideal—cleanliness, innocence, spirituality, and submission—not manifest sexual arousal and discharge. Men perform virility; women perform purity. Kaplan "blames" gender stereotyping, not biology, for the difference in the way perversion is carried out by men and by women. But by eliminating the pursuit of actual sexual sensation as a required criterion for perversion, she may be confusing them with ordinary compulsions. Also, she does not fully explain *why* these differences in desire developed in the first place. Any way you slice the data, anatomical females do not rape, pore over pornography, or cross-dress to the same extent as anatomical males. Gender role conditioning certainly seems to be a necessary component of an explanation for the development of so-called paraphilias, but is it sufficient? Would women engage in these practices as frequently as men in the absence of gender stereotyping? Again, we do not know.

To be sure, most people are not interested in the causes of paraphilia. Many people claim that they do not think about perversion at all. Nor do they claim to care. There is, of course, a small group openly interested in its practice, a large group *secretly* interested in its practice, a vocal group interested in its elimination and punishment, and a tiny cohort of queer theorists interested in its politics. But, even among these groups, causation is not a burning issue. The official psychiatric definition says nothing about how or why perverse desire develops. It is descriptive, not explanatory. There is hardly a constituency lobbying for research into its etiology. But therapists in the trenches of clinical work do not have the conceptual luxury of dismissing causation. Etiology is too closely related to mechanisms for treatment to be ignored. Besides, psychoanalytic therapists are, in a sense, professional snoops.

Ever the conquistador, Freud tackled the subject in his famous 1905 essay, "Three Essays on the Theory of Sexuality." There, he cleverly noted that perversions in adults—such as spanking, coprophilia, walking on all fours—resemble the polymorphous perversity of childhood, that blissful Arcadian period in human life when sexuality might be enacted via many means and erotic value could be freely and flamboyantly attached to any object. So, he conjectured, perversion might be the direct expression of infantile sexuality. It is sexuality that has failed to succumb to repression. It is raw sex. It is within us all. Queer critics such as Dollimore and de Lauretis seized on this idea to support their contention that perversion is central to human functioning (see Chapter 4). Freud goes on to suggest that neurosis, in contrast to perversion, is the "disguised" expression of infantile sexuality, that is, sexuality that has been repressed and defended against. Alluding to a certain oppositeness in their construction is the Freudian dictum: Neuroses are the negative of perversions. Both the neurotic and the pervert are propelled by the same infantile sexual aim. The difference is that in the neurotic the aim is unconscious, whereas in the pervert it is conscious.

Thus far in Freud's theorizing, he did not engage in sex/gender type-casting. But in his 1927 essay, "Fetishism," Freud girded the topic with a phallic-infused underlay.[78] Baldly stated, the fetish, for him, is a sub-stitute for the penis: the mother's missing penis that the little boy believed in and does not want to give up, even though he sees it's not there. For to acknowledge the reality of his mother's castration would make it possible for him to suffer the same fate. Presumably, in the unconscious—if you don't know about something, it doesn't happen. The creation of a fetish allows him, in a single gesture, to both affirm and deny his mother's penis-less condition. The fetishist disavows what he observes—the lack of a penis—and, at the same time, he positions a substitute in its place (so he must know on some level about castration, lest he wouldn't supply a replacement). He simultaneously represses and recognizes castration; he knows and doesn't know—his ego is thereafter split. Put differently, perversion involves a precarious denial of sexual difference, a denial that is prone to disintegration The sub-stitute (the fetish) commemorates his last perception prior to the moment of truth, that is, prior to his discovery of his mother's "mutila-tion." It is usually something like lingerie, shoes, fur—the last thing the boy sees before the horror of the *absence*. Freud, Lacan, and Foucault all viewed fetishism as the foundational perversion.

The disavowal of mother's castration became the hallmark of the Freudian understanding of fetishism. From this, Chasseguet-Smirgel concluded that all perverts are liars.[79] She, along with McDougall, sug-gested that perverts are attempting to deceive themselves and others; that they fool themselves into believing that their sexuality is superior to straight, vanilla, genital sex.[80] In fantasy, they reinvent the primal scene. They do this because an awareness of the difference between the two sexes as *the* condition of desire—that which the scene repre-sents—is too painful to bear. In the Freudian view, the reality of hetero-sexual coupling suggests the possibility of castration for, by definition, one member of the pair is missing a penis. The fetishist must never know that mother is penis-less.

Interestingly, the "lit-crit" crowd has conspicuously zeroed in on Freud's use of the mechanism of "disavowal," while at the same time disputing the importance of what Freud said was disavowed—sexual difference. Freud had linked disavowal to only one form of perversion—fetishism. Lacan, on the other hand, made it the fundamental opera-tion in all forms of perversion. And feminist critics, influenced by

French theory, realizing that there is nothing inherently masculine about the play of disavowal, have enthusiastically purloined the mechanism as a useful explanatory tool. They use the term metaphorically. (Recall that many are, after all, literature professors.) They argue, for example, that it is not only mother's castration that may be disavowed, it may be the culturally imposed feminine role. These feminists portray the female hysteric, not as a needy, pathetic, annoying loser as has been the wont of many traditional analysts, but as a feminist heroine—as one who resists patriarchy with her symptoms. The hysterical woman, via disavowal, simultaneously accepts and refuses the organization of her sexuality required by male-dominated capitalism. Her conversion symptom, let's say tremors, articulates, albeit nonverbally, that which society requires her to repress—active sexual desire. It doesn't take too much imagination to connect tremors with ecstatic release. So the hysteric affirms her active sexuality in the same gesture (tremors) with which she denies it. Hysteria, explained by disavowal, may be seen as a strategy of protest, a creative alternative to the suffocating options available for women prior to feminism.

Disavowal has also been used by cultural critics to explain the curious ubiquity of the "money shot" in hardcore straight and male gay porn flicks. The "money shot," or "cum shot," refers to the close-up filming of a penis ejaculating. This particular visual flourish has been de rigueur in skin flicks since the '70s. While the camera lingers on the male's orgasm, it overlooks the female's. As critic Linda Williams (in this instance an unrepentant Freudian) notes, this shot attempts to disavow difference—that the female orgasm is any different from the male's—offering up the spectacle of male ejaculation as a substitute for what is not there: the invisible female orgasm.[81] Contra Williams, I think it is more about the queerness of sex than a denial of difference. After all, the money shot often involves a straight male spectator jerking off as he is observing the pleasure of another man. Surely this dynamic contains homoerotic elements. If this is so, it represents yet another contradiction in an exclusively binary view of sex/gender.

Back to fetishism. According to Freudian logic, fetishism saves the boy from becoming a homosexual by endowing women with a characteristic that makes them tolerable as sexual objects. Put differently, the fetishist is a failed homosexual. The practice of fetishism is, for Freud, a uniquely masculine phenomenon. Followers of Freud, like Chasseguet-Smirgel, shackle the fetishist to the anal period of development, a time when the male does not know about the scary business of sex/gender difference. She thereby banishes him from maturity.[82] Girls presumably have no need to disavow their mother's castration because they have no castration anxiety, in that they do not have a penis to lose. Obviously you could not expect a penis substitute to reassure a female of her possession of a penis. Girls, for old-fashioned Freudians, resolve their Oedipus complex by having daddy's babies inside themselves. Alluding to this idea, psychoanalyst Estela Welldon trenchantly remarked that "women can't have perversions because they can have babies."[83] Still, Freud's hypothetical scenario, if accurate, could "explain" the lopsided data about incidence of perversion between anatomical males and females, though it takes for granted the universal presence of penis envy. Not a happy thought for feminists and queers.

For Lacan, in true Gallic phallic tradition, the girl becomes the phallus (see Chapter 4). In other words, she becomes a signifier of desire. This, presumably, explains her role as object of the male gaze (recall Mulvey's early theorizing) and her propensity for engaging in "masquerade," that is, in posing as helpless and adorable, which Riviere sees as the key to femininity (again, see Chapter 4).

Attempting to tilt these concepts in a feminist direction, critical theorists of the '80s and '90s "played" with the phallus. Or, more accurately, they "played" with who is allowed to assign phallic (that is, erotic) status to things, and to what things they may assign them. Now this is a phallus; now that is a phallus. Now it is here. Now it is there. In doing so, they expanded the repertoire of both the subjects and objects of desire. You can see the beginning of PoMo stirrings here. Their re-conceptualizing project required some contorting of traditional theory but served to "legitimize" fetishism for women. For example, the aforementioned critic Elizabeth Grosz, pointing out the reverse dynamics of fetishism (which is supposedly predominantly male) and hysteria (which is supposedly predominantly female) suggested that, in fetishism, the male turns a part of *another's* body or a thing (*not* himself) into a phallus; whereas in hysteria, the female makes *herself* (or a part of *herself*) into a phallus. In this scenario, a lesbian may be seen as a successful female fetishist because she turns someone other than herself into a phallus.[84] (This is in contrast to the male homosexual, who is a failed fetishist.) In plainer English, what Grosz does, following in the footsteps of Irigaray, is to portray the lesbian as the master of her own desire, not the mistress of another's. But note that her argument still privileges the phallus as the signifier of desire.

Feminist convolutions of Freudian/Lacanian theory abound. Recall de Lauretis (Chapter 4): For her, a girl's "loss" of a penis merely reworks an earlier, more profound castration, the loss of her own lovable woman's body, that is, a body that is lovable to her mother, from whom she must separate. De Lauretis's "fetish," which might be a tattoo or piercing, signals an active sexual attraction (by the wearer of the fetish) to another's female body. Ultimately her theory gestures toward a different explanation of the causal mechanisms of perversity, but it does not quite jettison the phallus as the über constructor of desire and language.

Neither does Sara Kofman's. In her rereading of Freud, she argues that the most salient point about fetishism is *not* castration anxiety (though castration anxiety and penis envy exist) but rather *uncertainty* over whether the mother is castrated or not. Kofman is among those post-Lacanian critics who forefront the mechanism of disavowal. Freud's deliberate use of the term "disavowal" (rather than "denial" or "repression") renders the boy uncertain of mother's castration, for it suggests an incomplete, tentative denial of difference. Disavowal involves the unconscious defense mechanism of "*doing*" and "*undoing*." Though girls do not have castration anxiety for obvious reasons, they, like boys, may be *uncertain* about their mother's anatomy; that is, they may disavow; they may mentally *do* and *undo* their ideas about their mother's castration; hence, they too may fetishize.[85] Like Kaplan, Kofman looks at the underlying dynamics of perversion, the metaphoric potential of the behavior rather than the gymnastics of the act. In other words, she too looks at perverse strategy, which in Kofman's view involves a generalized oscillation between the two contradictory beliefs that mother is, or is not, castrated, rather than perversion per se. Like Kaplan, she de-sexualizes fetishism, detaching it from the realm of lust. Perverse behavior for her, as with Kaplan, does not necessarily include arousal or orgasm. Other critics, using logic akin to Kofman's, troll through literature, ferreting out instances of female "fetishism"—Naomi Schor in George Sand's novel *Valentine*, Emily Apter in nineteenth-century French literature, and Marjorie Garber in Shakespeare.[86–88]

But, by and large, these theorists see female fetishism in terms of the elusive, illusive phallus. True, they put the topic of female perversion on people's radar screens, but they do not completely reckon with some awkward axioms of psychoanalytic theory: the concept of penis envy, castration anxiety, the monopoly of the phallus as the signifier of desire. Much of their theorizing ties perversions to "having" or "being" a phallus, or dealing with their mothers' lack of one. They are using the phallic jargon even as they are trying to minimize the importance of the phallus. To a certain extent, their writing depends upon the idea of sexuality with which they argue. In the '80s, the closest feminists came to a woman-centered alternative to the phallus as a signifier— and I credit Lorraine Gamman and Merja Makinen for pointing this out—may be contained in the work of critic Parveen Adams.[89,90] She allows lesbian sadomasochists—but only lesbian sadomasochists—a sexuality that is detached from any penile references. In doing so, she divorces sexuality from gender—a move in the direction of queer theory. Unfortunately, straight women or ordinary lesbians cannot inhabit this territory of active, mobile, playful female libido. Their sexuality is still organized around the paternal phallus. But the lesbian sadomasochist enjoys the same erotic prerogatives as the ordinary (i.e., male) pervert, and then some. She is not constrained, as he is, by castration anxiety. Her "fetish" is not used to disavow the mother's missing penis. She accepts that the mother doesn't have a penis, so her desire is "cut off" from the phallus and may alight anywhere. Unlike the male pervert who is locked into a rigid, monotonous, ritualistic performance of perversion, she is free to construct many fetishes, many fantasies, which she may try on "like costumes."[91] Her fetishes are like postmodernist Baudrillard's simulacra (see Chapter 1). Adams does not, however, tell us how female sadomasochism develops in an individual.

Adams was not writing in a political vacuum. Her essay has been used to support the position that S/M is just one among many possible women's sexual practices. This is in opposition to the much-publicized "moral feminist" view that sadomasochism, even when enacted exclusively by and among females, is irrevocably linked to a power imbalance, violence, and the exploitation of women. To them, S/M inherently parodies oppressive heterosexual norms and is therefore always a toxic metaphor for straight male domination. The pro-S/M women's faction, which is also anticensorship of pornography, regards S/M as liberatory, as productive of erotic fantasy; the latter group regards it as an example of all that is wrong with society, a dynamic that must be eradicated. The female pro-S/Ms think of their opponents as prudes; the anti-S/Ms think of their female detractors as colluding in their own subordination. Like many therapists these days, I am in favor of "different strokes for different folks," as long as the "strokes" are consensual and controlled. And given my taste for irony and theater, I applaud the strategy of women taking on the signs of their victimization (e.g., "grrl" power) and putting them to new uses—as long as it does no harm.

Meanwhile, as critical theorists were offering copious insights—and spinning copious circumlocutions—about perversions, the psychoanalytic community remained largely oblivious, both to the proto-queer theorists and to perversions. There were not many data or speculations emanating from the clinical consulting room. Gradually, however, there has been a shift in thinking about perversions. The early exclusive interest in an unconscious denial of difference had been supplemented (in Anglo-American psychoanalytic circles, anyway) by a focus on their defensive nature. This change mirrored a general shift in psychoanalytic thinking. I have alluded to this transition before when I discussed psychoanalysts' interests from the '20s and '30s on early mothering and social reality as determinants of behavior. Over time, traditional psychoanalytic thinking segued into "ego psychology," which amended doctrine to make it compatible with developmental psychology, "object relations theory," which rejected the solipsism of Freud's theory of drives in favor of a "two-persons psychology," and Kohut's "self psychology," which blithely disregarded the rules of analytic neutrality and abstinence in favor of an empathic understanding of the patient.[92] Perversions, never a priority interest, became less so.

The maverick, but highly respected analyst, Robert Stoller, one of the very few psychoanalysts dealing with the topic (Ethel Person is another) has called a fetish "a story masquerading as an object."[93] He meant that perversions might be seen as compact but highly complex compromises or strategies that attempt to resolve an individual's personal developmental drama. They are improvised mechanisms of damage control that become habit forming. Though perverse acts look like they are about sexual tension and discharge, they are really about repairing the self and the broken-down capacity to love. This damage may result from a web of multiple determinants, such as a person's thwarted struggle to emerge from fusion with a suffocating mother. Here is a paraphrased explanation of perversion from a glossary published by the American Psychoanalytic Association in 1990 that reflects the recent polyglot party line about etiology: Besides just resolving Oedipal conflict, it says, a perversion has important functions outside the phallic field.[94] It may sustain the ego. It may supply relief from having to separate from one's mother, control aggression, prop up one's body image, express feminine identification and triumph over it, dehumanize and neutralize people who are experienced as threatening, bridge gaps in one's sense of reality, and lessen painful feelings such as depression.

In this newer perspective, separation anxiety seems to trump castration anxiety. For example, Person—who drew her conclusions from field research as well from her patients' erotic fantasies and dreams—sees in some men's compulsive consumption of pornography not just anxiety about losing their penis but also intense neediness. Their use of porn enacts their yearning for the "omni-available" (that is, totally sexually available) woman, and/or the all-giving, all-nurturing pre-Oedipal mother. Oral needs are camouflaged as sexual wishes.[95] In so-called obscene media, as opposed to a real life, men may gratify their immature desires as they please, no holds barred. Consumers of porn need not suffer the sting of rejection.

Regarding another staple of pornography for straight men—the depiction of lesbian sex—Person points to an unconscious identification of the male spectator with one or the other of the female actors, perhaps as a way of repairing his enforced separation from his mother. In this fantasy, the viewer merges with his mother or incorporates her into himself.[96] If this seems preposterous, think of Hitchcock's infamous "mother's boy," Norman Bates. In *Psycho*'s startling climax, the viewer discovers that Bates has long been impersonating his mom who, in fact, he may have murdered. He literally incorporated her into himself. The lasting prominence of this scene in the public imagination testifies to its psychological resonance.

Stoller, who, like Person, did field research—and drew on the empirical work of now-notorious John Money, the advisor to the parents of a boy who was raised as a girl (see Chapter 2)—as well as psychoanalysis, termed perversion "an erotic form of hatred."[97] To be sure, he also maintained that all sexuality contains a degree of hatred, lest it wouldn't be very exciting; but perverse acts, as opposed to ordinary ones, overshoot the mark. Nonperverse people do not powerfully fear intimacy. But perverts, though they crave closeness, are desperate to avoid it. To them, true intimacy would render them vulnerable to being engulfed by another. Stoller saw in fetishism, rape, sex, murder, sadism, masochism, voyeurism, and pedophilia—but not homosexuality, which he viewed as nonperverse!—"hostility, revenge, triumph, and a dehumanized object." The act itself may be an attempt at retribution for past humiliation, in which "trauma becomes triumph."[98] You may recognize Stoller's influence on my analysis of Charlie (see Chapter 2). To Stoller, perversion is all about the fantasy that accompanies any given behavior. If the underlying fantasy does not contain hostility or the desire to injure the partner, then the behavior cannot be classified as perverse sexuality, but merely a variant of sexuality.

Queers might applaud Stoller for his activism in the psychiatric community on behalf of homosexuals. He was ahead of the bell curve in recognizing their mental health. A cohort of feminists might applaud him for partially removing perversity from an exclusively phallic field. He also presciently theorized about sex outside gender; that is, he detached gender identity issues ("I am male" vs. "I am female") from gender role ("I am masculine" vs. "I am feminine") and sexual orientation ("I lust after boys" vs. "I lust after girls")—a nod to queer theory *avant la lettre*. This was a considerable departure from the thinking of his contemporary colleagues; for example, McDougall's automatic conflation of lesbianism with gender identity disorder. But at the same time, he was no sexual romantic. To Stoller, there is a dark side to sexuality that should be held at bay and would sensibly suggest a limit to the complete liberalization of all sexual practices. Stoller, moreover, claimed that an unstable gender identity might lead to cross-dressing impulses and behaviors, such as those associated with trans-vestism and transsexualism, a claim that mutually contaminated each other with pathological spin.[99]

Like Person, Stoller suggested that gender identity precedes gender role and sexual orientation in development and that it organizes them, not the reverse. Both Stoller and Person are fans of early gender iden-tity consolidation. Both tend to see gender "disturbances" (which, as typically defined, are usually male) as arising from extreme separation anxiety in early life. Consider, for example, the three so-called cross-dressing disorders—transvestism (wherein "heteros" cross-dress for purposes of sexual arousal), practitioners of drag (wherein gays cross-dress out of a wish to parody the opposite gender role), and transsexu-alism (wherein individuals cross-dress because they wish to be the opposite sex). In those disorders, the man (as a child) supposedly alle-viated his anxiety by fusing with his mother in fantasy. He accom-plished this, like Norman Bates, by habitually incorporating some aspect of her into himself, or, in the most extreme instance, by revers-ing his gender identity from male to female. In this way, the mother and child become "one" and the danger of separation is nullified. Note that the child does not suffer from castration anxiety; on the contrary, he suffers from anxiety unless he is castrated!

A dyed-in-the-wool Freudian might view that idea as un-Freudian. The gender reversal supposedly takes place **before** the child is two years old, notably **before** the Oedipal period, **before** the child discovers ana-tomical differences. Stoller coined the term "core gender identity" to describe this early conviction of being either male or female, which Benjamin has since renamed "nominal gender identity" to accommo-date the newly minted conclusions of developmental research that gen-der identity (not only role) must be learned.[100,101] These data suggest that genital sensation stimulates an awareness of anatomical distinction between the sexes by the middle of the second year; only later do chil-dren know that having a certain genital means that they are male or female. Benjamin's relabeling of the concept has the advantage of purg-ing it of any essentialist tinge.

But even as a few psychoanalytic theorists and developmental psy-chologists are moving in the direction of regarding gender identity as something that is acquired, rather than as something that is bedrock, most clinicians hold fast to sex/gender binaries. This is where we are today. Psychoanalytical clinicians have not made the huge theoretical leap of acknowledging (no less accounting for) the mental health of people with fluid sex/gender identities—precisely the point that post-modern critics challenge. For Butler et al., there is no core identity. "But," therapists retort, "what about deviants' pain or the pain they inflict on others?" "What pain?" queers reply. Gender-bending, in their view, is not inherently painful or pain-inducing. Those with the power to define things—not sex/gender deviants—produce the pain. Without their categories, deviance would not hurt.

Psychoanalytic/Queer Theory Compatibility: F

THE RELATIONAL SCHOOL

It is hardly coincidental that many of the American psychoanalysts writing about postmodern gender reside or were trained in New York or northern California, hubs of multiculturalism and alternative lifestyles. But, as we shall see, it is also probably not coincidental that these coastal psychoanalysts tend to belong to the "relational" (aka, the "interpersonal") school, the school that takes very seriously the impact of actual relationships on psychic life, alongside instinct-driven fantasy. For it turns out that the relational model resonates more comfortably with postmodern theory than more classical models, thereby providing a far more fertile ground for deconstructing sex/gender binaries. The advent of the journal *Psychoanalytic Dialogues* in 1991 marks these theorists' serious entry into the psychoanalytic fray. Important contributors to the interpersonal oeuvre include Stephen Mitchell, Virginia Goldner, Muriel Dimen, Adrienne Harris, Adria Schwartz, Jessica Benjamin, Lewis Aron, Thomas Ogden, and Owen Renik, among others.[102–110]

To be sure, the differences among the schools of psychoanalysis are more apparent than real, and in actual practice may blur. But, on the whole, relational therapists, compared to traditionalists, think a bit more specifically and deeply about the chemistry between therapist and patient and their mutual influence. Treatment is thought to occur in that couple, in the "intersubjective encounter," to use their jargon. Hypothetically speaking, relational therapists have more "permission" to disclose things about themselves to their patients than their forebears, who were instructed to be neutral and abstinent. So-called interpersonal clinicians believe that, despite therapists' efforts to be anonymous, their "vibes" are a ubiquitous presence in the consulting room anyway. Besides, a therapist's real persona may be therapeutically useful. It may work in service of a relationship that might facilitate treatment. Like their progenitors, the object relations theorists, relational therapists believe that individuals develop in and through relationships with others. They similarly view people as object-seeking rather than plea-sure-seeking—the original primary object being a person's mother. People want love and recognition.

Let me clarify my own position. To the extent that the object rela-tions theory devolved into an ideology that primarily blames mothers for causing psychopathology, I part company with its views. To the extent that it marginalizes the role of robust sexuality in the interac-tions between child and parent in favor of a treacly mother–child bond, I regard it as a bit sentimental. To the extent that it downplays the impor-tance of language and the unconscious in mediating reality, I see it as simplistic and naive. In some cruder derivations of the object/relations model, the psyche is no longer layered and contradictory but is pre-sumed to mechanically mirror what the child actually experiences. In that version, the theory seems to me to be hardly distinguishable from behaviorism. If a child's response were so easily connected to a stimu-lus, why not jettison the idea of an unconscious altogether? Yet, those unsophisticated endpoints are not the inevitable outcomes of object relations theorists' logic. There is much I applaud in the theory. It broke new ground by providing a plausible (albeit incomplete) alterna-tive to the Oedipus complex with its exaggerated emphasis on the penis and the father. I believe, as the theory asserts, that people deeply wish for loving relationships with others. Desire is not all about instinctual gratification. And I share the view of relational theorists (the heirs of object relations theorists) that therapists, in order to be effective, must convey their humanity in their sessions with patients.

More important to the task at hand, the relational model radically disputes the idea of objectivity, that a therapist can objectively interpret what a patient thinks and feels without influencing it. This has been called "one-person" theory. In contrast, there is the aforementioned "two-person" theory in which the therapists' contamination is acknowl-edged. In the latter, the patient and therapist coconstruct reality from moment to moment. The implication is that there is no one Truth. There is no single, essential, ultimate correct insight to explain a patient's psyche that only an expert—here, a psychoanalyst—gets to define. It is all a matter of perspective—and there are many possible perspectives. The goals of two-person treatment are less about insight and finding the underlying truth about symptoms and more about helping patients bear uncertainty and develop the capacity for critical reflection on how their reality is constructed.[111]

The relational model was conceived, in part, as a correction factor to the classical model with its supposedly top-down, authoritarian, analyst-dominated interpretations of the patient. In stating this, I do not mean to imply that classical analysts foist their interpretations on patients, but that traditional therapists are a bit more apt to assume that they are "right," or at least more "right" than their patient about the patient's unconscious. Relational therapists, on the other hand, are cultural relativists. They imply that they have less of a fix on things, but that this democratic, ambiguous stance is ultimately therapeutic. These ideas plainly tilt their model in the direction of postmodernism, which, as I have shown, is in the air and probably prompted the development of relational theory in the first place. No wonder binary sex/gender began to be deconstructed in that domain rather than in the halls of classical institutes. In fact, dismantling the sex/gender binary was probably an inevitable outcome of a theory and methodology that prides itself on its sensitivity to power inequities and oppressive cultural biases in the invention of reality. The binary is an obvious product of power inequities and oppressive cultural bias (e.g., homophobia). It was ripe for deconstruction.

Relational psychoanalysts began incorporating gender fluidity into their theorizing in the last decade. Benjamin, for example, has recently suggested that the sex/gender possibilities of our early bisexual period—when crossover identifications and attachments abound—need not be given up, even after we discover the reality of anatomical sexual difference. Despite the dictates of culture and the Oedipus complex, people may revive these attachments and identifications later on without untoward consequences. This may explain the recent small spike in prevalence of same-sex love among middle-aged women who had heretofore lived their lives as heterosexuals. In other words, ambisexual feelings may benignly oscillate in and out of people over their lifetime. In this model, rigid sexual and gender polarities are transformed into a tolerable ambiguity. Sex/gender becomes slippery. Erotic desire becomes more complicated, textured, multicultural, plural.[112] Clearly Benjamin's later thinking betrays the influence of PoMo gender theory. Indeed, she addresses Butler directly in her writing.[113]

But Benjamin does not swallow queer theory hook, line, and sinker. To Benjamin, straight people may be able to tolerate deviant thoughts and feelings without disavowing them, without, as Butler suggests, holding them inside as "abject, repudiated otherness," resulting in melancholy. They are able to recognize and accept difference in another. They are free to hate something without destroying it or becoming it (that is, being destroyed by it). To Butler, on the other hand, straight people are haunted by excluded same-sex desire (see Chapter 4). Butler's subject (i.e., person) is created via "exclusion," by splitting off things in the psyche; but Benjamin's subject, in contrast, is created via "inclusion," by recognizing forbidden thoughts and holding them in tension with the acceptable parts of the self. Despite these differences, relational therapists and queer theorists, in keeping with the democratic nature of their theorizing, seem to be carrying on an open-minded, polite, mutually supportive dialogue. Layton, for example, recently engaged with Butler in *Gender and Psychoanalysis* over the nature of subjectivity, which Butler sees as fragmented and dispersed, and Layton sees as needing a location.[114] Layton is a therapist, and, of course, as such, treats actual patients (hopefully, with billing addresses), not positions in discourse.

Psychoanalytic/Queer Theory Compatibility: B+

ALL THINGS CONSIDERED...

To psychoanalyst David Schwartz, even therapists like Benjamin and Layton are not queer enough.[115] His grievance: They fail to dislodge anatomy from its position as the central organizer of sexuality. They trip over the body. This is an idea of which Butler might approve. Schwartz, like Butler, questions any and all theories of etiology of any and all things. Like her, he does not categorize people according to the sex of their love objects, nor does he view anatomy as the determining factor in the way children negotiate sexual difference. He similarly dismisses all linear models of child development, for he believes that they unfairly mandate repressive norms of health and disease along dominant cultural lines. Like her, he is a radical constructivist.

And while I applaud Schwartz for his politics and postmodern purity, I do not share his utopianism. In the end, I am a not a philosopher but a practicing psychologist working with flesh-and-blood individuals with concrete complaints. Schwartz's view leaves me lost in limbo with no roadmap. In his model (or antimodel) there is no protocol for treatment, for there is no better or worse way to proceed. Insurance companies would have a field day with this. Clinical training would be pointless. Were we to embrace Schwartz's logic, we would have to abandon all therapeutic judgement and all technique. I am not sure how this would be useful to suffering patients. To his credit, I am not sure that Schwartz is entirely "Schwartzian" in his practice at all times. In one brief clinical vignette, for example, he indicated some slippage, though he later regretted it. According to Schwartz, he had conveyed sympathy for a wife who objected to her husband's fetishistic attachment to enemas during their lovemaking. In his *post hoc* formulation of the case,

Schwartz wished he had been more tolerant of the man's behavior. But I suspect that few therapists would have done otherwise. Clinicians, even queer-positive clinicians, are only human, and, like their patients, rooted in culture where everything is **not** okay. Here, again, we encounter the theory/practice contradiction—the inevitable flip-flop.

In the end, good therapy seems to preclude theoretical purity. I recall treating a young woman a number of years ago—pre-SSRIs—who might be considered a poster child for queer theory, except that she was miserable. Carol (a pseudonym) was a highly educated anatomical female in her late twenties working as an accountant when she came to me for treatment. Her problem: She had no sexual orientation. Indeed, she had no sexual desire, and, in retrospect, I believe she had no gender identity, though neither she nor I conceived of her without a gender identity at the time. She had never masturbated, never experienced orgasm, and was clueless about "performing" femininity. For example, she was unaware that a ring with a precious stone worn on the ring finger of the left hand of a woman indicates that the woman is engaged. She was surprised that belt hooks on the waistband of a dress suggests that a belt "should" be worn. When she attempted to use a tampon, she developed Reynaud's syndrome: her hand turned blue. It was not that she felt like a male, but that she did not feel like anything. More than once, she jokingly suggested that she came from outer space.

Carol was highly superego driven: She was a dutiful daughter, loyal sister, and hard worker. Oblivious to her own attractiveness, she was awkward, highly obsessional, actuarial minded, anxious, and painfully shy. Today, she might be described as somewhat Asperger-like. Interestingly, Carol wanted sexual desire not in and of itself (never having experienced it) but for its instrumental value, reasoning, sensibly enough, that it was necessary for finding a life mate. Above all, she was desperately lonely.

Carol reported being happiest when she attached herself to a group as a kind of comic tagalong, like when she joined a sorority in college and acted as a go-between at parties. She daydreamed about joining the military (though she was antiwar), or a convent (though she was not Catholic), or a commune—any place where she could function without having to pair off. Her fantasies, which were never explicitly sexual, were of "hanging out" with Elton John, or me, or Pierce Brosnan, or a young female secretary in her office. Not surprisingly, her first reported dream was about Peter Pan, the boy who never grew up. In fact, she dreamt repeatedly of this story and reported identifying with Tiger Lily, the Indian princess who was tied up. Interestingly, during the course of Carol's two-year-long, weekly psychotherapy, she began to engage very sporadically in playful S/M with men, during which her hands were tied. She was neither orgasmic nor even genitally aroused during these activities, but found them somewhat compelling and tilting toward sexual excitation.

We could never piece together a psychodynamic narrative to explain her sexual ambiguity. Her parents, though conventional, were not repressive, and they encouraged her to pursue any sexual orientation to which she might be inclined. The most salient aspect of her childhood, aside from her lifelong feeling of not fitting in, was the resentment she felt toward her parents for not favoring her—she, who was so well behaved—over her sister who acted out. She left therapy prematurely for financial reasons, though she was quite pleased with herself for engaging in a proto-sexual act. Contra queer theory, the closer Carol felt to a category, the happier she felt.

Juxtapose Carol's predicament with one of the most memorable last lines in film history, a line that resonates with many folks' psychic reality, in Billy Wilder's *Some Like It Hot*. Tony Curtis and Jack Lemmon, dressed in drag, join up with Marilyn Monroe in an all-girl band. Millionaire Joe Brown, not realizing that Lemmon is a "he," falls in love with him. When cross-dressed Lemmon tries to let Brown down gently by explaining that he's not really a girl, Brown shrugs, "Well, nobody's perfect." The audience laughs. Brown doesn't question the "perversity" of his object choice. Neither does the audience. They find it human, albeit ironic and amusing—certainly not repugnant or subversive. But this is a movie, not real life. Brown, a fictional character, is free to be oblivious to sexual categories. Living outside the norm for living and breathing Carol is not so easy. Carol's audience—socially conservative America—wouldn't laugh. There is no acceptable place for someone without a sex/gender classification.

Gender is not quite over, but sex/gender categories are well on their way out. They are no longer accurate organizers of life. Any explanation of gender identity and/or sexual orientation built on the false premise of an infallible binary must be reevaluated. Desire can no longer be reduced to instincts, or objects, or biological spasms, or linguistic points in the ether. Perhaps desire may be too elusive to ever pin down. Indeed, the closer we get to determining its origins, the more it recedes…like water ahead of you on a highway on a hot summer day that vanishes when you get near. Perhaps we may never make sense of it.

But because desire is hard to commandeer and dissect does not mean that we should abandon the inquiry into its determinants and meaning. Our past failure to question our presumptions about sex/gender has resulted in intellectual sloppiness and gross injustice. We can do better. We can swear off the cheap satisfaction of categorical judgments and confront head-on the complexity of sexual desire. We can learn to tolerate ambiguity, uncertainty, and contradiction.

Theorizing about sex/gender cuts across many fields, but these fields barely communicate with each other. If there is to be progress in understanding the dynamics of desire, there must be a sustained dialogue among the many disciplines dealing with sexuality. It is about time that therapists, scientists, and scholars pull together, critique each others' points of view, abandon stale biases, and brainstorm. We must cooperatively dismantle and oil our conceptual machinery and then put it back together in better condition. Rather than ignore each others' literature, we should capitalize on the broad-based intellectual ferment to rebuild our theories so that they are true and useful. Since we have no answers, I suggest that theoretical humility—including humility about the theory that there is no theory—is in order. Therapists should maintain an actively skeptical stance as they proceed with their clinical work. After all, the most compelling stories unfold when you don't start out with the answer. Humbly, collectively, we may, to quote Alexander Portnoy's psychoanalyst, "perhaps to begin."

NOTES

Notes to Chapter One: Psychoanalysis Meets Postmodern Sex

1. RuPaul, *Letting It All Hang Out: An Autobiography* (New York: Hyperion, 1995).
2. E. Laumann et al., *The Social Organization of Sexuality: Sexual Practices in the United States* (Chicago: University of Chicago Press, 1994).
3. A. Bakker et al., "The Prevalence of Transsexualism in the Netherlands," *Acta Psychiatrica Scandinavica* 87 (1993): 237–238.
4. Reported by Deidre McCloskey in *Crossing: A Memoir* (Chicago: The University of Chicago Press, 1999), 31. This information was confirmed in a survey: Bonnie Bullough and Vern Bullough, "Men Who Cross-Dress: A Survey" in *Gender Blending*, (eds.) Bonnie Bullough et al. (Amherst, NY: Prometheus Books, 1997), 185.
5. John Berendt, "High-Heel Neil," *New Yorker*, 16 January 1995, 38–45.
6. Joanne Meyerowitz, *How Sex Changed* (Cambridge: Harvard University Press, 2002); Amy Bloom, *Normal* (New York: Random House, 2002); and Jeffrey Eugenides, *Middlesex* (New York: Farrar, Straus and Giroux, 2002).
7. Judith Thurman, "Guides to Etiquette," *New Yorker*, 18 February 2002 and 25 February 2002, 188–192.
8. Reported by Cris Beam in a radio segment on *This American Life*, episode 190 entitled "Living the Dream—Girls, Girls, Girls," broadcast on August 3, 2001. The reporter had been researching a group of transsexual teenagers in Los Angeles for two years.
9. I draw here from commentary on sex and evolution including: Jerry A. Coyne, "The Fairy Tales of Evolutionary Psychology: Of Vice and Men," *The New Republic*, 3 April 2000, 27–34; and Margaret Talbot, "The Female Misogynist," *The New Republic*, 31 May 1999, 34–40. For primary source material, see the writings of biologists Donna Haraway, Anne Fausto-Sterling, and Sarah Harding.
10. A. T. Watters, "Heterosexual Bias in Psychological Research on Lesbianism and Male Homosexuality," *Journal of Homosexuality* 13 (1986): 35–58.
11. A particularly rich source of queer-friendly theorists hail from the New York University Postdoctoral Program in Psychotherapy and Psychoanalysis, including Jessica Benjamin, Adrienne Harris, Muriel Dimen, Thomas Dominici, Ronnie Lesser, Ken Corbett, Virginia Golden, and others. Not all are gay, but I suspect many might accept the label "queer." Also in New York is Elisabeth Young-Bruehl at the Columbia Center for Psychoanalytic Training and Research. Grappling with postmodern gender theory outside of New York are Jane Flax, Lynne Layton, Nancy Chodorow, and Lois Shawver, among others.

12. The primary sources from which I draw my ideas here include the writings of French philosophers Francois Lyotard and Jean Baudrillard, deconstructionists Jacques Derrida and the Yale School, sociologist Pierre Bourdieu, postcolonialists Edward Said and Henry Louis Gates, historian Thomas Laqueur, and American philosopher Richard Rorty, among others. Their thinking evolved from the so-called structuralists—Marxist critics Frederic Jameson and Terry Eagleton, Ferdinand de Saussure, Claude Levi-Strauss, Louis Althusser, Roland Barthes, and Jacques Lacan, among others. I explain more technical aspects of these postmodern theories in later chapters.

13. Big names in queer theory include: Michel Foucault, Judith Butler, Teresa de Lauretis (who probably coined the term), Eve Kosofsky Sedgwick, Alice Jardine, and John Dollimore, as well as anthropologist Gayle Rubin and activist Michael Warner, among others. I explain their ideas in later chapters.

14. I am indebted to Robert Stoller, who makes similar observations in Robert J. Stoller, *Sexual Excitement: Dynamics of Erotic Life* (New York: Pantheon, 1979), 3–35.

15. I draw here from commentary on queer theory, including: Lee Siegel, "Queer Theory, Literature, and the Sexualization of Everything: The Gay Science," *The New Republic*, 9 November 1998, 30–42; and Martha Nussbaum, "The Hip Defeatism of Judith Butler: The Professor of Parody," *The New Republic*, 22 February 1999, 37–46.

16. Luce Irigaray, *This Sex Which Is Not One*, trans. Catherine Porter with Carolyn Burke (Ithaca, NY: Cornell University Press, 1977).

17. For a good discussion of the incidence and prevalence of intersexuality, see: Alice Domurat Dreger, *Hermaphrodites and the Medical Invention of Sex* (Cambridge: Harvard University Press, 1998), 40–43.

Notes to Chapter Two: Postmodernism for Those Who Missed It

1. Quoted in Annie Le Brun, *Sade: A Sudden Abyss*, trans. Camille Nash (San Francisco: City Lights Books, 1990), 45.

2. Discussed by Jean Baudrillard in *Symbolic Exchange and Death*, trans. Iain Hamilton Grant (London: Sage, 1976); and in his *Simulacra and Simulations*, trans. Nicola Dufresne (New York: Semiotext(e), 1983).

3. These ideas derive from the Frankfurt School—Theodor Adorno, Max Horkheimer, and Herbert Marcuse.

4. The best attempts I've seen at pinning down postmodernism (from whom I draw) are popular critic Todd Gitlin's article "Postmodernism Defined At Last!," *Utne Reader* July/August 1989, 52–58; Bruce Handy, "A 'Spy' Guide to Postmodern Everything," *Utne Reader* July/August 1989, 50–76; Andrew Boyd, *Life's Little Deconstruction Book* (New York: W. W. Norton, 1999); Vivien Burr, *An Introduction to Social Constructionism* (London: Routledge, 1995); Charles Lemert, *Postmodernism Is Not What You Think*, (Malden, MA: Blackwell, 1997); Karen Endicott, "Post-What?!?," *Dartmouth Alumni Magazine*, December 1998, 38–41; Stuart Sim, (ed.), *The Routledge Critical Dictionary of Postmodern Thought* (New York: Routledge, 1999); and Jim Powell, *Postmodernism for Beginners* (New York: Writers and Readers Publishing, 1998).

5. Jean-Francois Lyotard, *The Postmodern Condition: A Report on Knowledge*, trans. Geoff Bennington and Brian Masumi (Minneapolis: University of Minnesota Press, 1979).

6. Deborah Soloman, "How to Succeed in Art," *New York Times Magazine*, 27 June 1999, 38–41.

7. David Lehman describes the scandal at Yale in *Signs of the Times: Deconstruction and the Fall of Paul de Man* (New York: Poseidon Press, 1991).

8. Roberta Smith, "Body of Evidence," *Vogue*, August 1994, 152; and Hilarie Sheets, "The Mod Bod," *Art News*, June 1991, Vol. 100, no. 6, 98–101.

9. See Jacques Derrida, *Speech and Phenomenon*, trans. Alan Bass (Chicago: University of Chicago Press, 1978); *Of Grammatology*, trans. Gayatri Spivak (Baltimore: Johns Hopkins University Press, 1976); *Writing and Difference*, trans. Alan Bass (Chicago: University of Chicago Press, 1978).

10. Judith Butler, *Gender Trouble: Feminism and the Subversion of Identity* (New York: Routledge, 1990), viii.

11. See Sigmund Freud, "The Most Prevalent Form of Degradation in Erotic Life" in *Sexuality and the Psychology of Love*, (ed.), Philip Rieff (New York: Simon Schuster, 1963), 48–60, originally published in *International Journal of Psychoanalysis*, trans. Joan Riviere, Vol. 9, 1928, 161–171; and Sigmund Freud, "Fetishism" (1924) in James Strachey (ed.) *The Standard Edition of the Complete Psychological Waves of Sigmund Freud* (London: Hogarth, 1953–1974) Vol. 21, 149–157; and Sigmund Freud, *Three Essays on the Theory of Sexuality* (1905) in James Strachey (ed.) The Standard Edition of the Complete Psychological Works of Sigmund Freud (London: Hogarth, 1953–1974) Vol. 7, 125–254.

12. Susan Suleiman, "Surrealism," in *Feminism and Psychoanalysis: A Critical Dictionary*, (ed.) Elizabeth Wright (Cambridge, MA: Blackwell, 1992).

13. As quoted in David Morris, *Illness and Culture in the Postmodern Age* (Berkeley and Los Angeles: University of California Press, 1998), 161. Postmodern theorists who propose that the concrete biological body lacks any tangible essence include Jean-Luc Nancy in his essay "Corpus," in *Re-Thinking Technologies*, (ed.) Verena Andermatt Conley (Minneapolis: University of Minnesota Press, 1993); and Elizabeth Grosz, *Volatile Bodies: Toward a Corporeal Feminism* (Bloomington: Indiana University Press, 1994).

14. Joan Riviere, "Womanliness as a Masquerade," *International Journal of Psychoanalysis* 10, (1929): 35–44.

15. Lee Siegel, "The Gay Science," *The New Republic*, 9 November 1998, 30–42.

16. Michel Foucault, *The History of Sexuality: An Introduction* (New York: Vintage, 1990), 43.

17. Jean-Paul Sartre, *Being and Nothingness* (New York: Washington Square Press, 1996), as described in Susan Bordo, *The Male Body* (New York: Farrar, Straus and Giroux, 1999), 172.

18. Sara Corbett, "When Debbie Met Christina, Who Then Became Chris," *New York Times Magazine*, 14 October 2001, 84–87.

19. Freud, "Degradation," 48–60.

20. Marjorie Garber discusses this with respect to cross-dressers and transsexuals in Marjorie Garber, *Vested Interests: Cross-Dressing and Cultural Anxiety* (New York: Routledge, Chapman and Hall, 1992).

21. Steve Hogan and Lee Hudson, (eds.) *Completely Queer: The Gay and Lesbian Encyclopedia* (New York: Henry Holt and Co., 1998), 92–93. Also discussed by Alan Mansfeld and Barbara McGinn, "Pumping Iron: The Muscular and the Feminine," in *Body Matters*, (eds.) Sue Scott and David Morgan (London: The Falmer Press, 1993), 49–59.

22. Anne Hollander, *Feeding the Eye* (New York: Farrar, Straus and Giroux, 1999), 158.

23. John DiCarlo, "The Gym Body and Heroic Myth," *Harvard Gay and Lesbian Review* 8, no. 4 (2002): 14–16; Michael Shernoff, "Steroids and the Pursuit of Bigness," *Harvard Gay and Lesbian Review* 8, no. 4 (2002), 32–33; D. Carlat et al., "Eating Disorders in Males," *American Journal of Psychiatry*, 154, no. 8 (1997), 1127–1131.

24. Susan Bordo, *The Male Body* (New York: Farrar, Straus and Giroux, 1999), 181.

25. Susan Sontag, "Notes on Camp," in *Against Interpretation* (New York: Delta Books, Dell Publishing, 1967),, first published in *Partisan Review* 31, no. 4 (fall 1964): 515–530.

26. Ken Plummer, "Speaking its Name" in *Modern Homosexualities: Fragments of Lesbian and Gay Experience* (London: Routledge, 1992), 3–25.

27. Stephen Murray, *Homosexualities* (Chicago: University of Chicago Press, 2000), 199–200.

28. Joan Nestle, *The Persistent Desire: A Femme-Butch Reader* (Boston: Alyson Press, 1992).

29. Murray, *Homosexualities*, 220–227; Neil Miller, *Out of the Past: Gay and Lesbian History from 1869 to the Present* (New York: Vintage, 1995), 319–326.

30. Rita Mae Brown, "The Shape of Things to Come," in Miller, *Out of the Past*, 388.

31. Murray, *Homosexualities*, 385; and Miller, *Out of the Past*, 368–371 and 399.

32. Miller, *Out of the Past*, 421–426.

33. Marjorie Garber, *Vice Versa: Bisexuality and the Eroticism of Everyday Life* (New York: Simon and Schuster, 1995), 16–67.

34. John Harlow, "Hollywood Actresses Find It Pays To Be Gay," *Sunday Times* (London), 9 July 2000, p. 27.

35. Terry Stein, "A Critique of Approaches to Changing Sexual Orientation," in *Textbook of Homosexuality and Mental Health*, (eds.) Robert Cabaj and Terry Stein (Washington, DC: American Psychiatry Press, 1996), 526.

36. John Colapinto, *As Nature Made Him: The Boy Who Was Raised As a Girl* (New York: HarperCollins, 2000), 214.

37. Heather Findlay, "Freud's 'Fetishism' and the Lesbian Dildo Debates," in *Out In Culture: Gay, Lesbian, and Queer Essays on Popular Culture*, (eds.) Corey Creekmur and Alexander Doty (Durham, NC: Duke University Press, 1995), 328–342.

38. Data from a Carnegie Mellon study reported by Philip Elmer-Dewitt, "On a Screen Near You: Cyberporn," *Time*, 3 July 1995, 40.

39. Paraphrased from Bordo, *The Male Body*, 170. Also discussed in J. Michael Bailey, *The Man Who Would Be Queen: The Science of Gender-Bending and Transsexualism* (Washington, DC: Joseph Henry Press, 2003), 94.

40. John Berger, *Ways of Seeing* (London: BBC and Penguin Publishing, 1972), 47. These arguments were elaborated by film critics Laura Mulvey in "Visual Pleasure and Narrative Cinema," *Screen* 16, no. 3, (1975): 6–18; and Mary Ann Doane, "Masquerade Reconsidered: Further Thoughts on the Female Spectator," *Discourse* 11 (fall/winter 1988/89): 42–54. Both used a Lacanian perspective in formulating their position. They subsequently revised their position.

41. See Mikhail Bakhtin, *Rabelais and His World*, trans. Helene Iswolsky (Cambridge: MIT Press, 1968) and Mikhail Bakhtin, *The Dialogical Imagination*, trans. Caryl Emerson and Michael Holquist (Austin: University of Texas Press, 1981).

42. Sigmund Freud, "The 'Uncanny'" (1919) in James Strachey (ed.) in *The Standard Edition of the Complete Psychological Works of Sigmund Freud* (London: Hogarth, 1953–1974), 17:217–252.

43. The film was based on J.G. Ballard's 1973 novel of the same name.

44. Elizabeth Grosz, "The Body," in *Feminism and Psychoanalysis: A Critical Dictionary*, (ed.) Elizabeth Wright (Cambridge, MA: Blackwell Publishers, 1992), 38.

45. This idea derives from Donna J. Haraway, "Cyborg Manifesto: Science, Technology, and Socialist-Feminism in the Late Twentieth Century," in *Simians, Cyborgs, and Women: The Reinvention of Nature* (New York: Routledge, 1991), 183–202.

Notes to Chapter Three: Facts and Factoids

1. Shari Thurer, "Homosexual Panic in the Postmodern Age" (paper presented at the American Psychological Association, Spring Meeting Div. 19, New York, NY, April 1999).

2. Jacqueline Zita, *Body Talk: Philosophical Reflections on Sex and Gender* (New York: Columbia University Press, 1998), 16–19.

3. I rely here on excellent critiques of research by: Anne Fausto-Sterling, *Sexing the Body: Gender Politics and the Construction of* Sexuality (New York: Basic Books, 2000); Edward Stein, *The Mismeasure of Desire: The Science, Theory, and Ethics of Sexual Orientation* (New York: Oxford University Press, 1999); Judith Lorber, *Paradoxes of Gender* (New Haven, CT: Yale University Press, 1994); Sandra Lipsitz Bem, *The Lenses*

of Gender: Transforming the Debate on Sexual Inequality (New Haven, CT: Yale University Press, 1993); Richard Horton, "Is Homosexuality Inherited?," *New York Review of Books*, 13 July 1995, 36–40; Andrew Hacker, "Gays and Genes," *New York Review of Books*, 27 March 2003, 14–16.

4. John Leland and Mark Miller, "Can Gays 'Convert'?" *Newsweek*, 17 August 1998, 46–52.
5. For example see: S. Marc Breedlove, "Sex on the Brain," *Nature* 389 (1997): 801.
6. Simon LeVay, "A Difference in Hypothalamic Structure between Heterosexual and Homosexual Men," *Science* 253, no. 5023 (1991): 1034–1037; Dean Hamer et al., "A Linkage between DNA Markers on the X Chromosome and Male Sexual Orientation," *Science* 261 (1993): 321–327.
7. Deborah Blum, *Sex on the Brain: The Biological Differences between Men and Women* (New York: Penguin, 1997).
8. LeVay, "A Difference in Hypothalamic Structure," 1034–1037.
9. Hamer, "DNA Markers," 321–327.
10. Jean-Francois Ferveur et al., "Genetic Feminization of Brain Structures and Changed Sexual Orientation in Male Drosophilia," *Science* 267 (1995): 902–905.
11. See, for example: Chandler Burr, *A Separate Creation: The Search for the Biological Origins of Sexual Orientation* (New York: Hyperion, 1996); Anne Fausto-Sterling and Evan Balaban, "Genetics and Male Sexual Orientation," *Science*, Vol. 33 (1993) 1257; William Byne, "Why We Cannot Conclude that Sexual Orientation Is Primarily a Biological Phenomenon," *Journal of Homosexuality* 34, no. 1 (1997): 73–80; Horton, "Is Homosexuality Inherited?," 36–40; Stein, *The Mismeasure of Desire*, 167–171; and J. Michael Bailey, *The Man Who Would Be Queen: The Science of Gender-Bending and Transsexualism* (Washington, DC: Joseph Henry Press, 2003).
12. Joan Roughgarden, *Evolution's Rainbow: Diversity, Gender and Sexuality in Nature and People* (Berkeley and Los Angeles: University of California Press, 2004).
13. Hacker, "Gays and Genes," 15. Hacker is extrapolating from data from the 2000 Bureau of Census.
14. J. Michael Bailey, *The Man Who Would Be Queen: The Science of Gender-Bending and Transsexualism* (Washington, DC: Joseph Henry Press, 2003), 109.
15. Horton, "Is Homosexuality Inherited?," 40.
16. Roughgarden, *Evolution's Rainbow*, 142–158.
17. I am paraphrasing Margaret Talbot, "The Female Misogynist: The Whole Woman by Germaine Greer," *The New Republic*, 31 May 1999, 36; and Jerry Coyne, "Of Vice and Men," *The New Republic*, 3 April 2000, 28.
18. Randy Thornhill and Craig Palmer, *A Natural History of Rape: Biological Bases of Sexual Coercion* (Cambridge: MIT Press, 2000).
19. Coyne, "Of Vice and Men," 27–29.
20. Steven Pinker, *The Blank Slate: The Modern Denial of Human Nature* (New York: Viking Publishers, 2002).
21. Deborah Blum, *Sex on the Brain: The Biological Differences between Men and Women* (New York: Penguin, 1997), 25–33; Linda Brannon, *Gender: Psychological Perspectives* (Needham Heights, MA: Allyn & Bacon, 1996), 41–70.
22. Heino Meyer-Bahlburg, "Psychoendocrinology and Sexual Pleasure: The Aspect of Sexual Orientation," in *Sexual Nature, Sexual Culture*, (eds.) Paul Abramson and Steven Pinkerton (Chicago: University of Chicago Press, 1995), 135–153.
23. J. Michael Bailey, "Biological Perspectives on Sexual Orientation," in *Lesbian, Gay, and Bisexual Identities over the Lifespan*, (eds.) Anthony D'Augelli and Charlotte Patterson (New York: Oxford University Press, 1995), 112–113.
24. Brannon, *Gender*, 56.
25. Roger A. Gorski et al., "Evidence for a Morphological Sex Difference within the Medial Preoptic Area of the Rat Brain," *Brain Research* 148 (1978): 333–346.

26. Gunter Dormer, *Hormones and Brain Differentiation* (Amsterdam: Elsevier, 1976), 229, as quoted in Simon LeVay, *Queer Science: The Use and Abuse of Research into Homosexuality* (Cambridge: MIT Press, 1996), 118–119.

27. Fausto-Sterling, *Sexing the Body* (New York: Basic Books, 2000), 195–232.

28. Byne, "Biological Phenomenon," 73–80.

29. Ray Blanchard and Anthony Bogaert, "Homosexuality in Men and Number of Older Brothers," *American Journal of Psychiatry* 153 (1996): 27–31.

30. Alice Dreger, *Hermaphrodites and the Medical Invention of Sex* (Cambridge: Harvard University Press, 1998), 7–8.

31. Brannon, *Gender*, 69.

32. LeVay, *Queer Science*, 111.

33. Natalie Angier, *Woman: An Intimate Geography* (New York: Anchor Books, 1999), 263.

34. I am paraphrasing Margaret Talbot, "The Female Misogynist," 36–37.

35. Donald Symons, *The Evolution of Human Sexuality* (New York: Oxford University Press, 1979), as quoted in Deborah Blum, *Sex on the Brain: The Biological Differences between Men and Women* (New York: Penguin, 1997), 232.

36. Blum, *Sex on the Brain*, 233.

37. Camille Paglia, *Sexual Personae: Art and Decadence from Nefertiti to Emily Dickinson* (New York: Vintage, 1990), 26.

38. Philip Blumstein and Pepper Schwartz, *American Couples: Money, Work, Sex* (New York: Pocketbooks, 1983).

39. Diana Souhami, *Gertrude and Alice* (London: Pandora Press, 1991).

40. I am quoting myself here: Shari Thurer, *The Myths of Motherhood: How Culture Reinvents the Good Mother* (New York: Penguin, 1994), 213–214.

41. Daryl Bem, "Erotic Becomes Erotic: Interpreting the Biological Correlates of Sexual Orientation," *Archives of Sexual Behavior* 29 (2000), no. 6: 531–548.

42. Edward Stein, *The Mismeasure of Desire*, 234–243.

43. Richard Green, *The "Sissy Boy" Syndrome and the Development of Homosexuality* (New Haven, CT: Yale University Press, 1987), as cited in Emily Nussbaum, "Dr. Strangelove: Does the Exotic Become Erotic?" *Lingua Franca* (June 1998): Vol. 8, no. 4, 38–44.

44. Eve Kosofsky Sedgwick, "How To Bring Your Kids up Gay," in *Tendencies* (Durham, NC: Duke University Press, 1993), 157.

45. J. Hall and D. Kimura, "Sexual Orientation and Performance on Sexually Dimorphic Motor Tasks," *Archives of Sexual Behavior* 24 (1995): 395–407.

46. Holly Brubach, *Girlfriends: Men, Women and Drag* (New York: Random House, 1999), 8–9.

47. Ibid., 102.

48. Gayle Rubin, "The Traffic in Women," in *Toward an Anthropology of Women*, (ed.) Rayna Reiter (New York: Monthly Review Press, 1975).

49. Will Roscoe, *Changing Ones* (New York: Palgrave Macmillan, 1998); and Gilbert Herdt, (ed.), *Third Sex, Third Gender* (New York: Zone Books, 1996), 21–81.

50. Terry Tafoya, "Native Two-Spirit People," in *Textbook of Homosexuality and Mental Health*, (eds.) Robert Cabaj and Terry Stein (Washington, DC: American Psychiatry Press, 1996), 603–617.

51. Serena Nanda, *Gender Diversity: Crosscultural Variations* (Prospect Heights, IL: Waveland Press, 2000), 27–43.

52. *BBC News, World Edition*, online, "India's First Eunuch Mayor Unseated," Charles Haviland, Thursday, 29 August 2002, www.bbc.co.uk/l/hi/south_asia/224164.stm

53. Stephen O. Murray, *Homosexualities* (Chicago: University of Chicago Press, 2000), 1–24. Other classifiers include: Gilbert Herdt, "Developmental Discontinuities and Sexual Orientation across Cultures," in *Homosexuality/Heterosexuality: Concepts of Sexual Orientation*, (eds.) D. P. McWhorter et al. (New York: Oxford University Press, 1990), 208–236.

54. Steve Hogan and Lee Hudson, "Greece," in *Completely Queer: The Gay and Lesbian Encyclopedia* (New York: Henry Holt and Company, 1998), 256–257.

55. Francisco Gonzalez and Olivia Espin, "Latino Men, Latina Women, and Homosexuality," in *Textbook of Homosexuality and Mental Health*, (eds.) Robert Cabaj and Terry Stein, (Washington, DC: American Psychiatric Association Press, 1996), 583–589.

56. Andrea Sankar, "Sisters and Brothers, Lovers and Enemies: Marriage, Resistance in Southern Kwangtung," in *Anthropology and Homosexual Behavior*, (ed.) Evelyn Blackwood (New York: Haworth, 1986).

57. Frederick Whitam, "Culturally Universal Aspects of Male Homosexual Transvestites and Transsexuals," in *Gender Blending*, (eds.) Bonnie Bullough et al. (Amherst, NY: Prometheus Books, 1997), 189–203.

58. Anne Fausto-Sterling, "The Five Sexes: Revisited," *The Sciences*, July 2000. Online. I also referred to Phyllis Burke, *Gender Shock: Exploding the Myth of Male and Female* (New York: Anchor Books, 1996), 206–207, 219–221.

59. Joan Stephenson, "Female Olympians' Sex Tests Outmoded," *JAMA* 276, no. 3 (1996): 177–178.

60. Anne Bolin, "Transforming Transvestism and Transsexuals: Polarity, Politics, and Gender," in *Gender Blending*, (eds.) Bonnie Bullough, et al. (Amherst, NY: Prometheus Books, 1997), 25–32.

61. Suzanne Kessler and Wendy McKenna, *Gender: An Ethnomethodological Approach* (Chicago: University of Chicago Press, 1978), 1–21.

62. Sandra Bem, "The Measurement of Psychological Androgyny," *Journal of Consulting and Clinical Psychology* 42 (1974): 320–335.

63. Kate Bornstein, *Gender Outlaw: On Men, Women, and the Rest of Us* (New York: Vintage, 1994), 37.

64. Edward Stein, *The Mismeasure of Desire*, 49–68.

65. Thomas Laqueur, *Making Sex: Body and Gender from the Greeks to Freud* (Cambridge: Harvard University Press, 1990).

Notes to Chapter Four: Queer Theory

1. Paraphrased from: Michael Rowe, "Walking with the Ghost of Barry Winchell," *The Advocate Online,* June 11, 2003; and David France, "An Inconvenient Woman," *New York Times Magazine*, 28 May 2000, 24–107.

2. Traditional Values Coalition Online, "Exposed: The Truth about Pfc. Barry Winchell." www.traditionalvalues.org/urban/eleven.php-25k

3. William Turner, *A Genealogy of Queer Theory* (Philadelphia: Temple University Press, 2000), 2.

4. Lee Siegel, "The Gay Science," *The New Republic*, 9 November 1998, 320.

5. Steve Hogan and Lee Hudson, "Queer," in *Completely Queer: The Gay and Lesbian Encyclopedia* (New York: Henry Holt and Co., 1998), 462.

6. Excerpted from *Northwest Passage* (March, 1985) in *Utne Reader* no. 12 (Oct./Nov. 1985): 38

7. Tamsin Spargo, *Foucault and Queer Theory* (Cambridge, UK: Icon Books, 1999), 38.

8. Annamarie Jagose, *Queer Theory: An Introduction* (New York: New York University Press, 1996), 127.

9. Ibid., 1.

10. Michael Warner, (ed.), *Fear of a Queer Planet* (Minneapolis: University of Minnesota Press, 1993).

11. Caleb Crain, "Pleasure Principles," *Lingua Franca* (October 1997): Vol. 7, no. 8, 26–37.

12. These include: Turner, *Genealogy*; Spargo, *Foucault*; Jagose, *Queer Theory*; Lynne Segal, *Straight Sex: Rethinking the Politics of Pleasure* (Berkeley and Los Angeles: University of

California Press, 1994); Vivien Burr, *An Introduction to Social Constructionism* (London: Routledge, 1995); as well as other authors as noted.

13. Simone De Beauvoir, *The Second Sex* (Toronto: Bantam, 1964), 249. 1st American edition, trans. and (ed.) by H.M. Parsley (New York: Knopf, 1952).

14. Wendy Kaminer, "Feminism's Identity Crisis," *Atlantic Monthly* (October 1993): Vol. 272, 51–68.

15. Carol Gilligan, *In a Different Voice: Women's Conception of the Self and Morality* (Cambridge: Harvard University Press, 1982).

16. Carol Gilligan et al., (eds.), *Making Connections: The Relational World of Adolescent Girls at the Emma Willard School* (Cambridge: Harvard University Press, 1990).

17. K. Kling et al., "Gender Differences in Self-Esteem: A Meta-Analysis," *Psychological Bulletin* 125 (1999): 143–151.

18. Margaret Talbot, "The Female Misogynist," *The New Republic*, 31 May 1999, 36.

19. Kaminer, "Identity Crisis," 64.

20. Nancy Chodorow, *The Reproduction of Mothering: Psychoanalysis and the Sociology of Gender* (Berkeley and Los Angeles: University of California Press, 1978) and Nancy Chodorow, *Feminism and Psychoanalysis* (New Haven, CT: Yale University Press, 1989).

21. Turner, *Genealogy.*

22. Ibid., 88.

23. Celia Kitzinger, "Social Constructionism: Implications for Lesbian and Gay Psychology," in *Lesbian, Gay, and Bisexual Identities over the Lifespan*, (eds.) Anthony D'Augelli and Charlotte Patterson (New York: Oxford University Press, 1995), 138–140.

24. Hogan and Hudson, *Completely Queer*, 323.

25. Michel Foucault, *The History of Sexuality, Volume 1: An Introduction*, trans. Robert Hurley (New York: Vintage, 1990; New York: Pantheon, 1978).

26. Spargo, *Foucault*, 10; and Jagose, *Queer Theory*, 5.

27. Michel Foucault, "On the Genealogy of Ethics: An Overview of Work in Progress," in *Michel Foucault: Beyond Structuralism and Hermeneutics*, 2nd (ed.), (eds.) Hubert Dreyfus and Paul Rabinow (Chicago: University of Chicago Press, 1983), 229.

28. David Halperin, *Saint Foucault: Towards a Gay Hagiography* (New York: Oxford University Press, 1995), 4, as quoted in Tamsin Spargo, *Foucault and Queer Theory* (Cambridge, UK: Icon Books, 1999), 13.

29. Vivien Burr, *Social Constructionism*, 52.

30. Ibid., 40.

31. Ibid.

32. Michel Foucault, *Madness and Civilization: A History of Insanity in the Age of Reason*, trans. Richard Howard (New York: Random House, 1965).

33. Chris Rohmann, *"Michel Foucault," A World of Ideas* (New York: Ballantine, 1999), 142–143.

34. Madan Sarup, *An Introductory Guide to Post-Structuralism and Postmodernism:* 2nd (ed.) (New York: Simon and Schuster, 1993), 39.

35. Lydia Fillingham, *Foucault for Beginners* (New York: Writers and Readers Publishing, 1993), 140–145.

36. Michel Foucault, *Discipline and Punish: The Birth of the Prison*, trans. Alan Sheridan (New York: Vintage Books, 1979).

37. Dana Cavallaro, *Critical and Cultural Theory* (New Brunswick, NJ: Althone Press, 2001), 91.

38. Foucault, *Discipline and Punish*, 201.

39. Vivien Burr, *Social Constructionism*, 68.

40. Ibid., 70.

41. Steve Hogan and Lee Hudson, *Completely Queer*, 221.

42. Michel Foucault, *The History of Sexuality, Volume 1: An Introduction*, trans. Robert Hurley (New York: Vintage, 1990; New York: Pantheon, 1978), 4–5; Spargo, *Foucault*, 11.

43. Foucault, *The History of Sexuality*, 18–19; Charles Lemert, *Postmodernism Is Not What You Think* (Malden, MA: Blackwell Publishers, 1997), 50.

44. Foucault, *The History of Sexuality*, 36–49.

45. Burr, *Social Constructionism*, 66.

46. Jim Powell, *Postmodernism for Beginners* (Village Station, NY: Writers and Readers Ltd., 1998), 110–111; Gilles Deleuze and Felix Guattari, *Anti-Oedipus: Capitalism and Schizophrenia*, trans. Robert Hurley et al. (Minneapolis: University of Minnesota Press, 1983).

47. Foucault, *The History of Sexuality*, 43.

48. Ibid., 101.

49. Spargo, *Foucault*, 21.

50. Foucault, *The History of Sexuality*, 71.

51. My secondary sources are: David Lehman, *Signs of the Times* (New York: Simon and Schuster, 1991); Jim Powell, *Derrida for Beginners* (Hyderabad, India: Orient Longman Limited, 2000); Burr, *Social Constructionism*; Madan Sarup, *An Introductory Guide to Post-Structuralism and Postmodernism* (Athens: University of Georgia Press, 1993); Donald Palmer, *Structuralism and Poststructuralism for Beginners* (Village Station, NY: Writers and Readers, Ltd., 1997); and Jim Powell, *Postmodernism for Beginners* (Village Station, NY: Writers and Readers, Ltd., 1998).

52. I shall focus on the three books Derrida published in French in 1967: Jacques Derrida, *Of Grammatology* trans. Gayatri Spirak (Baltimore: Johns Hopkins University Press, 1976); Jacques Derrida, *Speech and Phenomena* trans. David Allison (Evanston, IL: Northwestern University, 1973); and Jacques Derrida, *Writing and Difference* trans. Alan Bass (London: Routledge and Kegan Paul, 1978).

53. Palmer, *Structuralism and Poststructuralism*, 143.

54. Powell, *Derrida*, 100–101.

55. Sarup, *An Introductory Guide*, 6.

56. My secondary sources are Sarup, *An Introductory Guide*, 1–31; Stuart Sim, (ed.), *The Routledge Critical Dictionary of Postmodern Thought* (New York: Routledge, 1999), 300–301; Burr, *Social Constructionism*, 155–158; Darian Leader and Judy Groves, *Introducing Lacan* (New York: Totem Books, 1995); Dana Breen, *The Gender Conundrum* (London: Routledge, 1993); Rosalind Minsky, *Psychoanalysis and Gender: An Introductory Reader* (London: Routledge, 1996), 137–177; Lynne Segal, *Straight Sex: Rethinking the Politics of Pleasure* (Berkeley and Los Angeles: University of California Press, 1994); Palmer, *Structuralism and Poststructuralism*; and Dr. Mary Klages, University of Colorado, Home Page, www.Colorado.edu/English/ENG201Klages

57. Jacques Lacan, *Ecrits: A Selection*, trans. A. Sheridan (London: Tavistock, 1977), 40–46.

58. Dani Cavallaro, *The Body for Beginners* (New York: Writers and Readers Publishing, 1998), 82.

59. Mary Klages, "Queer Theory," *English 2010 Home Page for Dr Mary Klages*, University of Colorado, last revision 29 October 1997. www.Colorado.edu/English/Eng201Klages

60. Mary Klages, "Jacques Lacan," *English 2010 Home Page for Dr Mary Klages*, University of Colorado, last revision 29 October 1997; Lynne Segal, *Straight Sex*, 131. www.Colorado.edu/English/Eng201Klages

61. Jacques Lacan, *The Seminar, Book III. The Psychoses*, trans. Russell Grigg (London: Routledge, 1993), 146.

62. Sarup, *An Introductory Guide*, 15.

63. Bruce Fink, *The Lacanian Subject: Between Language and Jouissance* (Princeton: Princeton University Press, 1995), 6.

64. Rosalind Minsky, *Psychoanalysis and Gender*, 142.

65. Jacques Lacan, "The Meaning of the Phallus" originally published in *Ecrits* (Paris: Sevil, 1966) 93–100, in Minsky, Rosalind, (ed.) *Psychoanalysis and Gender: An Introductory Reader*, trans. Jacqueline Rose (London: Routledge, 1996), 269–280.

66. Laura Mulvey, "Visual Pleasure and Narrative Cinema," *Screen* 16, no. 3, (1975), 6–18.

67. Parveen Adams, "Of Female Bondage," in *Between Feminism and Psychoanalysis*, (ed.) Teresa Brennan (London: Routledge, 1989).

68. Juliet Mitchell, *Psychoanalysis and Feminism* (London: Macmillan, 1974); and Juliet Mitchell and Jacqueline Rose, (eds.), *Jacques Lacan and the Ecole Freudienne: Feminine Sexuality* (London: Macmillan, 1982).

69. Ellie Ragland-Sullivan, *Jacques Lacan and the Philosophy of Psychoanalysis* (Urbana: University of Illinois Press, 1986).

70. Sarup, *An Introductory Guide*, 95.

71. Guy Hocquenghem, *Homosexual Desire*, trans. Daniella Dangoor (London: Allison and Busby, 1978), 117.

72. Luce Irigaray, *Speculum of the Other Woman*, trans. G. C. Gill (Ithaca: Cornell University Press, 1985); and Luce Iragaray, *This Sex Which Is Not One*, trans. C. Porter and C. Burke (Ithaca: Cornell University Press, 1985).

73. Helen Cixous, "The Laugh of the Medusa," trans. K. Cohen and P. Cohen, *Signs* 1, no. 4 (1976): 875–893.

74. Julia Kristeva, *The Kristeva Reader*, (ed.) Toril Moi (Oxford: Blackwell, 1986).

75. Minsky, *Psychoanalysis and Gender*, 160.

76. Stephen Frosh, *Sexual Difference: Masculinity and Psychoanalysis* (London: Routledge, 1994), 76.

77. Jacques Lacan, "Encore (Seminar XX)" (1972–1973) in Juliet Mitchell and Jacqueline Rose, (eds.), *Jacques Lacan and the Ecole Freudienne: Feminine Sexuality* (London: Macmillan, 1982), 137–161, originally published (Paris: Sevil, 1975).

78. Monique Wittig, "One Is Not Born a Woman," *Feminist Issues* 1, no. 1 (1980): 447–454.

79. Leo Bersani, "Is the Rectum a Grave," in *AIDS: Cultural Analysis/Cultural Activism*, (ed.) Douglas Crimp (Cambridge: MIT Press, 1988), 197–223.

80. Idea taken from Lynne Segal, *Straight Sex: Rethinking the Politics of Pleasure* (Berkeley and Los Angeles: University of California Press, 1994), 294.

81. Ibid., 193.

82. Jonathan Dollimore, *Sexual Dissidence: Augustine to Wilde; Freud to Foucault* (Oxford: Clarendon Press, 1991), 28.

83. Sigmund Freud, "Three Essays on the Theory of Sexuality" (1905) in James Strachey (ed.) *The Standard Edition of the Complete Psychological Works* (London: Hogarth, 1953–1974) Vol. 7, 125–245.

84. Ibid., 231.

85. Sigmund Freud, "New Introductory Lectures," (1933) in James Strachey (ed.) *The Standard Edition of the Complete Psychological Works of Sigmund Freud* (London: Hogarth, 1953–1974) Vol. 21, 223–246; pointed out by Judith Roof in *A Lure of Knowledge: Lesbian Sexuality and Theory* (New York: Columbia University Press, 1991), 209.

86. As quoted in Tamsin Spargo, *Foucault and Queer Theory* (Cambridge, UK: Icon Books, 1999), 13.

87. Turner, *Genealogy*, 107.

88. Dinitia Smith, "'Queer Theory' Is Entering the Literary Mainstream," *New York Times*, 17 January 1998, p. A15.

89. Eve Kosofsky Sedgwick, *Epistemiology of the Closet* (Berkeley and Los Angeles: University of California Press, 1990), 182–213.

90. Eve Kosofsky Sedgwick, *Between Men: English Literature and Male Homosocial Desire* (New York: Columbia University Press, 1985), 83–96.

91. Sedgwick, *Epistemiology*, 21.

92. Ibid., 1.
93. Eve Kosofsky Sedgwick, "Jane Austen and the Masturbating Girl," *Critical Inquiry* 17 (1991): 818–837.
94. Eve Kosofsky Sedgwick, *A Dialogue of Love* (Boston: Beacon Press, 1999).
95. Teresa De Lauretis, "Habit Changes," *differences*, 6, no. 2 (1994): 297.
96. Teresa De Lauretis, "Queer Theory: Lesbian and Gay Sexualities," *differences*, 3, no. 2 (1992): v.
97. Segal, *Straight Sex*, 203.
98. Jean Laplanche and Jean-Bertrande Pontalis, "Fantasies and Origins of Sexuality," in *Formations of Fantasy*, (eds.) Victor Burgin et al. (London: Methuen, 1986), 5–34.
99. Sigmund Freud, "A Child is Beaten: A Contribution to the Theory of Perversions" (1919) in James Strachey (ed.) *The Standard Edition of the Complete Psychological Works of Sigmund Freud* (London: Hogarth Press, 1953–1974), 17:175–204.
100. Teresa De Lauretis, *The Practice of Love: Lesbian Sexuality and Perverse Desire* (Bloomington: Indiana University Press, 1994), 79–149.
101. De Lauretis, "Habit Changes," 297.
102. Adam Phillips, *On Kissing, Tickling, and Being Bored* (Cambridge: Harvard University Press, 1993), xix.
103. Sigmund Freud, "Psychogenesis of a Case of Female Homosexuality" (1920) in James Strachey (ed.) *The Standard Edition of the Complete Psychological Works of Sigmund Freud* (London: Hogarth Press, 1953–1974), 18:145–172.
104. Teresa De Lauretis, " Letter to an Unknown Woman," in *That Obscure Object of Desire: Freud's Female Homosexual Revisited*, (eds.) Ronnie C. Lesser and Erica Schoenberg (New York: Routledge, 1999), 50.
105. I am using Elizabeth Grosz's reading of De Lauretis here: Elizabeth Grosz, "The Labor of Love: Analyzing Perverse Desire," *differences* 22 June 1994. Obtained from the internet via e-Library, now www.highbeam.com/library/docO.asp?.DOCID=1P1
106. Marjorie Garber, "Fetish Envy," *October* 54 (fall 1990): 45–56.
107. Naomi Schor, "Female Fetishism: The Case of George Sand" in *The Female Body in Western Culture*, (ed.) Susan Suleiman (Cambridge: Harvard University Press, 1986), 363–372.
108. Grosz, "Labor of Love," online (see above).
109. Judith Butler, *Gender Trouble: Feminism and the Subversion of Identity* (New York: Routledge, 1990).
110. Judith Butler, *Bodies That Matter: On the Discursive Limits of "Sex"* (New York: Routledge, 1993).
111. Judith Butler, "Extracts from Gender As Performance: An Interview with Judith Butler" interview by Peter Osborne and Lynne Segal, *Radical Philosophy* 67 (summer 1994). Online at: www.theory.org.uk/but-int1.htm
112. Butler, *Gender Trouble*, 13.
113. Ibid., 25.
114. Ibid., 140.
115. Ibid., 22.
116. Ibid., 107–109.
117. Judith Butler, "Contingent Foundations," in *Feminist Orientations*, (eds.) Selya Benhabib et al. (New York: Routledge, 1995), 47.
118. Judith Butler, "Performative Acts and Gender Construction: An Essay in Phenomenolgy and Feminist Theory," in *Performing Feminism*, (ed.) Sue Ellen Case (Baltimore: Johns Hopkins University Press, 1990), 270–282.
119. Butler, *Bodies*, 244.
120. Ibid., 93.
121. Ibid., 231.

122. For example: Judith Butler, "Response to Lynne Layton's 'The Doer behind the Deed: Tensions and Intersections between Butler's Vision of Performativity and Relational Psychoanalysis'" *Gender and Psychoanalysis* 2, no. 2 (1997), 518.

123. Michael Levenson, "Speaking to Power: The Performances of Judith Butler," *Lingua Franca* Vol. 8, no. 7 (September 1998): 61.

124. Ibid., 62.

125. Lynne Layton, *Who's That Girl? Who's That Boy: Clinical Practice Meets Postmodern Gender Theory* (Northvale, NJ: Jacob Aronson, 1998), 209.

126. Ibid., 224.

127. Butler elaborates this idea in Judith Butler, "Melancholy Gender—Refused Identification," *Psychoanalytic Dialogues* 5, no. 2 (1995): 165–180.

128. Judith Butler, "Gender Trouble, Feminist Theory, and Psychoanalytic Discourse," in *Feminism/Postmodernism*, (ed.) Linda Nicholson (New York: Routledge, 1990), 330.

129. Brad Epps, "The Fetish of Fluidity," in Tim Dean and Christopher Lane, (eds.), *Homosexuality and Psychoanalysis* (Chicago: University of Chicago Press, 2001), 412–431.

Notes to Chapter Five: Men Are From Earth, Women Are From Earth, and So Are Queers

1. Andrew Sullivan, "Washington Diarist: Revolution, Televised," *The New Republic*, 1 March 2004, 34.

2. Laura Sessions Stepp, "Partway Gay: For Some Teen Girls, Sexual Preference Is a Shifting Concept," *Washington Post*, Sunday, 4 January 2004, p. D01.

3. A few recent books grapple with this convergence: Thomas Domenici and Ronnie Lesser, (eds.), *Disorienting Sexuality: Psychoanalytic Reappraisals of Sexual Identities* (New York: Routledge, 1995); Anthony Elliot and Charles Spezzano, (eds.), *Psychoanalysis At Its Limits: Navigating the Postmodern Turn* (New York: Free Association, 2000); Muriel Dimen and Virginia Goldner, (eds.), *Gender in Psychoanalytic Space* (New York: Other Press, 2002); Susan Fairfield et al., (eds.), *Bringing the Plague: Toward a Postmodern Psychoanalysis* (New York: Other Press, 2002); Tim Dean and Christopher Lane, (eds.), *Homosexuality and Psychoanalysis* (Chicago: University of Chicago 2001); and Adria Schwartz, *Sexual Subjects: Lesbians, Gender, and Psychoanalysis* (New York: Routledge, 1998).

4. Joanna Ryan, "Reflections on 'Disorienting Sexuality,'" *Gender and Psychoanalysis* 2 no. 2 (1997): 182.

5. Elizabeth Grosz, *Volatile Bodies: Toward a Corporeal Feminism* (Bloomington: Indiana University Press, 1994).

6. Jane Gallop, *Thinking through the Body* (New York: Columbia University Press, 1988).

7. Sigmund Freud, "New Introductory Lectures," (1933) in James Strachey (ed.) *The Standard Edition of the Complete Works of Sigmund Freud* (London: Hogarth Press, 1953–1974), 22:130.

8. Dana Breen, (ed.), "Introduction," *The Gender Conundrum: Contemporary Psychoanalytic Perspectives on Femininity and Masculinity* (New York: Routledge, 1993), 3.

9. Sigmund Freud, "The Ego and the Id" (1923) in James Stachey (ed.) *The Standard Edition of the Complete Works of Sigmund Freud* (London: Hogarth Press, 1953–1974), 19:26.

10. Freud, *Standard Edition*, Vol. 22, 130.

11. Breen, *The Gender Conundrum*, 37.

12. Sigmund Freud, "Three Essays on the Theory of Sexuality," (1905) in James Strachey (ed.) *The Standard Edition of the Complete Works of Sigmund Freud* (London: Hogarth Press, 1953–1974), 7:147–148.

13. Rosalind Mirsky, *Psychoanalysis and Gender: An Introductory Reader* (London: Routledge, 1996), 35.

14. Freud, *Standard Edition*, Vol. 7, 145.

15. Sigmund Freud, "An Outline of Psychoanalysis," (1940) in James Strachey (ed.) *The Standard Edition of the Complete Works of Sigmund Freud* (London: Hogarth Press, 1953–1974), 23:152.

16. Sigmund Freud, "Instincts and Their Vicissitudes," (1915) in James Strachey (ed.) *The Standard Edition of the Complete Works of Sigmund Freud* (London: Hogarth Press, 1953–1974), 14:182.

17. Idea from Jeffrey Weeks, "Homosexuality," in 157–161.

18. Lynne Segal, *Straight Sex: Rethinking the Politics of Pleasure* (Berkeley and Los Angeles: University of California Press, 1994), 117–122.

19. Freud, *Standard Edition*, Vol. 7, 142.

20. Sigmund Freud, "Leonardo da Vinci and a Memory of His Childhood," (1910) in James Strachey (ed.) *The Standard Edition of the Complete Works of Sigmund Freud* (London: Hogarth Press, 1953–1974), 11:59–137.

21. Sigmund Freud, "An Analysis Terminable and Interminable," (1937) in James Strachey (ed.) *The Standard Edition of the Complete Works of Sigmund Freud* (London: Hogarth Press, 1953–1974), 23:251.

22. Malcolm Bowie, "Bisexuality," in *Feminism and Psychoanalysis*, (ed.) Elizabeth Wright (Cambridge, MA: Blackwell, 1992), 29.

23. Breen, *The Gender Conundrum*, 232.

24. Nancy Chodorow, *The Reproduction of Mothering: Psychoanalysis and the Sociology of Gender* (Berkeley and Los Angeles: University of California Press, 1978).

25. Fritz Morgenthaler, "Introduction to the Panel on Disturbances of Male and Female Identity as Met with in Psychoanalytic Practice," *International Journal of Psychoanalysis* 50 (1969): 109–112.

26. Irene Fast, *Gender Identity* (Hillsdale, NJ: Analytic Press, 1984).

27. Sigmund Freud, "The Ego and the Id" (1923) in James Strachey (ed.) *The Standard Edition of the Complete Works of Sigmund Freud* (London: Hogarth Press, 1953–1974), 19:3–68.

28. Carolyn Stack, "Psychoanalysis Meets Queer Theory: An Encounter with the Terrifying Other," *Gender and Psychoanalysis* 4, no. 1 (January 1999): 74.

29. Freud, *Standard Edition*, Vol. 23, 141–207.

30. Jeffrey Weeks, "Homosexuality," in *Feminism and Psychoanalysis*, (ed.) Elizabeth Wright (Cambridge, MA: Blackwell, 1992), 157.

31. Ernst Freud, (Ed.), *Letters of Sigmund Freud 1873–1939* (London: Hogarth, 1961).

32. Jeffrey Weeks, "Homosexuality," in *Feminism and Psychoanalysis*, (ed.) Elizabeth Wright (Cambridge, MA: Blackwell, 1992), 158; Kenneth Lewes, *The Psychoanalytical Theory of Male Homosexuality* (London: Quartet, 1988, 1995), 24–35.

33. Irving Bieber et al., *Homosexuality: A Psychoanalytic Study of Male Homosexuals* (New York: Basic Books, 1962).

34. As quoted in Kenneth Lewes, *The Psychoanalytical Theory of Male Homosexuality* (London: Quartet, 1988, 1995), 182.

35. Ibid., 108.

36. Charles Socarides, *The Overt Homosexual* (New York: Grune and Stratton, 1968).

37. Charles Socarides, "The Psychoanalytic Theory of Homosexuality with Special Reference to Therapy," in *Sexual Deviation*, (ed.) Ismond Rosen (Oxford: Oxford University Press, 1979).

38. Jeffrey Weeks, "Homosexuality" in *Feminism and Psychoanalysis*, (ed.) Elizabeth Wright, (Cambridge, MA: Blackwell, 1992), 159; Jean Laplanche and Jean-Baptiste Pontalis, *The Language of Psychoanalysis* (London: Hogarth Press, 1980).

39. Chodorow, *Reproduction*.

40. Jessica Benjamin, *The Bonds of Love: Psychoanalysis, Feminism, and the Problem of Domination* (New York: Pantheon, 1988).

41. Lewes, *Male Homosexuality*, 226.
42. Richard Friedman, *Male Homosexuality: A Contemporary Psychoanalytic Perspective* (New Haven, CT: Yale University Press, 1988).
43. Eve Kosofsky Sedgwick, *Tendencies* (Durham, NC: Duke University Press, 1993), 156.
44. Richard Isay, "The Development of Sexual Identity in Homosexual Men," *Psychoanalytic Study of the Child* 41 (1986): 467–489; and "The Homosexual Analyst," *Psychoanalytic Study of the Child* 46 (1991): 199–216.
45. Ken Corbett, "Homosexual Boyhoods," *Gender and Psychoanalysis* 1, no. 4, (1996): 429–461 and "Speaking Queer," *Gender and Psychoanalysis* 2, no. 4 (1997): 495–514.
46. Jennifer Downey and Richard Friedman, "Female Homosexuality: Classical Psychoanalytic Theory Reconsidered," *Journal of the American Psychoanalytic Association* 46, no. 2 (1998): 471–506.
47. Juliet Mitchell, *Psychoanalysis and Feminism* (London: Allan Lane, 1974).
48. Chodorow, *Reproduction*.
49. Benjamin, *The Bonds of Love*,.
50. Sigmund Freud, "Fragment of an Analysis of a Case of Hysteria," (1905) in James Strachey (ed.) *The Standard Edition of the Complete Works of Sigmund Freud* 1905 (London: Hogarth Press, 1953–1974), 7:3–124.
51. Sigmund Freud, "The Psychogenesis of a Case of Homosexuality in a Woman," (1920) in James Strachey (ed.) *The Standard Edition of the Complete Works of Sigmund Freud* (London: Hogarth Press, 1953–1974), 18:146–174.
52. Diana Fuss, "Fallen Women," in *That Obscure Object of Desire: Freud's Female Homosexual Revisited*, (eds.) Ronnie Lesser and Erica Schoenberg (New York: Routledge, 1999), 73.
53. Dianne Chisholm, "Lesbianism," in *Feminism and Psychoanalysis*, (ed.) Elizabeth Wright (Cambridge, MA: Blackwell, 1992), 218.
54. For an excellent review of psychoanalytic thinking about lesbianism, which guided my inquiry, see Noreen O'Connor and Joanna Ryan, *Wild Desires and Mistaken Identities Lesbianism and Psychoanalysis* (New York: Columbia University Press, 1993); as well as Beverly Burch, *On Intimate Terms: The Psychology of Difference in Lesbian Relationships* (Urbana and Chicago: University of Chicago Press, 1993); Adria Schwartz, *Sexual Subjects*; Judith Glassgold and Suzanne Iasenza, (eds.), *Lesbians and Psychoanalysis: Revolutions in Theory and Practice* (New York: Free Press, 1995); and Maggie Magee and Diana Miller, *Lesbian Lives, Psychoanalytic Narratives Old and New* (Mahwah, NJ: Analytic Press, 1997).
55. O'Connor and Ryan, *Wild Desires*, 174.
56. Juliet Mitchell and Jacqueline Rose (eds.), *Feminine Sexuality* Jacques Lacan and the École Freudieme, trans. Jacqueline Rose (London: Macmillan Press, 1982), 1–10.
57. Luce Irigaray, *This Sex Which Is Not One*, trans. Catherine Porter with Carolyn Burke (Ithaca: Cornell University Press, 1985).
58. Joanna Ryan, "Can Psychoanalysis Understand Homophobia?" in Tim Dean and Christopher Lane, (eds.), *Homosexuality and Psychoanalysis* (Chicago: University of Chicago, 2001), 307–321.
59. Jeanne Lampl-de Groot, "The Evolution of the Oedipal Complex in Women," *International Journal of Psychoanalysis* 9 (1928): 332–345.
60. Joanna Ryan, "Can Psychoanalysis Understand Homophobia?" in Tim Dean and Christopher Lane, (eds.), *Homosexuality and Psychoanalysis* (Chicago: University of Chicago, 2001), 313.
61. Janine Chasseguet-Smirgel, *Feminine Sexuality* (Ann Arbor, MI: University of Michigan, 1966); and Maria Torok, "The Significance of Penis Envy in Women." In Janine Chasseguet-Smirgel (ed.) *Female Sexuality* (Ann Arbor, MI: University of Michigan Press, 1970).

62. Joyce McDougall, *Plea for a Measure of Abnormality* (New York: International Universities Press, 1980), as quoted in Beverly Decker, "How To Have Your Phallus and Be It Too" in Judith Glassgold and Suzanne Iasenza, (eds.), *Lesbians and Psychoanalysis: Revolutions in Theory and Practice* (New York: Free Press, 1995), 78.

63. Joyce McDougall, "The Dead Father: On Early Psychic Trauma and Its Relation to Disturbance in Sexual Identity and in Creative Activity," *The International Journal of Psychoanalysis* 67 (1989): 205–219.

64. Joyce McDougall, *The Many Faces of Eros* (New York: Norton, 1995).

65. For example, Adrienne Harris, Ronnie Lesser, as noted in Domenici and Lesser, *Disorienting Sexuality*, xi–xv, and April Martiñ as noted in Domenici and Lesser, *Disorienting Sexuality*, 255–264.

66. See Jessica Benjamin, *Like Subjects, Love Objects: Essays on Recognition and Sexual Difference* (New Haven, CT: Yale University Press, 1995); and Nancy Chodorow, *Femininities, Masculinities, Sexualities: Freud and Beyond* (Lexington: University of Kentucky Press, 1994).

67. Judith Roof, *A Lure of Knowledge: Lesbian Sexuality and Theory* (New York: Columbia University Press, 1991).

68. Lewes, *The Psychoanalytic Theory*.

69. O'Connor and Ryan, *Wild Desires*.

70. Alex Comfort, *The Joy of Sex: A Gourmet Guide to Lovemaking* (New York: Octopus, 2002), 233. Originally published by Dr. Alex Comfort's father, Dr. Alex Comfort (New York: Crown, 1972).

71. Muriel Dimen, "The Disturbance of Sex: A Letter to Michael Bronski," in Susan Fairfield et al., (eds.), *Bringing the Plague: Toward a Postmodern Psychoanalysis* (New York: Other Press, 2002), 295–308.

72. Michael Bronski, "Dr. Fell," in Susan Fairfield et al., (eds.), *Bringing the Plague: Toward a Postmodern Psychoanalysis* (New York: Other Press, 2002), 279–294.

73. Muriel Dimen, "The Disturbance of Sex: A Letter to Michael Bronski," in Susan Fairfield et al., (eds.), *Bringing the Plague: Toward a Postmodern Psychoanalysis* (New York: Other Press, 2002), 98.

74. Louise Kaplan, *Female Perversions: The Temptations of Emma Bovary* (New York: Doubleday, 1991), 6–7.

75. Paul Gebhard, "Sadomasochism" in *Dynamics of Deviant Sexuality: Scientific Proceedings of the American Academy of Psychoanalysis*, (ed.) Jules Masserman (New York: Grune & Stratton, 1969), 77–80.

76. Kaplan, *Female Perversions*, 8–9.

77. Ibid., 76.

78. Sigmund Freud, "Fetishism," (1924) in John Strachey *The Standard Edition of the Complete Works of Sigmund Freud* 1927 (London: Hogarth Press 1953–1974), 21:147–158.

79. Janine Chasseguet-Smirgel, *Creativity and Perversion* (London: Free Association Press, 1985).

80. Joyce McDougall, "Primal Scene and Sexual Perversion," *International Journal of Psychoanalysis* 53, no. 2 (1972): 371–384.

81. Linda Williams, "Pornographies On/Screen" in *Sex Exposed: Sexuality and the Pornography Debate*, (eds.) Lynne Segal and Mary McIntosh (New Brunswick, NJ: Rutgers University Press, 1993), 243.

82. Janine Chasseguet-Smirgel, "Reflexions on the Connexions between Perversion and Sadism," *International Journal of Psychoanalysis* 59 (1978): 27–35.

83. Estela Welldon, *Mother, Madonna, Whore: The Idealization and Denigration of Motherhood* (London: Free Association Press, 1988), 7.

84. Elizabeth Grosz, "Fetishization," in *Feminism and Psychoanalysis: A Critical Dictionary*, (ed.) Elizabeth Wright (Cambridge, MA: Blackwell, 1992), 117–118.

85. Sara Kofman, *The Enigma of Woman: Woman in Freud's Writings*, trans. Catherine Porter (Ithaca, NY: Cornell, 1985).

86. Naomi Schor, "Female Fetishism: The Case of George Sand" in *The Female Body in Western Perspectives*, (eds.) Susan Suleiman and Susan Rubin (Cambridge: Harvard University Press, 1986) pages?.

87. Emily Apter, *Feminizing the Fetish: Psychoanalysis and Narrative Obsession in Turn-of-the Century France* (Ithaca, NY: Cornell, 1991).

88. Marjorie Garber, *Vested Interests: Cross-Dressing and Cultural Anxiety* (London: Routledge, 1992).

89. Lorraine Gammen and Merja Makinen, *Female Fetishism* (New York: New York University Press, 1995), 109–110.

90. Parveen Adams, "Of Female Bondage," in *Between Feminism and Psychoanalysis*, (ed.) Teresa Brennan (London: Routledge, 1989), 247–266.

91. Mandy Merck, *Perversions: Deviant Readings* (New York: Routledge, 1993), 242.

92. I am paraphrasing Mikkel Borc-Jacobsen from "Little Brother, Little Sister" *London Review of Books* 3, no. 10, 24 May 2001. http:/www.lrb.co.uk/v23/n1o/borc01_.html

93. Robert Stoller, *Observing the Erotic Imagination* (New Haven, CT: Yale University Press, 1985), 155.

94. Burness Moore and Bernard Fine, (eds.), *Psychoanalytic Terms and Concepts* (New Haven, CT: The American Psychoanalytic Association and Yale University Press, 1990), 142.

95. Ethel Spector Person, "Sexuality as the Mainstay of Identity: Psychoanalytic Perspectives," *Signs* 5, no. 4 (1980): 619, as quoted in Lynne Segal, *Straight Sex: Rethinking the Politics of Pleasure* (Berkeley and Los Angeles: University of California Press, 1994), 145.

96. Ethel Spector Person, *The Sexual Century* (New Haven, CT: Yale University Press, 1999), 334.

97. Robert Stoller, *Perversion: The Erotic Form of Hatred* (New York: Delta, 1975).

98. Ibid., 9.

99. Robert Stoller, *Sex and Gender: The Development of Masculinity and Femininity* (New York: Science House, 1968).

100. Ibid. Page?

101. Jessica Benjamin, "Sameness and Difference: An 'Overinclusive' View of Gender Constitution," in Muriel Dimen and Virginia Goldner, (eds.), *Gender in Psychoanalytic Space* (New York: Other Press, 2002), 181–207.

102. Stephen Mitchell, *Relational Concepts in Psychoanalysis* (Cambridge: Harvard University Press, 1988); and "Contemporary Perspectives on Self: Toward an Integration," *Psychoanalytic Dialogues* 1, no. 2 (1991): 121–147.

103. Virginia Goldner, "Toward a Critical Theory of Gender," *Psychoanalytic Dialogues* 1, no. 3 (1991): 249–272.

104. Muriel Dimen, "Deconstructing Difference: Gender, Splitting and Transitional Space," *Psychoanalytic Dialogues* 1, no. 3 (1991): 335–352.

105. Adrienne Harris, "Gender as Contradiction," *Psychoanalytic Dialogues* 1, no. 2 (1991): 197–224.

106. Schwartz, *Sexual Subjects*, xiii–12.

107. Jessica Benjamin, *The Shadow of the Other 1: Intersubjectivity and Gender in Psychoanalysis* (New York: Routledge, 1998).

108. Lewis Aron, "The Internalized Primal Scene," *Psychoanalytic Dialogues* 5, no.1 (1991): 195–237.

109. Thomas Ogden, *Subjects of Analysis* (Northvale, NJ: Aronson, 1994).

110. Owen Renik, "Analytic Interaction: Conceptualizing Technique in Light of the Analyst's Irreducible Subjectivity," *Psychoanalytic Quarterly* 62 (1993): 553–571.

111. Susan Fairfield, "Introduction: Culture and Coach," in *Bringing the Plague: Toward a Postmodern Psychoanalysis*, (eds.) Susan Fairfield et al. (New York: Other Press, 2002), 7.

112. Jessica Benjamin, "In Defense of Gender Ambiguity," *Gender and Psychoanalysis* 1, no. 1 (1996): 27–43.

113. Benjamin, *The Shadow*, 87–89 and 101–104.

114. Judith Butler, "Response to Lynne Layton's 'The Doer Behind the Deed,'" *Gender and Psychoanalysis* 2, no. 4 (1997): 515–520; Lynne Layton, "Reply to Judith Butler," *Gender and Psychoanalysis* 2, no. 4 (1997): 521–524.

115. David Schwartz, "Current Psychoanalytic Discourses on Sexuality: Tripping over the Body," in *Disorienting Sexuality*, (eds.) Thomas Domenici and Ronnie Lesser (New York: Routledge, 1995), 115–126.

BIBLIOGRAPHY

Abramson, Paul and Steven Pinkerton, eds. *Sexual Nature/Sexual Culture*. Chicago: University of Chicago Press, 1995.

Adams, Parveen. "Of Female Bondage." In *Between Feminism and Psychoanalysis*, edited by Teresa Brennan. London: Routledge, 1989.

Angier, Natalie. *Woman: An Intimate Geography*. New York: Anchor, 1999.

Apter, Emily. *Feminizing the Fetish: Psychoanalysis and Narrative Obsession in Turn-of-the Century France*. Ithaca, NY: Cornell University Press, 1991.

Aron, Lewis. "The Internalized Primal Scene." *Psychoanalytic Dialogues* 5, no. 1 (1991).

Bailey, J. Michael. "Biological Perspectives on Sexual Orientation." In *Lesbian, Gay, and Bisexual Identities over the Lifespan*, edited by Anthony D'Augelli and Charlotte Patterson. New York: Oxford University Press, 1995.

———. *The Man Who Would Be Queen: The Science of Gender-Bending and Transsexualism*. Washington, DC: Joseph Henry, 2003.

Bakhtin, Mikhail. *Rabelais and His World*. Translated by Helene Iswolsky. Cambridge, MA: MIT Press, 1968.

———. *The Dialogical Imagination*. Translated by Caryl Emerson and Michael Holquist. Austin: University of Texas Press, 1981.

Bakker, A., P. van Kesteren, L. Gooren, and P. Bezemer. "The Prevalence of Transsexualism in the Netherlands." *Acta Psychiatrica Scandinavica* 87 (1993).

Baudrillard, Jean. *Symbolic Exchange and Death*. Translated by Iain Hamilton Grant. London: Sage, 1976.

———. *Simulacra and Simulations*. Translated by Nicola Dufresne. New York: Semiotext(e), 1983.

BBC News, World Edition. "India's First Eunuch Mayor Unseated." 29 August 2002. By Charles Haviland. Available from http://news.bbc.co.uk/1/hi/world/south_asia/2224164.stm

Beam, Chris. "Living the Dream—Girls, Girls, Girls." Segment of episode 190 of the radio program *This American Life*. Broadcast on 3 August 2001.

Bem, Daryl. "Exotic Becomes Erotic: Integrating Biological and Experiential Antecedents of Sexual Orientation." *Archives of Sexual Behavior* 29, no. 6 (2000).

Bem, Sandra Lipsitz. "The Measurement of Psychological Androgyny." *Journal of Consulting and Clinical Psychology* 42 (1974).

———. *The Lenses of Gender: Transforming the Debate on Sexual Inequality*. New Haven: Yale University Press, 1993.

Benjamin, Jessica. *The Bonds of Love: Psychoanalysis, Feminism, and the Problem of Domination*. New York: Pantheon, 1988.

209

———. *Like Subjects, Love Objects: Essays on Recognition and Sexual Difference.* New Haven: Yale University Press, 1995.

———. "In Defense of Gender Ambiguity." *Gender and Psychoanalysis* 1, no. 1 (1996).

———. *The Shadow of the Other: Intersubjectivity and Gender in Psychoanalysis.* New York: Routledge, 1998.

———. "Sameness and Difference: An 'Overinclusive' View of Gender Constitution." In *Gender in Psychoanalytic Space,* edited by Muriel Dimen and Virginia Goldner. New York: Other Press, 2002.

Berendt, John. "High Heel Neil." *New Yorker,* 16 January 1995.

Berger, John. *Ways of Seeing.* London: BBC and Penguin, 1972.

Bersani, Leo. "Is the Rectum a Grave?" In *AIDS: Cultural Analysis/Cultural Activism,* edited by Douglas Crimp. Cambridge, MA: MIT Press, 1988.

Bieber, Irving, Harvey Dain, Paul Dince, Marvin Drellich, Henry Grand, Ralph Grundlach, Malvina Kremer, Alfred Rifkin, Cornelia Wilbur, and Tony Bieber. *Homosexuality: A Psychoanalytic Study of Male Homosexuals.* New York: Basic Books, 1962.

Blackwood, Evelyn, ed. *Anthropology and Homosexual Behavior.* New York: Haworth, 1986.

Blanchard, Ray, and Anthony Bogaert. "Homosexuality in Men and Number of Older Brothers." *American Journal of Psychiatry* 153 (January 1996).

Bloom, Amy. *Normal: Transsexual CEOs, Crossdressing Cops, and Hermaphrodites with Attitude.* New York: Random House, 2002.

Blum, Deborah. *Sex on the Brain: The Biological Differences between Men and Women.* New York: Penguin, 1997.

Blumstein, Philip, and Pepper Schwartz. *American Couples: Money, Work, Sex.* New York: Pocket Books, 1983.

Bolin, Anne. "Transforming Transvestism and Transsexuals: Polarity, Politics, and Gender." In *Gender Blending: Transgender Issues in Today's World,* edited by Bonnie Bullough, Vern Bullough, and James Elias. Amherst, NY: Prometheus, 1997.

Borch-Jacobsen, Mikkel. "Little Brother, Little Sister." *London Review of Books* 3, no. 10 (2001). Available from http://www.lrb.co.uk.

Bordo, Susan. *The Male Body.* New York: Farrar, Straus, and Giroux, 1999.

Bornstein, Kate. *Gender Outlaw: On Men, Women, and the Rest of Us.* New York: Vintage, 1994.

Bowie, Malcolm. "Bisexuality." In *Feminism and Psychoanalysis: A Critical Dictionary,* edited by Elizabeth Wright. Cambridge, MA: Blackwell, 1992.

Boyd, Andrew. *Life's Little Deconstruction Book.* New York: Norton, 1999.

Brannon, Linda. *Gender: Psychological Perspectives.* Needham Heights, MA: Allyn and Bacon, 1996.

Breedlove, S. Marc. "Review: Sex on the Brain: The Biological Differences between Men and Women," *Nature* 389, 23 October 1997.

Brennan, Teresa, ed. *Between Feminism and Psychoanalysis.* London: Routledge, 1989.

Breen, Dana, ed. *The Gender Conundrum: Contemporary Psychoanalytic Perspectives on Femininity and Masculinity.* London: Routledge, 1993.

Bronski, Michael. "Dr. Fell." In *Bringing the Plague: Toward a Postmodern Psychoanalysis,* edited by Susan Fairfield, Lynne Layton, and Carolyn Stack. New York: Other Press, 2002.

Brown, Rita Mae. "The Shape of Things to Come." In *Out of the Past: Gay and Lesbian History from 1869 to the Present,* edited by Neil Miller. New York: Vintage, 1995.

Brubach, Holly. *Girlfriends: Men, Women, and Drag.* New York: Random House, 1999.

Bullough, Bonnie, and Vern Bullough. "Men Who Cross-Dress: A Survey." In *Gender Blending: Transgender Issues in Today's World,* edited by Bonnie Bullough, Vern Bullough, and James Elias. Amherst, NY: Prometheus, 1997.

Bullough, Bonnie, Vern Bullough, and James Elias, eds. *Gender Blending: Transgender Issues in Today's World.* Amherst, NY: Prometheus, 1997.

Burch, Beverly. *On Intimate Terms: The Psychology of Difference in Lesbian Relationships.* Urbana and Chicago: University of Chicago Press, 1993.

Burgin, Victor et al., eds. *Formations of Fantasy.* London: Methuen, 1986.

Burke, Phyllis. *Gender Shock: Exploding the Myth of Male and Female.* New York: Anchor, 1996.

Burr, Chandler. *A Separate Creation: The Search for the Biological Origins of Sexual Orientation.* New York: Hyperion, 1996.

Burr, Vivien. *An Introduction to Social Constructionism.* London: Routledge, 1995.

Butler, Judith. *Gender Trouble: Feminism and the Subversion of Identity.* New York: Routledge, 1990.

———. "Gender Trouble, Feminist Theory, and Psychoanalytic Discourse." In *Feminism/ Postmodernism*, edited by Linda Nicholson. New York: Routledge, 1990.

———. "Performative Acts and Gender Construction: An Essay in Phenomenology and Feminist Theory." In *Performing Feminism*, edited by Sue Ellen Case. Baltimore: Johns Hopkins University Press, 1990.

———. "Contingent Foundations: Feminism and the Question of 'Postmodernism.'" In *Feminists Theorize the Political*, edited by Judith Butler and Joan Scott. New York: Routledge, 1992.

———. *Bodies That Matter: On the Discursive Limits of "Sex."* New York: Routledge, 1993.

———. "Melancholy Gender—Refused Identification." *Psychoanalytic Dialogues* 5, no. 2 (1995).

———. "Response to Lynne Layton's 'The Doer behind the Deed: Tensions and Intersections between Butler's Vision of Performativity and Relational Psychoanalysis.'" *Gender and Psychoanalysis* 2, no. 4 (1997).

———. and Joan Scott, eds. *Feminists Theorize the Political.* New York: Routledge, 1992.

Byne, William. "Why We Cannot Conclude That Sexual Orientation Is Primarily a Biological Phenomenon." *Journal of Homosexuality* 34, no. 1 (1997).

Cabaj, Robert and Terry Stein, eds. *Textbook of Homosexuality and Mental Health.* Washington DC: American Psychiatry Press, 1996.

Carlat, D., C. Camargo, and D. Herzog. "Eating Disorders in Males." *American Journal of Psychiatry* 154, no. 8 (1997).

Case, Sue Ellen, ed. *Performing Feminism.* Baltimore: Johns Hopkins University Press, 1990.

Cavallaro, Dana. *Critical and Cultural Theory.* New Brunswick, NJ: Althone, 2001.

Cavallaro, Dani. *The Body for Beginners.* New York: Writers and Readers, 1998.

Chasseguet-Smirgel, Janine. *Feminine Sexuality.* Ann Arbor, MI: University of Michigan, 1966.

———. *Female Sexuality*, ed. Ann Arbor, MI: University of Michigan, 1970.

———. "Reflexions on the Connexions between Perversion and Sadism." *International Journal of Psychoanalysis* 59 (1978).

———. *Creativity and Perversion.* London: Free Association, 1985.

Chisholm, Dianne. "Lesbianism." In *Feminism and Psychoanalysis: A Critical Dictionary*, edited by Elizabeth Wright. Cambridge, MA: Blackwell, 1992.

Chodorow, Nancy. *The Reproduction of Mothering: Psychoanalysis and the Sociology of Gender.* Berkeley: University of California Press, 1978.

———. *Feminism and Psychoanalysis.* New Haven: Yale University Press, 1989.

———. *Femininities, Masculinities, Sexualities: Freud and Beyond.* Lexington: University of Kentucky Press, 1994.

Cixous, Helen. "The Laugh of the Medusa." Translated by K. Cohen and P. Cohen. *Signs* 1, no. 4 (1976).

Colapinto, John. *As Nature Made Him: The Boy Who Was Raised As a Girl.* New York: HarperCollins, 2000.

Comfort, Alex. *The Joy of Sex: A Gourmet Guide to Lovemaking.* New York: Octopus, 2002. Originally published by Alex Comfort's father, Dr. Alex Comfort. New York: Crown, 1972.

Conley, Verena A., ed. *Re-thinking Technologies*. Minneapolis: University of Minnesota Press, 1993.

Corbett, Ken. "Homosexual Boyhood: Notes on Girlyboys." *Gender and Psychoanalysis* 1, no. 4 (1996).

———. "Speaking Queer." *Gender and Psychoanalysis* 2, no. 4 (1997).

Corbett, Sara. "When Debbie Met Christina, Who Then Became Chris." *New York Times Magazine*, 14 October 2001.

Coyne, Jerry A. "The Fairy Tales of Evolutionary Psychology: Of Vice and Men." *New Republic*, 3 April 2000.

Crain, Caleb. "Pleasure Principles." *Lingua Franca*, October 1997.

Creekmur, Corey and Alexander Doty, eds. *Out In Culture: Gay, Lesbian and Queer Essays on Popular Culture*. Durham, NC: Duke University Press, 1995.

D'Augelli, Anthony and Charlotte Patterson, eds. *Lesbian, Gay, and Bisexual Identities Over the Lifespan*. New York: Oxford University Press, 1995.

De Beauvoir, Simone. *The Second Sex*. Toronto: Bantam, 1964. First American edition translated and edited by H.M. Parsley. New York: Knopf, 1952.

De Lauretis, Teresa. "Queer Theory: Lesbian and Gay Sexualities." *differences* 3, no. 2 (1992).

———. "Habit Changes." *differences* 6, no. 2 (1994).

———. *The Practice of Love: Lesbian Sexuality and Perverse Desire*. Bloomington: Indiana University Press, 1994.

———. "Letter to an Unknown Woman." In *That Obscure Object of Desire: Freud's Female Homosexual Revisited*, edited by Ronnie C. Lesser and Erica Schoenberg. New York: Routledge, 1999.

Dean, Tim, and Christopher Lane, eds. *Homosexuality and Psychoanalysis*. Chicago: University of Chicago, 2001.

Decker, Beverly. "How to Have Your Phallus and Be It Too." In *Lesbians and Psychoanalysis: Revolutions in Theory and Practice*, edited by Judith Glassgold and Suzanne Iasenza. New York: Free Press, 1995.

Deleuze, Gilles, and Felix Guattari. *Anti-Oedipus: Capitalism and Schizophrenia*. Translated by Robert Hurley, Mark Seem, and Helen Lane. Minneapolis: University of Minnesota Press, 1983.

Derrida, Jacques. *Of Grammatolgy*. Translated by Gayatri Spivak. Baltimore, MD: Johns Hopkins University Press, 1976.

———. *Speech and Phenomenon*. Translated by David Allison. Chicago: University of Chicago Press, 1978.

———. *Writing and Difference*. Translated by Alan Bass. Chicago: University of Chicago Press, 1978.

DiCarlo, John. "The Gym Body and Heroic Myth." *Harvard Gay and Lesbian Review* 8, no. 4 (2002).

Dimen, Muriel. "Deconstructing Difference: Gender, Splitting and Transitional Space." *Psychoanalytic Dialogues* 1, no. 3 (1991).

———. "The Disturbance of Sex: A Letter to Michael Bronski." In *Bringing the Plague: Toward a Postmodern Psychoanalysis*, edited by Susan Fairfield, Lynne Layton, and Carolyn Stack. New York: Other Press, 2002.

Dimen, Muriel, and Virginia Goldner, eds. *Gender in Psychoanalytic Space*. New York: Other Press, 2002.

Doane, Mary Ann. "Masquerade Reconsidered: Further Thoughts on the Female Spectator." *Discourse* 11 (Fall/Winter 1988/89).

Dollimore, Jonathan. *Sexual Dissidence: Augustine to Wilde; Freud to Foucault*. Oxford: Clarendon, 1991.

Domenici, Thomas, and Ronnie Lesser, eds. *Disorienting Sexuality: Psychoanalytic Reappraisals of Sexual Identities*. New York: Routledge, 1995.

Dormer, Gunter. *Hormones and Brain Differentiation.* Amsterdam: Elsevier, 1976.

Downey, Jennifer, and Richard Friedman. "Female Homosexuality: Classical Psychoanalytic Theory Reconsidered." *Journal of the American Psychoanalytic Association* 46, no. 2 (1998).

Dreger, Alice Dumurat. *Hermaphrodites and the Medical Invention of Sex.* Cambridge, MA: Harvard University Press, 1998.

Drescher, Jack: *Psychoanalytic Therapy and the Gay Man.* NJ: Analytic Press, 1998.

Elliot, Anthony, and Charles Spezzano, eds. *Psychoanalysis at Its Limits: Navigating the Postmodern Turn.* New York: Free Association, 2000.

Elmer-Dewitt, Philip. "On a Screen Near You: Cyberporn." *Time,* 3 July 1995.

Endicott, Karen. "Post-What?!?" *Dartmouth Alumni Magazine,* December 1998.

Epps, Brad. "The Fetish of Fluidity." In *Homosexuality and Psychoanalysis,* edited by Tim Dean and Christopher Lane. Chicago: University of Chicago, 2001.

Eugenides, Jeffrey. *Middlesex.* New York: Farrar, Straus, and Giroux, 2002.

Fairfield, Susan. "Analyzing Subjectivity: A Postmodern Perspective on Some Current Psychoanalytic Theories of Subjectivity." In *Bringing the Plague: Toward a Postmodern Psychoanalysis,* edited by Susan Fairfield, Lynne Layton, and Carolyn Stack. New York: Other Press, 2002.

Fairfield, Susan, Lynne Layton, and Carolyn Stack, eds. *Bringing the Plague: Toward a Postmodern Psychoanalysis.* New York: Other Press, 2002.

Fast, Irene. *Gender Identity.* Hillsdale, NJ: Analytic Press, 1984.

Fausto-Sterling, Anne. "The Five Sexes: Revisited." *The Sciences,* July/August 2000.

———. *Sexing the Body: Gender Politics and the Construction of Sexuality.* New York: Basic Books, 2000.

Fausto-Sterling, Anne, and Evan Balaban. "Genetics and Male Sexual Orientation." *Science* 261 (1993).

Ferveur, Jean-Francois, et al. "Genetic Feminization of Brain Structures and Changed Sexual Orientation in Male Drosophila." *Science* 267 (1995).

Fillingham, Lydia. *Foucault for Beginners.* New York: Writers and Readers, 1993.

Findlay, Heather. "Freud's 'Fetishism' and the Lesbian Dildo Debates." In *Out in Culture: Gay, Lesbian, and Queer Essays on Popular Culture,* edited by Corey Creekmur and Alexander Doty. Durham, NC: Duke University Press, 1995.

Fink, Bruce. *The Lacanian Subject: Between Language and Jouissance.* Princeton, NJ: Princeton University Press, 1995.

Foucault, Michel. *Madness and Civilization: A History of Insanity in the Age of Reason.* Translated by Richard Howard. New York: Random House, 1965.

———. *The History of Sexuality.* vol. 1, *An Introduction.* Translated by Robert Hurley. New York: Pantheon, 1978.

———. *Discipline and Punish: The Birth of the Prison.* Translated by Alan Sheridan. New York: Vintage, 1979.

———. "On the Genealogy of Ethics: An Overview of Work in Progress." In *Michel Foucault: Beyond Structuralism and Hermeneutics,* 2nd ed., edited by Hubert Dreyfus and Paul Rabinow. Chicago: University of Chicago Press, 1983.

France, David. "An Inconvenient Woman." *New York Times Magazine,* 28 May 2000.

Freud, Ernst, ed. *Letters of Sigmund Freud, 1873–1939.* London: Hogarth, 1961.

Freud, Sigmund. "The Most Prevalent Form of Degradation in Erotic Life." In *Sexuality and the Psychology of Love,* edited by Philip Rieff; translated by Joan Riviere. New York: Simon & Schuster, 1963, originally published in *International Journal of Psychoanalysis,* vol. 9, 128.

———. "An Analysis Terminable and Interminable" (1937). In *The Standard Edition of the Complete Psychological Works of Sigmund Freud,* edited by James Strachey, vol. 23. London: Hogarth, 1953–1974.

———. "A Child Is Beaten: A Contribution to the Theory of Perversions" (1919). In *The Standard Edition of the Complete Psychological Works of Sigmund Freud*, edited by James Strachey, vol. 17. London: Hogarth, 1953–1974.

———. "The Ego and the Id" (1923). In *The Standard Edition of the Complete Psychological Works of Sigmund Freud*, edited by James Strachey, vol. 19. London: Hogarth, 1953–1974.

———. "Fetishism" (1927). In *The Standard Edition of the Complete Psychological Works of Sigmund Freud*, edited by James Strachey, vol. 21. London: Hogarth, 1953–1974.

———. "Fragment of an Analysis of a Case of Hysteria" (1905). In *The Standard Edition of the Complete Psychological Works of Sigmund Freud*, edited by James Strachey, vol. 7. London: Hogarth, 1953–1974.

———. "Instincts and Their Vicissitudes" (1915) In The *Standard Edition of the Complete Psychological Works of Sigmund Freud*, edited by James Strachey, vol. 14. London: Hogarth, 1953–1974.

———. "Leonardo da Vinci and a Memory of His Childhood" (1910). In *The Standard Edition of the Complete Psychological Works of Sigmund Freud*, edited by James Strachey, vol. 11. London: Hogarth, 1973–1974.

———. "New Introductory Lectures" (1933). In *The Standard Edition of the Complete Psychological Works of Sigmund Freud*, edited by James Strachey, vol. 22. London: Hogarth, 1953–1974.

———. "An Outline of Psychoanalysis" (1940). In *The Standard Edition of the Complete Psychological Works of Sigmund Freud*, edited by James Strachey, vol. 23. London: Hogarth, 1973–1954.

———. "The Psychogenesis of a Case of Homosexuality in a Woman" (1920). In *The Standard Edition of the Complete Psychological Works of Sigmund Freud*, edited by James Strachey, vol. 18. London: Hogarth, 1953–1974.

———. *Three Essays on the Theory of Sexuality* (1905). In *The Standard Edition of the Complete Psychological Works of Sigmund Freud*, edited by James Strachey, vol. 7. London: Hogarth, 1953–1974.

———. "The 'Uncanny'"(1917). In *The Standard Edition of the Complete Psychological Works of Sigmund Freud*, edited by James Strachey, vol. 17. London: Hogarth, 1953–1979.

Friedman, Richard. *Male Homosexuality: A Contemporary Psychoanalytic Perspective*. New Haven: Yale University Press, 1988.

Frosh, Stephen. *Sexual Difference: Masculinity and Psychoanalysis*. London: Routledge, 1994.

Fuss, Diana. "Fallen Women." In *That Obscure Object of Desire: Freud's Female Homosexual Revisited*, edited by Ronnie Lesser and Erica Schoenberg. New York: Routledge, 1999.

Gallop, Jane. *Thinking through the Body*. New York: Columbia University Press, 1988.

Gammen, Lorraine, and Merja Makinen. *Female Fetishism*. New York: New York University Press, 1995.

Garber, Marjorie. "Fetish Envy." *October* 54 (Fall 1990).

———. *Vested Interests: Cross-Dressing and Cultural Anxiety*. London and New York: Routledge, 1992.

———. *Vice Versa: Bisexuality and the Eroticism of Everyday Life*. New York: Simon and Schuster, 1995.

Gebhard, Paul. "Sadomasochism." In *Dynamics of Deviant Sexuality: Scientific Proceedings of the American Academy of Psychoanalysis*, edited by Jules Masserman. New York: Grune and Stratton, 1969.

Gilligan, Carol. *In a Different Voice: Women's Conception of the Self and Morality*. Cambridge, MA: Harvard University Press, 1982.

Gilligan, Carol, N. Lyons, and T. Hanmer, eds. *Making Connections: The Relational World of Adolescent Girls at the Emma Willard School.* Cambridge, MA: Harvard University Press, 1990.

Gitlin, Todd. "Postmodernism Defined at Last!" *Utne Reader* (July/August, 1989).

Glassgold, Judith, and Suzanne Iasenza, eds. *Lesbians and Psychoanalysis: Revolutions in Theory and Practice.* New York: Free Press, 1995.

Goldner, Virginia. "Toward a Critical Theory of Gender." *Psychoanalytic Dialogues* 1, no. 3 (1991).

Gonzalez, Francisco, and Olivia Espin. "Latino Men, Latina Women, and Homosexuality." In *Textbook of Homosexuality and Mental Health,* edited by Robert Cabaj and Terry Stein. Washington, DC: American Psychiatric Association Press, 1996.

Gorski, Roger A., J. H. Gordon, J. E. Shryne, and A. M. Southam. "Evidence for a Morphological Sex Difference within the Medial Preoptic Area of the Rat Brain." *Brain Research* 148 (1978).

Green, Richard. *The "Sissy Boy" Syndrome and the Development of Homosexuality.* New Haven: Yale University Press, 1987.

Grosz, Elizabeth. "The Body." In *Feminism and Psychoanalysis: A Critical Dictionary,* edited by Elizabeth Wright. Cambridge, MA: Blackwell, 1992.

———. "Fetishization." In *Feminism and Psychoanalysis: A Critical Dictionary,* edited by Elizabeth Wright. Cambridge, MA: Blackwell, 1992.

———. "Labors of Love: Analyzing Perverse Desire." *differences* 6, nos. 2 and 3 (1994).

———. *Volatile Bodies: Toward a Corporeal Feminism.* Bloomington, IN: Indiana University Press, 1994.

Hacker, Andrew. "Gays and Genes." *New York Review of Books,* 27 March 2003.

Hall, J., and D. Kimura. "Sexual Orientation and Performance on Sexually Dimorphic Motor Tasks." *Archives of Sexual Behavior* 24 (1995).

Halperin, David. *Saint Foucault: Towards a Gay Hagiography.* New York: Oxford University Press, 1995.

Hamer, Dean, et al. "A Linkage between DNA Markers on the X Chromosome and Male Sexual Orientation." *Science* 261 (1993).

Handy, Bruce. "A *Spy* Guide to Postmodern Everything." *Utne Reader,* (July, August 1989).

Haraway, Donna J. "Cyborg Manifesto: Science, Technology, and Socialist-Feminism in the Late Twentieth Century." In her *Simians, Cyborgs, and Women: The Reinvention of Nature.* New York: Routledge, 1991.

Harlow, John. "Hollywood Actresses Find It Pays to Be Gay." *Sunday Times (London),* 9 July 2000.

Harris, Adrienne. "Gender as Contradiction." *Psychoanalytic Dialogues* 1, no. 2 (1991).

Herdt, Gilbert. "Developmental Discontinuities and Sexual Orientation across Cultures." In *Homosexuality/Heterosexuality: Concepts of Sexual Orientation,* edited by D. P. McWhorter, S. Sanders, and J. M. Reinisch. New York: Oxford University Press, 1990.

———, ed. *Third Sex, Third Gender.* New York: Zone, 1996.

Hocquenghem, Guy. *Homosexual Desire.* Translated by Daniella Dangoor. London: Allison and Busby, 1978.

Hogan, Steve, and Lee Hudson, eds. *Completely Queer: The Gay and Lesbian Encyclopedia.* New York: Holt, 1998.

Hollander, Anne. *Feeding the Eye.* New York: Farrar, Straus, and Giroux, 1999.

Horton, Richard. "Is Homosexuality Inherited?" *New York Review of Books,* 13 July 1995.

Irigaray, Luce. *This Sex Which Is Not One.* Translated by Catherine Porter with Carolyn Burke. Ithaca, NY: Cornell University Press, 1977.

———. *Speculum of the Other Woman.* Translated by G. C. Gill. Ithaca, NY: Cornell University Press, 1985.

Isay, Richard. "The Development of Sexual Identity in Homosexual Men." *Psychoanalytic Study of the Child* 41 (1986).

———. "The Homosexual Analyst." *Psychoanalytic Study of the Child* 46 (1991).

Jagose, Annamarie. *Queer Theory: An Introduction.* New York: New York University Press, 1996.

Kaminer, Wendy. "Feminism's Identity Crisis." *Atlantic Monthly,* October 1993.

Kaplan, Louise. *Female Perversions: The Temptations of Emma Bovary.* New York: Doubleday, 1991.

Kessler, Suzanne, and Wendy McKenna. *Gender: An Ethnomethodological Approach.* Chicago: University of Chicago Press, 1978.

Kitzinger, Celia. "Social Constructionism: Implications for Lesbian and Gay Psychology." In *Lesbian, Gay, and Bisexual Identities over the Lifespan,* edited by Anthony D'Augelli and Charlotte Patterson. New York: Oxford University Press, 1995.

Klages, Mary. "Jacques Lacan." *English 201: Modern Critical Thought.* University of Colorado at Boulder. Available from http://www.colorado.edu.

———. "Queer Theory." *English 201: Modern Critical Thought.* University of Colorado at Boulder. Available from http://www.colorado.edu.

Kling, K., J. Hyde, C. Showers, and B. Buswell. "Gender differences in Self-Esteem: A Meta-Analysis." *Psychological Bulletin* 125 (1999).

Kofman, Sara. *The Enigma of Woman: Woman in Freud's Writings.* Translated by Catherine Porter. Ithaca, NY: Cornell University Press, 1985.

Kristeva, Julia. *The Kristeva Reader.* Edited by Toril Moi. Oxford: Blackwell, 1986.

Lacan, Jacques. *Ecrits: A Selection.* Translated by A. Sheridan. London: Tavistock, 1977.

———. "Encore (Seminar XX)." In *Jacques Lacan and the Ecole Freudienne: Feminine Sexuality,* edited by Juliet Mitchell and Jacqueline Rose. London: Macmillan, 1982.

———. *The Seminar, Book III: The Psychoses.* Translated by Russell Grigg. London: Routledge, 1993.

———. "The Meaning of the Phallus." Translated by Jacqueline Rose. In *Psychoanalysis and Gender: An Introductory Reader,* edited by Rosalind Minsky. London: Routledge, 1996.

Lampl-de Groot, Jeanne. "The Evolution of the Oedipal Complex in Women." *International Journal of Psychoanalysis* 9 (1928).

Laplanche, Jean, and Jean-Baptiste [Jean-Bertrand] Pontalis. *The Language of Psychoanalysis.* London: Hogarth, 1980.

———. "Fantasies and Origins of Sexuality." In *Formations of Fantasy,* edited by Victor Burgin, James Donald, and Cora Kaplan. London: Methuen, 1986.

Laqueur, Thomas. *Making Sex: Body and Gender from the Greeks to Freud.* Cambridge, MA: Harvard University Press, 1990.

Laumann, E., J. Gagnon, R. Michael, et al. *The Social Organization of Sexuality: Sexual Practices in the United States.* Chicago: University of Chicago Press, 1994.

Layton, Lynne. "Reply to Judith Butler." *Gender and Psychoanalysis* 2, no. 4 (1997).

———. *Who's That Girl? Who's That Boy: Clinical Practice Meets Postmodern Gender Theory.* Northvale, NJ: Jason Aronson, 1998.

Le Brun, Annie. *Sade: A Sudden Abyss.* Translated by Camille Nash. San Francisco: City Lights, 1990.

Leader, Darian, and Judy Groves. *Introducing Lacan.* New York: Totem, 1995.

Lehman, David. *Signs of the Times: Deconstruction and the Fall of Paul de Man.* New York: Poseidon, 1991.

Leland, John, and Mark Miller. "Can Gays 'Convert'?" *Newsweek,* 17 August 1998.

Lemert, Charles. *Postmodernism Is Not What You Think.* Malden, MA: Blackwell, 1997.

Lesser, Ronnie and Erica Schoenberg, eds. *That Obscure Object of Desire: Freud's Female Homosexual Revisited.* New York: Routledge, 1999.

LeVay, Simon. "A Difference in Hypothalamic Structure between Heterosexual and Homosexual Men." *Science* 253 (1991).

———. *Queer Science: The Use and Abuse of Research into Homosexuality.* Cambridge, MA: MIT Press, 1996.

Levenson, Michael. "Speaking to Power: The Performances of Judith Butler." *Lingua Franca,* September 1998.

Lewes, Kenneth. *The Psychoanalytical Theory of Male Homosexuality.* London: Quartet, 1988.

Lorber, Judith, *Paradoxes of Gender.* New Haven: Yale University Press, 1994.

Lyotard, Jean-Francois. *The Postmodern Condition: A Report on Knowledge.* Translated by Geoff Bennington and Brian Massumi. Minneapolis: University of Minnesota Press, 1979.

Magee, Miller, and Diana Miller. *Lesbian Lives: Psychoanalytic Narratives Old and New.* Mahwah, NJ: Analytic Press, 1997.

Mansfeld, Alan, and Barbara McGinn. "Pumping Iron: The Muscular and the Feminine." In *Body Matters,* edited by Sue Scott and David Morgan. London: Falmer, 1993.

Masserman, Jules, ed. Dynamics of Deviant Sexuality: Scientific Proceedings of the American of Psychoanalysis. New York: Grune & Stratton, 1969.

McCloskey, Deirdre. *Crossing: A Memoir.* Chicago: University of Chicago Press, 1999.

McDougall, Joyce. "Primal Scene and Sexual Perversion." *International Journal of Psychoanalysis* 53, no. 2 (1972).

———. *Plea for a Measure of Abnormality.* New York: International Universities Press, 1980.

———. "The Dead Father: On Early Psychic Trauma and Its Relation to Disturbance in Sexual Identity and in Creative Activity." *International Journal of Psychoanalysis* 67 (1989).

———. *The Many Faces of Eros.* New York: Norton, 1995.

McWhirter, D.P. et al., eds. *Homosexuality/Heterosexuality: Concepts of Sexual Orientation.* New York: Oxford University Press, 1990.

Merck, Mandy. *Perversions: Deviant Readings.* New York: Routledge, 1993.

Meyer-Bahlburg, Heino. "Psychoendocrinology and Sexual Pleasure: The Aspect of Sexual Orientation." In *Sexual Nature, Sexual Culture,* edited by Paul Abramson and Steven Pinkerton. Chicago: University of Chicago Press, 1995.

Meyerowitz, Joanne. *How Sex Changed.* Cambridge, MA: Harvard University Press, 2002.

Miller, Neil. *Out of the Past: Gay and Lesbian History from 1869 to the Present.* New York: Vintage, 1995.

Minsky, Rosalind, ed. *Psychoanalysis and Gender: An Introductory Reader.* London: Routledge, 1996.

Mitchell, Juliet. *Psychoanalysis and Feminism.* London: Macmillan, 1974.

Mitchell, Juliet, and Jacqueline Rose, eds. *Jacques Lacan and the Ecole Freudienne: Feminine Sexuality.* London: Macmillan, 1982.

Mitchell, Stephen. *Relational Concepts in Psychoanalysis.* Cambridge, MA: Harvard University Press, 1988.

———. "Contemporary Perspectives on Self: Toward an Integration." *Psychoanalytic Dialogues* 1, no. 2 (1991).

Moore, Burness, and Bernard Fine, eds. *Psychoanalytic Terms and Concepts.* New Haven: American Psychoanalytic Association and Yale University Press, 1990.

Morgenthaler, Fritz. "Introduction to the Panel on Disturbances of Male and Female Identity as Met with in Psychoanalytic Practice." *International Journal of Psychoanalysis* 50 (1969).

Morris, David. *Illness and Culture in the Postmodern Age.* Berkeley: University of California Press, 1998.

Mulvey, Laura. "Visual Pleasure and Narrative Cinema." *Screen* 16, no. 3 (Autumn 1975).

Murray, Stephen O. *Homosexualities.* Chicago: University of Chicago Press, 2000.

Nancy, Jean-Luc. "Corpus." In *Re-Thinking Technologies,* edited by Verena Andermatt Conley. Minneapolis: University of Minnesota Press, 1993.

Nanda, Serena. *Gender Diversity: Crosscultural Variations*. Prospect Heights, IL: Waveland, 2000.

Nestle, Joan. *The Persistent Desire: A Femme-Butch Reader*. Boston: Alyson, 1992.

Nicholson, Linda, ed. *Feminism/Postmodernism*. New York: Routledge, 1990.

"Northwest Passage (March 1985)." *Utne Reader*, no. 12 (October/November 1985).

Nussbaum, Emily. "Dr. Strangelove: Does the Exotic Become Erotic?" *Lingua Franca*, June 1998.

Nussbaum, Martha. "The Hip Defeatism of Judith Butler: The Professor of Parody." *New Republic*, 22 February 1999.

O'Connor, Noreen, and Joanna Ryan. *Wild Desires and Mistaken Identities: Lesbianism and Psychoanalysis*. New York: Columbia University Press, 1993.

Ogden, Thomas. *Subjects of Analysis*. Northvale, NJ: Aronson, 1994.

Osborne, Peter, and Lynne Segal. "Extracts from Gender as Performance: An Interview with Judith Butler." *Radical Philosophy* 67 (Summer 1994).

Paglia, Camille. *Sexual Personae: Art and Decadence from Nefertiti to Emily Dickinson*. New York: Vintage, 1990.

Palmer, Donald. *Structuralism and Poststructuralism for Beginners*. New York: Readers and Writers, 1997.

Person, Ethel Spector. "Sexuality as the Mainstay of Identity: Psychoanalytic Perspectives." *Signs* 5, no. 4 (1980).

———. *The Sexual Century*. New Haven: Yale University Press, 1999.

Phillips, Adam. *On Kissing, Tickling, and Being Bored*. Cambridge, MA: Harvard University Press, 1993.

Pinker, Steven. *The Blank Slate: The Modern Denial of Human Nature*. New York: Viking, 2002.

Plummer, Ken. "Speaking Its Name." In *Modern Homosexualities: Fragments of Lesbian and Gay Experience*, edited by Ken Plummer. London: Routledge, 1992.

Powell, Jim. *Postmodernism for Beginners*. New York: Writers and Readers, 1998.

———. *Derrida for Beginners*. Hyderabad, India: Orient Longman, 2000.

Ragland-Sullivan, Ellie. *Jacques Lacan and the Philosophy of Psychoanalysis*. Urbana: University of Illinois Press, 1986.

Reiter, Rayna, ed. *Toward An Anthropology of Women*. New York: Monthly Review Press, 1975.

Renik, Owen. "Analytic Interaction: Conceptualizing Technique in Light of the Analyst's Irreducible Subjectivity." *Psychoanalytic Quarterly* 62 (1993).

Riviere, Joan. "Womanliness as a Masquerade." *International Journal of Psychoanalysis* 10 (1929).

Rohmann, Chris. "Michel Foucault." In his *A World of Ideas: A Dictionary of Important Theories, Concepts, Beliefs, and Thinkers*. New York: Ballantine, 1999.

Roof, Judith. *A Lure of Knowledge: Lesbian Sexuality and Theory*. New York: Columbia University Press, 1991.

Roscoe, Will. *Changing Ones*. New York: Palgrave Macmillan, 1998.

Rosen, Ismond, ed. *Sexual Deviation*. Oxford: Oxford University Press, 1979.

Roughgarden, Joan. *Evolution's Rainbow: Diversity, Gender, and Sexuality in Nature and People*. Berkeley: University of California Press, in press.

Rowe, Michael. "Walking with the Ghost of Barry Winchell." *Advocate Online*, 11 June 2003. Available from http://www.advocate.com

Rubin, Gayle. "The Traffic in Women." In *Toward an Anthropology of Women*, edited by Rayna Reiter. New York: Monthly Review Press, 1975.

RuPaul. *Letting It All Hang Out: An Autobiography*. New York: Hyperion, 1995.

Ryan, Joanna. "Reflections on *Disorienting Sexuality*." *Gender and Psychoanalysis* 2, vol. 2 (1997).

———. "Can Psychoanalysis Understand Homophobia?" In *Homosexuality and Psychoanalysis*, edited by Tim Dean and Christopher Lane. Chicago: University of Chicago, 2001.

Sankar, Andrea. "Sisters and Brothers, Lovers and Enemies: Marriage Resistance in Southern Kwangtung." In *Anthropology and Homosexual Behavior*, edited by Evelyn Blackwood. New York: Haworth, 1986.

Sartre, Jean-Paul. *Being and Nothingness*. New York: Washington Square, 1996.

Sarup, Madan. *An Introductory Guide to Post-Structuralism and Postmodernism*. 2nd ed. New York: Simon and Schuster, 1993.

Schor, Naomi. "Female Fetishism: The Case of George Sand." In *The Female Body in Western Culture: Contemporary Perspectives*, edited by Susan Rubin Suleiman. Cambridge, MA: Harvard University Press, 1986.

Schwartz, Adria. *Sexual Subjects: Lesbians, Gender, and Psychoanalysis*. New York: Routledge, 1998.

Schwartz, David. "Current Psychoanalytic Discourses on Sexuality: Tripping over the Body." In *Disorienting Sexuality: Psychoanalytic Reappraisals of Sexual Identities*, edited by Thomas Domenici and Ronnie Lesser. New York: Routledge, 1995.

Sedgwick, Eve Kosofsky. *Between Men: English Literature and Male Homosocial Desire*. New York: Columbia University Press, 1985.

———. *Epistemology of the Closet*. Berkeley: University of California Press, 1990.

———. "Jane Austen and the Masturbating Girl." *Critical Inquiry* 17 (1991).

———. *Tendencies*. Durham, NC: Duke University Press, 1993.

———. *A Dialogue of Love*. Boston: Beacon, 1999.

Segal, Lynne. *Straight Sex: Rethinking the Politics of Pleasure*. Berkeley: University of California Press, 1994.

Segal, Lynne and Mary McIntosh, eds. *Sex Exposed: Sexuality and the Pornography Debate*. New Brunswick, NJ: Rutgers University Press, 1993.

Sheets, Hilarie. "The Mod Bod." *Art News*, June 1991.

Shernoff, Michael. "Steroids and the Pursuit of Bigness." *Harvard Gay and Lesbian Review* 8, no. 4 (2002).

Siegel, Lee. "Queer Theory, Literature, and the Sexualization of Everything: The Gay Science." *New Republic*, 9 November 1998.

Sim, Stuart, ed. *The Routledge Critical Dictionary of Postmodern Thought*. New York: Routledge, 1999.

Smith, Dinitia. "'Queer Theory' Is Entering the Literary Mainstream." *New York Times*, 17 January 1998.

Smith, Roberta. "Body of Evidence." *Vogue*, August 1994.

Socarides, Charles. *The Overt Homosexual*. New York: Grune and Stratton, 1968.

———. "The Psychoanalytic Theory of Homosexuality with Special Reference to Therapy." In *Sexual Deviation*, edited by Ismond Rosen. Oxford: Oxford University Press, 1979.

Soloman, Deborah. "How to Succeed in Art." *New York Times Magazine*, 27 June 1999.

Sontag, Susan. "Notes on Camp." In her *Against Interpretation and Other Essays*. New York: Delta, 1967. First published in *Partisan Review* 31, no. 4 (Fall 1964).

Souhami, Diana. *Gertrude and Alice*. London: Pandora, 1991.

Spargo, Tamsin. *Foucault and Queer Theory*. Cambridge, UK: Icon, 1999.

Stack, Carolyn. "Psychoanalysis Meets Queer Theory: An Encounter with the Terrifying Other." *Gender and Psychoanalysis* 4, no. 1 (January 1999).

Stein, Edward. *The Mismeasure of Desire: The Science, Theory, and Ethics of Sexual Orientation*. New York: Oxford University Press, 1999.

Stein, Terry. "A Critique of Approaches to Changing Sexual Orientation." In *Textbook of Homosexuality and Mental Health*, edited by Robert Cabaj and Terry Stein. Washington, DC: American Psychiatry Press, 1996.

Stephenson, Joan. "Female Olympians' Sex Tests Outmoded." *JAMA* 276, no. 3 (17 July 1996).

Stepp, Laura Sessions. "Partway Gay: For Some Teen Girls, Sexual Preference Is a Shifting Concept." *Washington Post*, 4 January 2004.

Stoller, Robert. *Sex and Gender: The Development of Masculinity and Femininity.* New York: Science House, 1968.

———. *Perversion: The Erotic Form of Hatred.* New York: Delta, 1975.

———. *Sexual Excitement: Dynamics of Erotic Life.* New York: Pantheon, 1979.

———. *Observing the Erotic Imagination.* New Haven: Yale University Press, 1985.

Suleiman, Susan, ed. *The Female Body in Western Culture.* Cambridge, MA: Harvard University Press, 1986.

Sullivan, Andrew. "Washington Diarist: Revolution, Televised." *New Republic,* 1 March 2004.

Symons, Donald. *The Evolution of Human Sexuality.* New York: Oxford University Press, 1979.

Tafoya, Terry. "Native Two-Spirit People." In *Textbook of Homosexuality and Mental Health,* edited by Robert Cabaj and Terry Stein. Washington, DC: American Psychiatric Association Press, 1996.

Talbot, Margaret. "The Female Misogynist: *The Whole Woman* by Germaine Greer." *New Republic,* 31 May 1999.

Thornhill, Randy, and Craig Palmer. *A Natural History of Rape: Biological Bases of Sexual Coercion.* Cambridge, MA: MIT Press, 2000.

Thurer, Shari. *The Myths of Motherhood: How Culture Reinvents the Good Mother.* New York: Penguin, 1994.

———. "Homosexual Panic in the Postmodern Age." Presentation at the American Psychological Association, Div. 19, 15 April 1999, New York, NY.

Torak, Maria. "The Significance of Penis Envy in Women." In *Female Sexuality,* edited by Janine Chasseguet-Smirgel. Ann Arbor, MI: University of Michigan, 1970.

Thurman, Judith. "Guides to Etiquette." *New Yorker,* 18 and 25 February 2002.

Traditional Values Coalition. "Exposed: The Truth about Pfc. Barry Winchell." Available from http://www.traditionalvalues.org.

Turner, William. *A Genealogy of Queer Theory.* Philadelphia: Temple University Press, 2000.

Warner, Michael, ed. *Fear of a Queer Planet.* Minneapolis: University of Minnesota Press, 1993.

Watters, A. T. "Heterosexual Bias in Psychological Research on Lesbianism and Male Homosexuality." *Journal of Homosexuality* 13 (1986).

Weeks, Jeffrey. "Homosexuality." In *Feminism and Psychoanalysis,* edited by Elizabeth Wright. Cambridge, MA: Blackwell, 1992.

Welldon, Estela. *Mother, Madonna, Whore: The Idealization and Denigration of Motherhood.* London: Free Association Press, 1988.

Whitam, Frederick. "Culturally Universal Aspects of Male Homosexual Transvestites and Transsexuals." In *Gender Blending: Transgender Issues in Today's World,* edited by Bonnie Bullough, Vern Bullough, and James Elias. Amherst, NY: Prometheus, 1997.

Williams, Linda. "Pornographies On/Screen." In *Sex Exposed: Sexuality and the Pornography Debate,* edited by Lynne Segal and Mary McIntosh. New Brunswick, NJ: Rutgers University Press, 1993.

Wittig, Monique. "One Is Not Born a Woman." *Feminist Issues* 1, no. 1 (1980).

Wright, Elizabeth, ed. *Feminism and Psychoanalysis: A Critical Dictionary.* Cambridge, MA. Blackwell, 1992.

Zita, Jacqueline. *Body Talk: Philosophical Reflections on Sex and Gender.* New York: Columbia University Press, 1998.

INDEX

A

Absence, presence containing, 119, 176
Academia and postmodernism, 32
Activism, Foucault's (Michel) views on, 115
Actresses, bisexuality and Hollywood, 54–55
Adams, Parveen, 129, 179–180
Addams, Calpernia, 95–97
Admixture perspective, 71
Advertising, 3, 45–46, 49
Aesthetic sensibility crossing sex/gender lines, 50
Age-structured homosexuality, 88
Aggression differences between the sexes, 80–81
AIDS (acquired immune deficiency syndrome), 54
Ambiguous genitalia, 23–25, 90
American Psychoanalytic Association, 181
Andreas-Salome, Lou, 9–10
Androgen insensitivity syndrome (AIS), 78
Androgyny, 3, 6
Animals and evolutionary theory/homosexuality, 74–75
Anthropological studies, 85–89
Anti-Oedipus: Capitalism and Schizophrenia (Guattari & Deleuze), 114
Anus ignored in favor of the phallus, 129
Anything That Moves, 54
Arbitrary categories, reality organized into, 29–30
Aron, Lewis, 184
Art
    body, 2–3, 38–43
    good and bad, juxtaposition of, 29
    Lacan's (Jacques) influence on, 120

postmodernism and the theater, 32
psychoanalysis/psychology, original alliance with, 9–10

B

Bailey, Michael, 73, 84
Bakhtin, Mikhail, 63
Barney, Matthew, 39
Barthes, Roland, 56–57
Baudrillard, Jean, 28, 180
"Beast in the Jungle, The" (Sedgwick), 136
Beauty, social construction of, 45–46
Beauvoir, Simone de, 101
Behavioral acts, contexts/meaning of, 68–69, 98; *see also* Research on origins/development of identity/orientation/behavior
Bellmer, Hans, 40
Bem, Daryl, 83–84
Benedict, Ruth, 86
Benjamin, Jessica, 165, 166, 171, 184, 186–187
Bersani, Leo, 133–134
Bieber, Irving, 163–164
Binaries, body/identity/orientation, 39, 119; *see also* French theory; Postmodern gender theory; Queer theory
Biological determinism, 15, 70, 103, 131–132
Bisexuality
    actresses, Hollywood, 54–55
    compatibility quotient, psychoanalytic/queer theory, 157–159
    relational model and, 186
    role-playing, history of, 54
    visibility of, new, 2, 6